Hamburg

Bremen

Berlin

Zuider
Zee

m

NETHERLANDS

XXXXX
H

XXXX
TWENTY-
FIFTH

Elbe R.

G E R M A N Y

XXXX
FIRST

Weser R.

Leipzig

R.  XXXX
SECOND

Düsseldorf

Dresden

XXXX
NINTH

Cologne

XXXXX
B

U M   Liége

Bonn

XXXX
FIRST

Frankfurt

CZECHOSLOVAKIA

Rhine R.

OB WEST

XXXXX
12

LUXEMBOURG

XXXX
FIRST

XXXXX
G

Saarbrücken

XXXX
THIRD

Metz

XXXX
SEVENTH

Stuttgart

Strasbourg

XXXXX
OBERRHEIN

Munich

FR.  XXXX
FIRST

XXXX
NINETEENTH

XXXXX
6

Mulhouse

on

Saone R.

S W I T Z E R L A N D

A U S T R I A

Geneva

Milan

Venice

I T A L Y

Genoa

### NORTHWESTERN EUROPE
### 15 December 1944

— Front line 15 December 1944

➤ Proposed axis of 6th Army Group
  attack north of Strasbourg

Nice

0          75          150 Miles

0        75        150 Km

Marseille

Toulon

D I T E R R A N E A N   S E A

Endsheet map: Route the Seventh Army might have taken into the German heartland.

# DECISION
## AT
# STRASBOURG

Other military histories by David P. Colley

*The Road to Victory: The Untold Story of*
*World War II's Red Ball Express*

*Blood for Dignity: The Story of the First*
*Integrated Combat Unit in the U.S. Army*

*Safely Rest*

*Faces of Victory, Europe:*
*Liberating a Continent (coauthor)*

# DECISION
## AT
# STRASBOURG

Ike's Strategic Mistake to Halt the
Sixth Army Group at the Rhine in 1944

## By DAVID P. COLLEY

Naval Institute Press
*Annapolis, Maryland*

Naval Institute Press
291 Wood Road
Annapolis, MD 21402

Library of Congress Cataloging-in-Publication Data

Colley, David.
  Decision at Strasbourg : Ike's strategic mistake to halt the Sixth Army Group at the
Rhine in 1944 / David Colley.
     p. cm.
  Includes bibliographical references and index.
  ISBN 978-1-59114-133-4 (alk. paper)
  1. United States. Army. Army Group, 6th. 2. World War, 1939–1945—Campaigns—
Western Front. 3. Rhine River—Strategic aspects. 4. Devers, Jacob L. (Jacob
Loucks), 1887–1979—Military leadership. 5. Eisenhower, Dwight D. (Dwight
David), 1890–1969—Military leadership. I. Title.
D769.2556th .C65 2008
940.54'2439—dc22
                    2008015583

Printed in the United States of America on acid-free paper

14  13  12  11  10  09  08      9  8  7  6  5  4  3  2

First printing

For my wife, Mary Liz, for her unfailing support,
and for my family: Pad, Chris, Erin, Bo, and Lilly

# CONTENTS

Acknowledgments                                                    ix

Introduction                                                       xi

Chapter 1.    Victory Assured                                       1

Chapter 2.    First to the Rhine                                    7

Chapter 3.    What History Doesn't Tell Us                         17

Chapter 4.    Devers Gets in the Act                               21

Chapter 5.    From Marseille to Alsace                             30

Chapter 6.    To the Siegfried Line                                40

Chapter 7.    Broad Front or Single Thrust?                        44

Chapter 8.    The Enemy Waits for the 6th Army Group               55

Chapter 9.    Into the Vosges                                      61

Chapter 10.   Logistics                                            68

Chapter 11.   On to Strasbourg                                     77

Chapter 12.   Whither the 6th Army Group?                          85

Chapter 13.   The Prickly French                                   89

Chapter 14.   The Greatest Obstacle                                94

Chapter 15.   Cross the Rhine!                                     97

Chapter 16.   Planning the Crossing                               101

Chapter 17.   The River-Crossing Schools                          109

Chapter 18.   Moving Up                                           114

Chapter 19.   Moving Out                                              120

Chapter 20.   Finally, the Attack                                     129

Chapter 21.   Ike Balks                                               134

Chapter 22.   Why Not Cross the Rhine?                                145

Chapter 23.   Enemies in High Places                                 152

Chapter 24.   A Cautious and Inexperienced Commander                 158

Chapter 25.   What If Devers Had Crossed in November?                165

Chapter 26.   Breakthrough at Wallendorf                             172

Chapter 27.   New Orders for the 6th Army Group                      178

Chapter 28.   Northwind—Devers Saves the Day                         182

Chapter 29.   The Colmar Pocket                                      190

Chapter 30.   "Bayonets Will Be Sharpened"                           195

Chapter 31.   Finally, the Rhine and into the National Redoubt       199

Chapter 32.   Could the French Have Crossed the Rhine?               207

Epilogue                                                             211

Notes                                                                213

Bibliography                                                         231

Index                                                                241

# ACKNOWLEDGMENTS

★ ★ ★ ★

I wish to express my thanks to the people and organizations that helped me realize this book: the staff at the U.S. Army Military History Institute in Carlisle, Pennsylvania; the staff at the library and archives of the York County Heritage Trust, York, Pennsylvania, the repository for the papers of Gen. Jacob Devers; the staff of the National Archives, College Park, Maryland; Dottie Patoki at the Easton, Pennsylvania, Area Public Library; the staff of the Lafayette College libraries; Susan Lintelmann and the staff at the U.S. Military Academy Library; Richard Curtis, my agent, for his efforts on my behalf; Lt. Col. Roger Cirillo (Ret.), Director of the Association of the U.S. Army Book Program, Institute of Land Warfare, for his advice and suggestions; and my wife, Mary Liz, for her unfailing support and assistance.

# INTRODUCTION

★ ★ ★ ★

"History is bunk," Henry Ford once said. A more refined interpretation is that of the French author La Rochefoucauld, who reportedly said: "History never embraces more than a small part of reality." So it is with the American experience in western Europe during World War II. More than sixty years after the guns fell silent, the chronicle of that struggle has been largely interpreted and determined by a few of its major players. Eisenhower, Bradley, Patton, and Montgomery have become, in large part by their own hand, somewhat outsized figures in the European war. Historians have reiterated their interpretations of events, and these interpretations have become the popular memory of the war. Likewise, Normandy, Falaise, Bastogne, and Remagen are considered the principal battles. These men and these battles provide the lens through which Americans view the history of the war in the European theater of operations (ETO).

Other interpretations and perspectives on the history of the European war are seldom discussed. The names and accomplishments of generals who contributed significantly to the final victory are virtually lost today, and other crucial battles and maneuvers are now forgotten. How many Americans have heard of such generals as "Ted" Brooks, "Ham" Haislip, and "P" Wood? All three were considered great generals, and all three won major battles.

*Decision at Strasbourg* deals with a part of that unknown tapestry of the war in the ETO in 1944 and 1945 that historians have virtually ignored. It relates the remarkable story of Lt. Gen. Jacob L. Devers, who, technically, ranked second only to Eisenhower in the command structure, but who presented so modest a public persona that as late as 1944 most Americans did not know how to pronounce his name correctly. Devers' 6th Army Group made successful amphibious landings near Marseille, advanced rapidly through France while destroying the German Nineteenth Army, and then held down the southern end of the western front. This volume particularly addresses Devers' lost opportunity to win the war in late 1944, months before it finally ended in May 1945.

The contributions of the U.S. Seventh Army and the French First Army, which constituted the 6th Army Group, are largely unknown, yet the two armies advanced as fast and as far as any of the other Allied armies in France. Devers landed with his men in the south of France on August 15, 1944, from a vast naval invasion fleet and drove some four hundred miles, as the crow flies, into Alsace. They reached the Rhine five months before Generals Patton, Bradley, and Montgomery did, yet the latter trio has always received the accolades for first reaching and then crossing the Rhine.

The Rhine was the major objective of the Allied armies fighting in France in the summer and fall of 1944, and American and British generals alike recognized its strategic importance. The German generals also understood the military significance of this swift-flowing river; Germany was doomed if the Allies crossed its waters. The German army was depleted and badly demoralized at this point; a sizable combat force of Allies could have enveloped and destroyed it and then advanced eastward. The road to Berlin, the symbol of Nazi power, would have been open and the city virtually defenseless. But no such force existed on the eastern side of the river.

No other American or British army or general had reached the Rhine when Devers stood on its western bank near Strasbourg, France, on November 24, 1944, and quizzed members of patrols who had just returned from across the river, where they found German defenses unmanned. Devers looked into Germany and saw not just the enemy's homeland but an unparalleled opportunity to cross and seize a bridgehead on the opposite side. If he breached the Rhine, he could seal off the German Nineteenth Army in Alsace and come in behind the German First Army fighting Gen. George S. Patton Jr. in Lorraine. Devers' army group could disrupt the left wing of the German line and possibly cause the collapse of the entire enemy front west of the Rhine from Switzerland to the Netherlands. He ordered his engineers to begin preparations to launch a crossing on or before the first week in December; amphibious trucks (DUKWs) and army bridging equipment, long readied for this event, were moved up from the rear.

Devers never made that Rhine crossing in 1944. Eisenhower stopped the advance a day before it was scheduled to proceed. But historians have not told us why Ike canceled the operation; nor have they analyzed the consequences of Eisenhower's decision or the possible outcome of such an attack. No one has explored this question of why and what might have been—not even General Devers, who declined to write his memoirs after the war.

The Allies did not advance over the Rhine until March 1945, five months and thousands of American casualties after Devers planned his crossing. Many young men's lives might have been spared had Devers crossed the river in late

November or early December 1944; almost certainly the war would have been shortened. Instead, the Germans were given a free hand to continue their massive troop buildup in the Ardennes in preparation for the Battle of the Bulge, which began on December 16, 1944, three weeks after Devers' planned operation. The enemy generals knew they did not have to fear an attack across the river along the upper Rhine just north of Strasbourg; Eisenhower had made it plain in public and private pronouncements that the Allies would not come from that direction. But even a failed crossing attempt or a feint on Devers' front would have forced the Germans to divert thousands of troops to counter a 6th Army Group penetration across the Rhine. And this possibility raises a question: Would the Battle of the Bulge have taken place or have been as damaging had Devers crossed?

*Decision at Strasbourg* explores Devers' plans in detail, from the river-crossing schools established to train troops to negotiate the swift-moving Rhine to the order to begin transporting DUKWs and boats to the river. It also examines why Eisenhower suddenly ordered Devers not to cross the Rhine and the consequences of that order. Devers' bold plan has been lost to history because of a near-obsessive focus on other areas of the western front and on other generals who have been elevated to the pantheon of heroes of World War II. This book also examines the interplay between the Allied commanders—between Eisenhower and Devers, and between Devers and other generals such as Bradley and Patton. All were competing to be first over the Rhine, and their personal interactions affected Eisenhower's decision on which general would carry out this major operation and where the attack would be made. *Decision at Strasbourg* relates this remarkable and unknown story.

CHAPTER 1.

# Victory Assured

★ ★ ★ ★

M*arch 7, 1945.* It was early evening when Gen. Omar N. Bradley, commander of the U.S. 12th Army Group, answered the telephone in his office in Namur, Belgium. The Wallonian provincial capital, located some forty miles southeast of Brussels, was an appropriate place for an army headquarters. It had been battered by the crosscurrents of war and had witnessed invading armies since the Roman era. Strategically located at the confluence of the Sambre and Meuse Rivers, Namur was the hub of a road network that led into and out of France. Julius Caesar's legions had tamed the local Aduatici people in the first century BC, and the Merovingians had constructed a fortress on the rocky outcropping overlooking the city in the tenth century AD. Time and again Namur's citadels had been besieged and the city destroyed. Just thirty years before, in the summer of 1914, the Germans had blasted Namur into submission by lobbing shells from their massive "Big Bertha" guns into its rim of forts. Now, in this latest European war, Namur became Bradley's headquarters because of its proximity to the German frontier, where his troops had been fighting since the fall of 1944.

Despite all the signs of war—the bullet- and shell-pocked buildings, the comings and goings of thousands of soldiers, and the drone of Allied bombers destined for Germany filling the sky high above—Bradley's surroundings belied the conflict that was ravaging Europe. His office was in the Château de Namur, a splendid baroque palace, in what had once been the provincial governor's ornate drawing room. Clusters of smirking cherubs looked down on the tall, bespectacled, and balding commander from the vaulted ceiling; frescoes adorned the walls; a crystal chandelier hung above Bradley's desk, around which were placed several large leather chairs; and a sumptuous Oriental carpet covered the floor. The large windows looked out toward the Sambre River as it flowed lazily into the Meuse.[1] Only the brightly lit twenty-foot-tall map board displaying the positions of Bradley's troops along the western front was evidence that this was the headquarters of the most massive and powerful American army ever assembled.[2]

The previous minutes had not been good ones for the tall, reserved four-star general, who commanded four separate American armies holding a 150-mile sector of the front from Wesel, Germany, to the northern edge of the Black Forest far to the south. Bradley's mood was as dark as the blackout curtains drawn over his office windows. The man across his desk, Maj. Gen. Harold R. "Pink" Bull, trusted tactical and operational adviser to the supreme Allied commander, Gen. Dwight D. Eisenhower, had just arrived from Ike's headquarters in Versailles to inform Bradley that Ike was transferring four of his combat divisions to Gen. Jacob Devers' 6th Army Group in Alsace. Bradley fumed. He did not like Devers, and the 6th Army Group had been stealing his troops for the past month. Bradley had just sent several divisions to Alsace so that Devers could eradicate the Colmar Pocket, an enemy salient that Bradley believed Devers should have dealt with himself weeks before. Furthermore, Eisenhower had promised Bradley's Ninth Army to British field marshal Bernard L. Montgomery to cover Monty's right flank in the upcoming cross-Rhine attack set to begin in two weeks. Montgomery had also asked Ike for the use of a reserve of ten more of Bradley's divisions in the U.S. First Army that were to be diverted north to assist the British 21st Army Group should Montgomery need additional help crossing the Rhine.[3]

Bradley seemed to be losing control of his 12th Army Group, and he was furious. His troops had spent the last seven months in bitter fighting to break through the Siegfried Line, the protective belt of thousands of concrete bunkers guarding the German frontier with interlocking fields of fire, mines, and tank traps. Bradley now believed he was finally in position to push his four armies forward to the Rhine, leapfrog the river, and carry the war into the German heartland.[4] Instead he was being robbed of divisions so that other generals could have the glory of crossing the Rhine and defeating the enemy.

The Germans were now in full retreat through the Rhineland, ironically the homeland of General Eisenhower's forebears, who had emigrated to Pennsylvania in the mid-1700s.[5] Entire enemy divisions, or what was left of them, were fleeing over the Rhine or stranded on the river's west bank. American tanks rumbled into deserted villages where the somber brick or stone houses were shuttered and many of the windows displayed white bed sheets to signify surrender. The GIs called these towns "shirttail allies" and approached them warily, edging down deserted streets with rifles at the ready and their pockets and chest harnesses loaded down with hand grenades to blast any remaining enemy soldiers from cellars.[6] It was a slow, steady march to Germany's defeat.

All along the Rhine, the Germans were blowing the bridges as the vanguard of U.S. armored columns reached their western approaches. Nevertheless, Bradley dared to hope that his men might capture at least one bridge intact. Otherwise, his engineers would have to erect pontoon bridges across the Rhine to continue the pursuit of the fleeing Wehrmacht.[7]

If Bradley harbored ill will toward Eisenhower for stealing his troops, it was not apparent to Pink Bull. "Brad" and Ike were old friends from their West Point days. Both were members of the class of 1915, known years later as "the class the stars fell on" because so many of its graduates became generals in World War II. Fifty-nine attained the rank of brigadier general or higher, three achieved the four stars of a full general, and Ike and Bradley received a fifth star to become General of the Army. Bradley had been the first among his classmates to wear a star when he was appointed commandant of the Infantry School at Fort Benning, Georgia, in February 1941.[8]

Both Brad and Ike were good athletes, and both had played football for West Point, Brad as a substitute center and Ike as a running back so talented that the *New York Times* touted him as one of the most promising backs in the East. On one memorable day in 1913, Army tangled with the Carlisle Indian School and the legendary Jim Thorpe. To win, Army had to knock Thorpe out of the game and the Cadets "high-lowed" Thorpe on every occasion; Eisenhower would hit him high while another teammate hit him around the ankles. Thorpe went down hard every time, but always picked himself up and rejoined the huddle. He dashed for two touchdowns—one for ninety-five yards—and passed for another, and kicked three field goals and three extra points to crush the Army team, which scored only six points.[9]

Ike's athletic career was cut short by a knee injury that plagued him even as supreme commander thirty years later, but Bradley continued as a center and was on the 1915 team that logged a perfect season. It was in baseball, however, that Bradley truly excelled. He was a star left fielder on the 1915 team that won eighteen games and was considered one of the best teams ever to represent the academy. Their affinity for sports sealed Ike's and Brad's friendship, but each respected the other's achievements off the athletic field as well. Eisenhower penned a note in Bradley's yearbook that seemed to foretell this moment so many years later in Belgium: "Brad's most important characteristic is 'getting there' and if he keeps up the clip he's started some of us will someday be bragging that, 'Sure, General Bradley was a classmate of mine.'"[10]

Everyone praised Bradley, a shy midwesterner who eschewed alcohol and found profanity offensive. Maj. Gen. George S. Patton Jr., once Bradley's superior in North Africa but now his subordinate in Europe, opined that Bradley was just "too damned sound."[11] Bradley's aide, Maj. Chester B. Hansen, described him as a man of "great modesty" who "clung to the background."[12] But looks can be deceiving. Bradley was a determined and forceful commander, and an ambitious man. His natural reserve may have come from the fact he was descended from hardscrabble Missouri farmers and he had developed, even cultivated, an image of "homespun humility." He was known as the "GI's General," and like many of his soldiers, his passion was hunting. When he was an infantry instructor at Fort Benning, Georgia, he often rose early and headed for nearby swamps where he shot the heads off water moccasins.[13] During the North Africa campaign, Bradley would draw his pistol to pick off rocks tossed into the air by aides.

While attending the Army's Infantry School in 1929, Bradley impressed Lt. Col. George C. Marshall, the school's assistant commandant, who placed him on his famous list of up-and-coming officers who would fight the next war. Eleven years later Bradley became commandant of the school, and when war was declared, Marshall, now the army chief of staff, selected him to command the 28th Infantry Division.[14]

When Ike was appointed to command the Allies' North African invasion forces in 1942, he named Bradley assistant commander of the 2nd Corps under General Patton. When Patton was reassigned to prepare for and command American forces in the invasion of Sicily, Bradley took over the 2nd Corps and matched wits with the "Desert Fox," Erwin Rommel, the commander of the German Afrika Corps, which had plagued the British and Americans in Tunisia, Libya, and Egypt for more than two years.

Following the Allied conquest of Sicily in 1943, Ike appointed Bradley to command the U.S. First Army in England and to lead Americans troops into France. Once ashore in France, Bradley assumed command of the 12th Army Group, which grew to include the First, Third, Ninth, and Fifteenth armies. No American general had ever commanded so large a military force; it numbered around a million men in forty-three divisions and included hundreds of thousands of vehicles. By March 1945 Bradley had built a magnificent fighting force and was among Ike's most trusted lieutenants.[15]

In his Namur office, Bradley picked up the ringing telephone on his desk. The caller was Lt. Gen. Courtney Hodges, Bradley's subordinate and commander of the U.S. First Army, which at that moment was advancing along a wide stretch of the western front.

"Brad, we've gotten a bridge," Hodges said.

"A bridge? You mean you've got one intact on the Rhine?" Bradley asked, sitting forward in his chair. The bleakness of the day's events suddenly vanished. If Hodges truly had captured a bridge over the Rhine, the Germans were finished and American troops—all Bradley's troops—would pour into the Reich.

"Yep. The 9th Armored Division nailed one at Remagen before they blew it up," Hodges said.

"Hot dog, Courtney!" Bradley paused momentarily to absorb the news. "This will bust him wide open. Are you getting your stuff across?" Bradley asked.

"Just as fast as we can push it over. . . ."

"Shove everything you can across it, Courtney, and button up the bridgehead tightly. It'll probably take the other fellow a couple of days to pull enough stuff together to hit you."[16]

That morning, lead elements of Combat Command B (CCB) of the 9th Armored Division had reached the town of Remagen on the west bank of the Rhine and were amazed to peer through a thick haze and see the Ludendorf Railroad Bridge linking Remagen to Erpel on the east bank still intact. The Ludendorf Bridge at Remagen had been planned with its destruction in mind. Its architects had designed large chambers within its two main supports to be filled with explosives and detonated if an invading army appeared. During the Allied occupation of the Rhineland following World War I, however, French troops filled the chambers with concrete. In 1945 German engineers improvised and planted explosives elsewhere along the span as the Americans approached. As American tanks and infantry rushed to capture the span, the German defenders set off a series of powerful explosions that lifted the steel superstructure from its stone foundations. When the smoke cleared, the Americans were astonished to see the bridge still standing; many of the charges had failed to detonate, and the structure held together. The Americans immediately realized their prize, and infantry led by Sgt. Alex Drabik from Dayton, Ohio, rushed across and fanned out on the east bank of the Rhine to establish a bridgehead in the hills above Erpel.[17]

Hanging up the phone after receiving the news from General Hodges, the elated Bradley grinned broadly at General Bull. "There goes your ball game, Pink," he said as he thumped Bull on the shoulder. Bradley understood the immense significance of the bridge's capture not only for the war but also for his reputation, and within minutes he ordered his commanders to rush American troops over the Rhine. The Germans fought desperately to stop them. They sent planes to bomb the bridge, some of them the new twin-jet Messerschmitt 262, which the Americans had not yet seen, but all missed the target. The enemy fired V-2 rockets into the stratosphere, hoping the rockets would come down close enough to destroy the Ludendorf Bridge, but all were wide of the mark and did nothing more than set off huge explosions that rocked the countryside. Thousands of artillery rounds rained down around the span; enemy frogmen swam downriver in an attempt to attach demolition charges to the caissons, but the infiltrators were killed or captured.[18]

Richard Ralston, a young American infantry lieutenant, remembered crossing the Rhine at Remagen and watching enemy artillery shells explode in ugly black bursts in the water near his convoy. *Stars and Stripes* correspondent Andy Rooney described the artillery and mortar shells hitting around the bridge in the Rhine as falling "like huge raindrops, exploding . . . as they struck the water."[19]

American engineers erected several pontoon bridges next to the Ludendorf Bridge to carry the vast American army that was racing to Remagen from other parts of the Rhineland. American infantrymen, lost in their singular, seemingly inconsequential contribution to the war, looked behind them as they made their way across the river on the precarious floating bridges and saw an endless column of infantry, tanks, and trucks that was the tip of a hastily formed spearhead making the final push into Germany. Backing it was a force of some 4.5 million Allied soldiers, 3 million of them Americans, in 91 combat divisions, 21 corps, 8 armies, and 3 army groups.[20] Victory in Europe was now assured.[21] Newspapers all across America heralded the capture of the Remagen bridge. "The crossing itself was one of the most brilliant coup de mains of the war and it caught the enemy entirely by surprise," Howard Cowan wrote in the *New York Times*. His colleague Gladwin Hill noted in a companion piece, "German prisoners . . . casually predicted the defeat of Germany within three weeks or even ten days as a result." They were nearly right.[22]

After Bull left his office, Bradley immediately telephoned Eisenhower, who was elated that his old friend was first over the Rhine. "Get right on across with everything you've got," Ike said, and he ordered Bradley to rush as many as five divisions over the river. Eisenhower added a brief warning to his old pal, "Make sure you hold that bridgehead. It's the best break we've had."[23]

CHAPTER 2.

# First to the Rhine

★ ★ ★ ★

"The best break we've had." Gen. Jacob Loucks Devers snorted at the irony of the statement years after the war when he was reminded of Ike's comment to Bradley the day the Remagen bridge was captured in March 1945. That was all long past in 1969 when the old general reminisced about the war, his career, and his old boss, the supreme commander in Europe, Dwight D. Eisenhower, who had just died at age seventy-nine.[1]

Although history books barely mention it, Devers had contributed immensely to victory in the ETO in 1944 and 1945. Then, in June 1945, barely a month after the shooting stopped, he was appointed commander of Army Field Forces, a post that took him back to Washington, D.C., and wrapped him in relative obscurity. He was not counted among the "great" generals returning home after the war. Four years later, with no prospects of advancing further in the ranks, Devers retired from the military and returned to private life.

Devers had logged forty years of service and stepped down as a four-star general, a rank achieved by very few. Technically, he had been the second-highest-ranking Army officer in Europe during the war and was one of only two Americans to command an army group. Did he feel slighted at not being appointed Army chief of staff or even chairman of the Joint Chiefs? Always reticent and modest, Devers never publicly complained about being passed over for these top posts. But his sister, Catherine "Kit" Devers, spoke for him: "I never heard him talk about it, but every man who gets near the top, as he did, would have wanted to finish his career as chief of staff."[2] Unfortunately for Devers, there were too many other candidates for the chief's position who had made bigger names for themselves as dashing commanders during the war.

Devers remained active in a number of public and private posts during his retirement, before dying in 1979 at the age of ninety-two. In his early eighties, when he was interviewed about his participation in the war, he was still energetic and vital and still flashed the infectious smile that was his trademark as commander of the Allied 6th Army Group. Modest as Devers was, though, talk of politics and war could still arouse underlying passions a quarter century after World War II, particularly talk of the way historians interpreted the war in Europe. Generals Eisenhower, Patton, and Bradley had been named the heroes, eclipsing everyone else who participated. Devers was given no credit for the final victory, nor were the British and Canadians serving under Field Marshal Bernard Montgomery. And history says that General Bradley reached the Rhine first at Remagen.

Bradley's account in *A Soldier's Story* tells in great detail about being first to the Rhine and seizing the Remagen bridge. Ike praised him for it, and Bradley and his troops achieved worldwide acclaim.[3] Books were written about his stroke of military genius and exceptional generalship. A movie, *The Bridge at Remagen*, depicts the bridge's capture. The principal generals portrayed in these books and films are Eisenhower and Bradley. Such distortion of these important events irritated Devers. "I know all the books I read," Devers said, and even uttered a rare, yet tame, expletive. "Well, hell, we crossed the Rhine first—if you want to talk about it—because we were on the Rhine first." The "we" was the Seventh Army of his 6th Army Group, and the date was November 24, 1944.[4]

One might conclude that age had clouded Devers' mind when he said that his 6th Army Group was first on the Rhine and the first to send men across the river. That is not what the history books tell us. It was Bradley who crossed first at Remagen in March 1945, they say, followed by Patton's U.S. Third Army, and then by Montgomery's British and Canadian 21st Army Group, which crossed north of Cologne. But "Jake" Devers was not slipping into senility, despite his advanced age. The Seventh Army really was the first American unit to reach the Rhine, and Seventh Army patrols were the first to venture across the river into Nazi Germany. The 6th Army Group had raced up through southern France, wrecking the German Nineteenth Army as it pushed north with a speed that matched or bettered Patton's celebrated armored advance across northern France into Lorraine in late August 1944. But while Patton was stopped well short of the Rhine at Metz, Devers' troops pushed on to the strategic river and prepared to cross. The old adage that history is agreed-upon fiction could not be more accurate when it comes to interpreting the war in Europe in 1944 and 1945. The Seventh Army led the way to the Rhine, and but for a stroke of fate and questionable leadership by Eisenhower, Devers' troops would have established a bridgehead on the east bank and might have ended the war in January instead of May 1945. Had that been the case, no one would ever have heard of the Remagen bridge.

Devers' military career began almost by accident. He had never contemplated a position in the Army when he enrolled at Lehigh University in Bethlehem, Pennsylvania. He had already been assigned a room and a roommate when his local congressman sought him out as a candidate for West Point who could make the grade in a curriculum heavy in math and engineering. Devers was proficient in the sciences and was amenable to the appointment. He was nominated, passed the entrance examinations, and was accepted into the Corps of Cadets, class of 1909.

"Jamie" Devers came from sturdy German French (Alsatian) stock. He experienced a wholesome upbringing in the lush, rolling green hills and inviting glens of Pennsylvania Dutch country, where his ancestors had settled in the early 1800s. He was born in 1887 in the city of York and grew up in this bustling, small manufacturing town in south-central Pennsylvania one hunred miles west of Philadelphia. In the latter part of the nineteenth century, York spun in its own universe, as many small American cities did. The unpaved streets ran to the edge of the country and pedestrians got around town on boardwalks.

There were four Devers children: three boys, born one year apart, and one girl, Catherine, whom the family nicknamed "Kit." Jamie was the oldest. Their mother, Ella Kate, was a semi-invalid who needed help to manage her household. Raising three boys so close in age, the nanny once said, was like having to take care of triplets.

Jamie was a hardworking child from an industrious and strict family. He cut grass in summer, shoveled snow in winter, had a year-round newspaper route, and even picked unburned nuggets of coal from the furnace ashes for ten cents an hour. Every harvest season he was pressed to work on his grandfather's farm baling hay along with his two brothers, Frank and Philip. Jamie was irked that his grandfather Loucks paid him half the wages the hired hands received although he believed he worked twice as hard. Nevertheless, the reward at the end of a hard day of farm labor was a visit to Bierman's Ice Cream Parlor, where the brothers were allowed all the ice cream they could eat. Years later, Devers fondly remembered the huge gatherings of Devers and Loucks families during holidays in the rambling Bull Road farmhouse owned by Grandfather Loucks, a businessman turned farmer, after whom Devers was named. Ironically, many of the Loucks hailed from Strasbourg, the city Devers' armies would retake from the Germans a half century later.

Jamie's father, Philip Devers, a robust five feet ten inches tall and weighing 220 pounds, had worked his way up from store clerk to partner in Sievers & Devers jewelry store, and he demanded discipline and punctuality from all his children, including Catherine. If they were late for meals, they did not eat; if they were late getting dressed for an outing, they were left behind. Philip Devers was determined to instill dependability, honesty, hard work, and integrity in his children.

Jamie was class president in high school, a top student, and, like Omar Bradley, had a passion for sports. He was the quarterback of York High School's 1904 football team, known as an opportunist who waited for the moment when the opponent was off guard. He pitched for the school's baseball team as well, and had a mean curveball. But it was basketball that Jamie loved best, and he studied the moves and played the game for hours at the local YMCA.[5]

The Deverses were a close-knit family, and Kit recalled that when the day came for Jamie to leave for West Point, his departure came as a blow to her and her mother. "I can still remember mother and I standing in the kitchen trying not to cry."[6] West Point was a world away for a country boy used to the freedom of rural York County, and Jamie's first experiences there were humbling and humiliating, particularly the hazing. His slight build was a disadvantage when it came to the demanding physical requirements for plebes. There was not an ounce of fat on his 120-pound, five-foot-ten-inch frame, and he was so pigeon-toed that he was easily identified marching among the ranks of look-alike cadets with their caps pushed down over their brows and chinstraps tugging at their jaws. His visiting mother easily picked him out as the one with the awkward gait.

When Devers became an army group commander, observers always remarked on his friendly, boyish grin, but at West Point it occasionally got him in trouble. He would smile at an inopportune moment to give the impression to an upbraiding up-perclassman that he was amused when he was not supposed to be. But the grin also got him out of trouble, when he would flash a smile and all might be forgiven.

Devers was known for his clean living at the academy; he did not gamble and seldom drank. Years later, these traits would stand in contrast to those of his boss, Supreme Allied Commander Dwight Eisenhower, who both enjoyed his drinks and was a master poker player. The caption that accompanies his photo in the West Point yearbook of 1909 reveals much about Jamie Devers: "An exceedingly earnest youth with rather Puritanical views. Jamie is the model of the well-bred Kadet. For many moons we have watched his actions and have concluded that for purity, propriety and precision, Jacob is hard to beat." The inscription concludes, "He is a wonderfully clever young man." "Clever" was a word used to describe Devers throughout his career, and it was not always meant as a compliment.[7]

Regardless of his slight build, Devers made a name for himself as an athlete at West Point. He played four years of basketball and was named team captain his senior year, and he played shortstop on the baseball squad. Wherever he went at the academy, he rubbed shoulders with men who would become famous thirty years later during World War II. George S. Patton Jr. was a classmate, and "Vinegar Joe" Stillwell was Devers' basketball coach. Stillwell also became a general and served with distinction in China. Had American land forces invaded Japan in 1946, Stillwell would have been their leader.

Devers was commissioned a second lieutenant on graduation and chose the artillery as his specialty branch. He selected a "pack outfit" as his first assignment because the artillery had all the latest communications systems and emphasized training. He would be able to work with horses and mules and would have to be well conditioned mentally and physically.[8] He went west to join the 4th Mountain Artillery at Vancouver Barracks in Washington. Three months later, the 4th was amalgamated into a regiment and he was assigned to Fort D. A. Russell, an old cavalry post in Wyoming.

"We packed all over the Rocky Mountains," Devers recalled years later. "We went on a thousand-mile march from Cheyenne, south to Denver, down to Colorado Springs, to Canyon City, to the southern border of Colorado, crossing the Continental Divide seven times or more. These were paths that hadn't been gone over for maybe a couple of years—all with packs." His experiences with pack animals taught him a great deal about the psychology of commanding men. Both man and beast have needs, he noted, and a commander, like a handler, must be attuned to their sensitivities. Devers quickly learned that a mule is often smarter than a horse because it will let you know when something is wrong; a horse won't. When a mule gets caught in barbed wire, it will stand and wait to be pulled free. A horse will panic and tear itself to shreds trying to escape.

A horse "has a way of telling you when you're not on the right wavelength. . . . If you went out to mount your horse on a cold day and you were stiff and rigid, he's very liable—even if he's an old plow horse—to give you a good buck to let you know you're to loosen up and relax so he could do his job. I think the people that were in the cavalry and the field artillery, and the horse game [polo] could do anything," Devers said later. "They had to shoe those horses. They had to know when they were sick. They watched to see that they had their proper feed." Devers translated his experiences with animals to his men. "If you had a fractious horse, nervous and high strung, it taught you something about handling high-strung men. You had to handle that horse with care and kindness, and also discipline." Mules are more amiable, less difficult and sometimes had a sense of humor and mischief. Once while leading a pack train, Devers' men secretly taught the lead mule to pluck off a man's hat if he got too close. Every time Devers approached the head of the column the mule tried to bite off his campaign hat.[9]

Duty at Fort Russell was harsh, and in letters home Devers complained about the wind that blew incessantly across the landscape. Then suddenly the complaints stopped. He had met a young lady from Washington, D.C., named Georgie Hayes Lyon when she was visiting her uncle, the post's commanding officer. The couple fell in love, and they were married in 1911. Her uncle's Army career had taught Georgie how to be an Army wife, and she understood her role throughout their lives together. "She was a marvelous asset as far as his Army career," Kit said. "I don't think she was ever terribly ambitious for him. I think really what she wanted was to be with him."[10]

A year later Devers was assigned to West Point to teach mathematics and artillery tactics to a cadet corps that included Dwight Eisenhower and Omar Bradley. His four years of basketball at the academy also made him a natural to coach basketball. He was assigned to Hawaii in 1917, and was stationed there when the United States entered World War I. He quickly rose to the rank of major, but an overseas assignment eluded him. Like many of his fellow officers who "missed" the Great War, Devers thought his career was doomed for lack of combat experience. But he did he make it to Germany for a stint of occupation duty.

Between his assignments at West Point and at various artillery bases, Devers was accepted at the Army's Command and General Staff School at Fort Leavenworth, Kansas. It was an important step in his career. The school's candidates were rising young officers who someday hoped to wear a general's star. He changed his name from Jamie to "Jake" at the insistence of one of his commanding officers, who noted that "Jamie" was an unprofessional name for a military officer with aspirations of being a general.

Devers displayed two dominant characteristics as a young commander: he plunged into his work and his play, and he pursued objectives with tremendous vigor and enthusiasm. No detail was too small for his attention, and he was an excellent planner. He once tested the comfort level of a new steel helmet by wearing it in bed while recuperating from pneumonia. As an artilleryman he studied the results of hundreds of practice firings and streamlined the artillery's methods by reducing from eight to six the number of shots to achieve a direct hit. "When he started something he knew what he was doing," Kit recalled. "He didn't go off half-cocked."[11] Devers remained an avid athlete as well. During a posting at Fort Myers, Virginia, he would often skip lunch to play polo with George Patton, and he was notorious on the golf course for jogging from shot to shot to stay physically fit.

Devers met George Marshall in the late 1920s and impressed the future army chief of staff with his administrative and organizational skills. Marshall followed Devers' career closely and in 1940 advanced him to brigadier, over 474 officers with more seniority, and assigned him, with President Roosevelt's blessing, to command Fort Bragg, North Carolina. At the time, Devers was one of only fifty generals in the U.S. Army.

Fort Bragg was in the throes of a major construction program that had fallen behind schedule, and the project needed an innovator who could reinvigorate it. Devers proved right for the task; he supervised more than 31,000 workers, managed more than seven hundred lumber mills, administered a budget of $44,681,309, and oversaw the construction of some 2,500 new buildings on the sprawling base.

He finished the job within a year by doing away with red tape. By the time the job was completed in 1941, the number of military personnel stationed at Bragg had risen from 5,400 to 67,000.[12]

Despite his heavy responsibilities, Devers never forgot his troops. When the men in a newly arrived battalion at Fort Bragg complained that they had not showered in days, Devers guaranteed the men hot showers within twenty-four hours—even though the base did not have adequate hot water facilities. He prodded his staff and solved the problem by hooking two steam locomotives to the base water system.

In 1941 Marshall reassigned Devers to Fort Knox, Kentucky, to take charge of the nation's armored forces. It was a plum assignment, one Eisenhower must have coveted because of his fascination with armored warfare. Under Devers, America's tank forces grew from a few ragtag units to fourteen full-fledged armored divisions that saw action in World War II. He pioneered the development of armored tactics, elevating the tank from a subsidiary unit role on the battlefield to a primary instrument of attack. It was under Devers' watch that the United States developed the M-4 Sherman tank, the principal armored vehicle of American forces during World War II. The Sherman was not the best tank on the battlefield, but it was produced by the thousands and was mechanically reliable—something German tanks often were not—and it gave the Allies numerical superiority over the enemy. In the end, tens of thousands of Shermans overpowered a few thousand German panzers. While he was chief of armored forces Devers revealed how he would direct his armies three years later in Alsace. "The tank is nothing but a mechanism to carry firepower to the enemy position, utilizing mobility for tactical and strategic purpose." By the time Devers left the armored force, syndicated newspaper columnist Roscoe Drummond noted, he was "America's outstanding panzer expert."[13]

Devers was of a somewhat different cut than many of the other generals who would lead armies in Europe. During World War II, *New York Times* correspondent Hanson W. Baldwin likened him to a small-town businessman, a Chamber of Commerce type rather than a three-star general in command of two armies. Baldwin also described him as "a Pennsylvania Dutchman with Irish charm" and "a very infectious smile."[14] A man with Irish charm as a hard-nosed commander of troops? He just did not fit the picture. The "wide grin" and ageless, smooth face never seemed to reflect the worries that lined the faces of the other commanders, and gave Devers a boyish look not altogether appropriate for his serious and lofty position. He was always neatly dressed and often wore a high-crowned garrison cap that gave him the appearance of a grinning doorman. Even his nickname seemed inappropriate for an army group commander. True, he was no longer "Jamie," but his comrades and President Roosevelt, with whom he often consulted, had started calling him "Jakie." Somehow the nickname reflected his stature among the generals in the ETO. There was something about Devers and his army group that no one took seriously.

The fame and praise Devers deserved for his accomplishment eluded him, and he was as little remembered twenty-five years after World War II as he is today. In 1944 and 1945, however, he had been one of the top commanders in the ETO. Only one man in that theater outranked him—Devers' boss, General of the Army Dwight Eisenhower—and only two other generals, Bradley and Field Marshal Montgomery, who held the same status as army group commanders, were his equals. In time of service Devers was senior to all other American field commanders in Europe, including Eisenhower, and he had been a general longer than any of them. He was awarded his first star in 1940. By 1943 he had risen to the rank of lieutenant general. He got his fourth star in March 1945, the year after he took command of the 6th Army Group. All other field generals in Europe were subordinate to Devers, Bradley, and Montgomery; even Patton, who has been elevated to near Olympian status, held a lesser command. Patton led one army, the Third, while Devers was in charge of two, the American Seventh Army under Lt. Gen. Alexander M. Patch and the French First Army under Gen. Jean de Lattre de Tassigny. All told, Devers' 6th Army Group comprised nearly a half million men by the war's end.

How could a general of such high rank and such stellar accomplishments be so ignored and forgotten? Devers himself was largely responsible for the oversight. He was a modest man who either failed to understand or failed to deal with the reductive nature of history. He should have spoken out about his achievements and taken an active role in shaping and interpreting past events—as Eisenhower, Bradley, and Montgomery did. When he did not, others recorded his accomplishments for him, in the process diminishing the importance of the role he played. Devers never did speak out publicly. It was simply not in his nature to celebrate himself and disparage others—even commanders such as Eisenhower, with whom he often disagreed about how to conduct the war—and no one has ever written a substantive biography focused on his military achievements.

Kit Devers noted that reserve was a family trait of all the Devers children. Their mother despised showmanship, and the children were taught to be "very reticent" about their accomplishments. "Jake would never toot his own horn anywhere, anytime to anyone, " Kit said. "He would never even state the things that were true accomplishments."[15]

Another factor explaining Devers' anonymity was his location in the wings, so to speak, on the southern end of the western front. The press and historians were always more interested in what transpired at center stage, always eager to relate Patton's latest antics or an Eisenhower news conference. In a November

1944 letter to radio newscaster Lowell Thomas, an unknown writer tried to raise Devers' profile. "Although [Devers is] the second ranking general on the western front," he wrote, "little or no public recognition has been given him, in fact, so little that commentators do not even know how to correctly pronounce his name, which is not *Dee-vers*, but *Devers*, the *Dev* as in devil."[16]

Unlike his counterparts, who were experts at public relations, Devers avoided publicity. He praised generals who put substance before form and he eschewed press conferences. Reporters who visited Devers' command had to work for their stories. Devers would take them into the field to show them the real situation. "When the public press and people come to get something [he would] say, 'Well, come on. I haven't got time to talk to you but come out here and see for yourself. . . . Don't stage it. Don't print all those press releases.'"[17]

Devers' 6th Army Group performed well—often brilliantly—in France after making amphibious landings near Marseille on August 15, 1944. The U.S. Seventh and First French armies pushed north through the Rhone Valley to Lyon and Dijon over the rugged and often rain-soaked or snowbound Vosges Mountains and across the Alsace Plain to the Rhine River. Its location on the southern wing of the Allied front, far from the Ruhr industrial area farther to the north—the stated Allied objective—meant that the 6th Army Group received little publicity back home, but his fellow Allied commanders were well aware of Devers' performance; they were both envious and angry. Patton, accustomed to headlines for his lightning advance across northern France in August 1944, cursed Devers' luck and obvious competence as a field commander. Patton once complained in a letter to his wife, Beatrice, that the 6th Army Group "seem[s] to have made a monkey of me." Devers was stealing Patton's limelight, and the 6th Army Group's relatively easy advances threatened to eclipse Patton's reputation as the Allies' best fighting general.[18] Devers' achievements seemed only to diminish his standing with Eisenhower and Bradley, though, and left his 6th Army Group the orphan of the western front.

By mid-September 1944, Devers' armies had linked with Allied forces under Eisenhower's command that had landed at Normandy on D-day, June 6, 1944. From that moment, the 6th Army Group, now a force of several hundred thousand, anchored the southern end of the Allied line in Alsace. Despite its excellent performance, Eisenhower and his Supreme Headquarters Allied Expeditionary Force (SHAEF) anticipated that the 6th Army Group would play only a supporting role in the defeat of the enemy. SHAEF had no plans for Devers to spearhead the Allied drive into Germany.[19] In fact, SHAEF had no plans for the 6th Army Group whatsoever.

The 6th Army Group started off as a small invasion force of only three U.S. divisions—albeit the best and most veteran in the U.S. Army (the 3rd, 45th, and 36th divisions had fought through North Africa and Italy)—and a motley collection of French divisions. SHAEF had little expectation that this force would grow much larger or be very effective. It was afforded a quasi-independent status on the right wing and was seen more as diversionary force and a flank guard to the Third Army than an aggressive expeditionary force.

SHAEF was also wary of the fighting capabilities of the army group's contingent of French troops. They had lost their reputation as reliable soldiers in France's sudden and total defeat in 1940, and the new French 1st Army of 1944 comprised tattered remnants of that once-proud force, African colonials who were unused to the colder climate of Europe, and untrained and undisciplined members of the French Resistance.[20]

# CHAPTER 3

# What History Doesn't Tell Us

★ ★ ★ ★

Eisenhower's lack of respect for Jake Devers and his 6th Army Group was never more evident than on November, 24, 1944, the day Devers was prepared to send his Seventh Army across the Rhine to invade Nazi Germany. The supreme commander was suddenly presented with a remarkable and long-awaited opportunity to shorten World War II and perhaps even alter the history of the future Cold War. The 6th Army Group had effectively neutralized the German Nineteenth Army in Alsace and was poised to cross the Rhine and come in behind the left wing of the German front. They could smash the German First Army fighting Patton's Third Army in Lorraine or at least force it to withdraw behind the Rhine. Devers calculated that the entire German front could crumble from a Seventh Army attack that might also unleash an Allied sweep through Germany to take Berlin before the Russians got there.

The Allies' objectives had been clear ever since the landings at Normandy in June 1944 and near Marseille in August 1944. Ike's orders to all his generals were precise: the armies were to advance to the Rhine, cross it, and establish bridgeheads on the opposite bank.[1] Bradley, Montgomery, and Patton made no secret of their intention to follow Ike's orders to the letter, and neither did Devers. The top generals had discussed cross-Rhine attacks at SHAEF meetings, and written orders had been issued for the armies to establish bridgeheads on the east bank.

If Eisenhower had no sense of the capabilities, aggressiveness, and vigor of the 6th Army Group, Devers certainly did. He was present at 15th Corps headquarters on November 22, 1944, when its commander, Maj. Gen. Wade Haislip, ordered his French 2nd Armored Division, commanded by Gen. Jacques Leclerc, to advance on Strasbourg. "I was up there listening . . . when Haislip finally gave him the 'go ahead,'" Devers recalled.[2] The French armored division hastily moved out, ignoring the German defenses and the heavy gray storm clouds hovering low over the Alsatian plain that unleashed torrents of rain on the sodden and war-shattered terrain. Villages and towns were in ruins, torched and demolished by the retreating Germans, and enemy dead lay unattended in water-filled abandoned trenches.

Leclerc was one French general whom the Americans admired and liked to have among their ranks, and he made no secret of his preference for serving with the Americans rather than the French. He was a driving, no-nonsense commander whom the Germans feared because his troops often took revenge for their defeat in 1940 and for the years of terror during the Occupation by summarily shooting Wehrmacht soldiers they found in their way.[3]

Leclerc's tanks rolled out of Saverne and blasted their way through German roadblocks into Haguenau on November 22. The 2nd Armored Division was now only eight miles northwest of Strasbourg, the ancient French provincial capital known for its architectural beauty and as a center of commerce on the Rhine. Seventh Army intelligence reported that there was little to stop Leclerc's advance, and that same morning Leclerc received additional orders from General Patch, commander of the U.S. Seventh Army, to "attack Strasbourg, employing armored elements to assist the Sixth Corps in the capture of the city."[4]

Leclerc needed no prodding, and at 7:15 AM on the twenty-third his tanks began to roll southeast in four armored groups.[5] Task Force (TF) Rouvillois took up the attack against Strasbourg from the north, and TF Massu was to move in from the south. Along with Combat Command L (CCL) and CCV, Leclerc's troops would encircle the city and drive the Germans across the two bridges to the German city of Kehl, 650 yards away on the east bank of the Rhine.

TF Massu's tanks encountered stiff opposition as they approached the city, but TF Rouvillois raced through the rain-soaked countryside, smashing through German barricades and strong points with ease. The stunned Germans looked up to see American-built Sherman tanks bearing French insignias charging through the ancient cobbled streets of Strasbourg. The French tanks were now on the Rhine. Frantic enemy troops scrambled to reach safety and pulled back to defend the railway and highway bridges over the Rhine that led to Kehl. Unless defended, these bridges would provide the Allies with an open pathway into the Nazi Reich. The pop of rifles, staccato bursts from machine guns, and tank and artillery fire echoed through the streets for the next twenty-four hours as the French battled bands of surrounded and desperate Germans. The fate of beautiful Strasbourg, a city that had existed for nearly two thousand years, lay in the balance.

The city would survive. A contingent of Leclerc's troops pushed on to the Strasbourg Cathedral, which dated to the twelfth century, and hoisted the Tricolour from one of the magnificent spires that rose above the city. The flag waved in an autumn wind made heavy by the sounds of war. The capture of Strasbourg was so swift that Devers himself was surprised. He quickly moved to consolidate his gains and sent in American infantry, who advanced cautiously through the streets

Lt. Gen. Lucian K. Truscott Jr. (left), Lt. Gen. Alexander Patch (center), and Lt. Gen. Jacob Devers meeting on October 9, 1944.

Maj. Gen. Jacques Leclerc, commander of the French 2nd Armored Division.

Gen. George Marshall (left) confers with Gen. Jean de Lattre de Tassigny, French 1st Army commander (center), and Lt. Gen. Jacob Devers in October 1944.

American infantrymen move forward to assault a town near Raon l'Étape,
November 17, 1944.

French infantrymen advance in the Belfort area, November 20, 1944.

An American machine-gun crew awaits further German assaults during German Operation Northwind, January 17, 1945.

Maj. Gen. Wade Hampton Haislip, commander of the 15th Corps.

An American infantryman receives a bottle of wine from a young French girl in Luxeuil, France, September 17, 1944.

Troops of the 45th Division land near Saint-Maxime in southern France, August

German general Frederich Wiese.

Gen. Jacob Devers, 1943.

Yearbook photo of Jacob Devers, 1909.

German tanks move to the front through Toulouse, France, in August 1944.

Infantrymen of the 45th Division practice on the Doubs River in France for a cross-Rhine attack in November–December 1944.

Railroad bridge destroyed in southern France and repaired by American engineers using the undercarriage of a German railroad gun.

Lt. Gen. Alexander M. Patch.

to reinforce Leclerc's forces. One of the first U.S. units to arrive was the 324th Regiment of the U.S. 44th Infantry Division.[6]

While the capture of Strasbourg was critical, the terrain to the north was of greater strategic importance to Devers and Patch. It was here that the 6th Army Group planned a cross-Rhine attack, hoping to unhinge the German front from Switzerland to the Netherlands and open a passageway deep into the German heartland. Once Leclerc's troops took Strasbourg, Patch ordered elements of the U.S. 79th, 3rd, and 45th divisions to consolidate positions north and northwest of Strasbourg.[7] Also moving north of the city and along the Rhine, the 117th Cavalry Reconnaissance Squadron encountered only spotty resistance.[8]

Generals Devers and Patch understood the significance and dangers of a Rhine crossing as well as anyone. It would not be a piece of cake. The Wehrmacht troops on the Alsace front were a far cry from Hitler's superbly trained legions of 1941 and 1942; for the most part, they were the very young and the old. Nevertheless, on Devers' insistence, Patch issued orders to the units moving north up the Rhine to send patrols across the river to reconnoiter the landscape and test the defenses on the east bank in Germany. Battered, yes, but the Wehrmacht was still an army that could inflict heavy casualties on any enemy that took it lightly. The troops may have lacked experience, but many of their officers were competent veterans.[9]

U.S. infantry patrols immediately slipped across the river to undertake reconnaissance probes to assess the enemy's strength along the east bank of the river. Among the spots targeted for observation was the area around the German city of Rastatt, a small industrial town of about 25,000 that invading armies had trampled for centuries. The French destroyed the town in 1689, and it was the site of the Treaty of Rastatt, which, as part of the treaties signed at Utrecht and Baden in 1713 and 1714, ended the War of the Spanish Succession.

The American scouts stealthily moved out from the river's edge as night descended, paddling hard to keep the swift current from sweeping them downstream. Beyond the narrow edge of the Rhine Valley on the east bank loomed the aptly named Black Forest, and the scouts scanned the darkened terrain for evidence of German sentries and defenses as they reached the east bank and stepped into Germany. They looked warily about and slowly moved out, not speaking, communicating with sign language and whispers, weapons held low and at the ready. The silence was perturbing. Where were the expected buzz saw blasts from MG-42 machine guns, the pop of Mauser rifles, and the deafening explosions of grenades and mortars?

But there were no firefights, no artillery or mortar attacks, and no encounters with enemy troops; there was only an eerily empty landscape. Bunkers and defensive positions were unmanned, and there was little sign of the Wehrmacht that had used this area to launch troops of its own Seventh Army across the Rhine in the final days of the Battle of France in 1940.

Near Rastatt, at least, the German army could do nothing to stop Devers' troops if he sent them across the river to establish a bridgehead. The Germans had made a grave error. Gambling that the 6th Army Group would become bogged down in the Vosges Mountains and be unable to take Strasbourg until the spring of 1945, they had left the east bank of the Rhine south of Karlsruhe virtually un-defended. The Germans also calculated that the Americans would not cross the Rhine in the 6th Army Group's sector because their high command knew that this area of the front was not the Allies' primary military or political objective. That was farther to the north around the Ruhr industrial zone.

Home to industries that produced more than 50 percent of Germany's arms, the Ruhr was vital to the German war effort. The industrial zone lay along the Ruhr River, which rises in the hills of central Germany and flows westward to the Rhine at Duisburg. Vast coal deposits brought steel manufacturing to the region in the nineteenth century when Krupp and Thyssen built large integrated coal and steel empires. Essen, Düsseldorf, and Dortmund, the region's principal cit-ies, were regular targets for British and American bombers. By the war's end, all three had been churned into rubble. But the air raids failed to completely halt war production; only ground troops could do that.[10] The Germans also expected the 6th Army Group to regroup and resupply before launching a major attack across the Rhine.

Devers himself met some of the infantry patrols as they returned and ques-tioned them about what they had learned.[11] He frequently visited frontline units, on occasion getting too close to combat for his aides' comfort. The infantry scouts told Devers what he expected to hear: "There's nobody in those pillboxes." Devers knew that the French had sent patrols across the Rhine farther south near Mulhouse and had found it undefended, too.[12] The east bank of the Rhine from Mulhouse to Rasttat was defenseless, and the commander of the 6th Army Group saw an opportunity he had been planning for two months. The 15th Corps of the U.S. Seventh Army, 6th Army Group, was going to cross the Rhine.

CHAPTER 4.

# Devers Gets in the Act

★ ★ ★ ★

Lt. Gen. Jacob Devers became a major player in the unfolding drama of World War II in the spring of 1943, a year and a half before his armies reached the Rhine, when he was named Commanding General, European Theater of Operations. This critical assignment was the same post Eisenhower had held before being named overall commander of the Allied invasion of North Africa in August 1942. Had Eisenhower lost the confidence of the American and British Combined Chiefs of Staff in North Africa, as he almost did, Devers might have remained supreme commander in Europe in 1944 and 1945, and history would have enshrined the nickname "Jake" instead of "Ike."

Devers came to the new assignment in Europe by chance on May 10, 1943, when Eisenhower's successor, Lt. Gen. Frank M. Andrews of the U.S. Army Air Corps, was killed in a plane crash while returning to London from Washington. Devers was well known and respected in military and political circles, and his appointment was welcomed. Syndicated columnist Roscoe Drummond wrote of Devers' promotion, "His presence in London spells invasion."[1]

England in 1943 was a burgeoning island fortress and staging area for the Allies' planned invasion of continental Europe. U.S. air bases spotted the countryside, and the U.S. Army Air Corps was mounting daily bombing raids against targets in France, Germany, and the Low Countries. American infantry and armored units poured into the British Isles.

Devers remembered London as a "gray and battered city" with thousands of American troops filling the streets. The windows of Kensington Palace Gardens were boarded up, "fences were broken down, lawns grown rank and wild. . . . In winter it was bitterly cold; the windows and curtains failed to keep out the northeast wind."[2] The Blitz with its nightly raids had ended, but pockets of destruction blemished the proud British capital. The Germans still managed sporadic bombing attacks, and war damage was evident everywhere. Saint Paul's Cathedral was badly damaged; so too were the Parliament buildings, the palace at Westminster, and

Westminster Abby. The German raiders that did make it through to London were always met by a hail of antiaircraft fire from the big guns spotted throughout the city and in the countryside, and the noisy barrages could be more dangerous to the city's inhabitants than enemy bombs. Shards of shrapnel from exploding shells rained down, sometimes with lethal force, and slammed onto rooftops like a hard rain.[3]

Devers found his new job demanding, but he approached it with his usual energy and optimism. Much of his work dealt was public relations to show U.S. resolve and bolster the Allied will for the upcoming invasion. "We are eager to fight," he told the Anglo-American Press Association, "and we want to get at the enemy as quickly as possible. Weather and water may slow us up, but nothing will prevent the final victorious battle."[4]

The European command held only modest powers in early 1943. The focal point of the war had shifted to North Africa, where Eisenhower had established himself in Algiers as America's most promising up-and-coming commander and the leader of the Anglo-American forces fighting the Germans in Tunisia. A cross-channel attack against the enemy in France was not even a certainty as the Americans and British argued over the best strategy to defeat the enemy. Would the landings be in France, in Italy, or even the Balkans, the region Churchill called the Germans' "soft underbelly"? The Americans, led by Chief of Staff George Marshall, favored France.

Devers' job in England was to lay the foundation and develop preliminary plans and studies for a cross-channel attack somewhere between Calais and Normandy. He immediately encountered British resistance. "I came to the conclusion," Devers reported, "that the British didn't intend to cross that English Channel unless somebody took some positive action." He realized the Americans would have to lead if the invasion were to take place.[5] One of his principal objectives was to acquire as many landing craft as possible to carry the invasion troops to the French shore, and he badgered Churchill to encourage British shipyards to produce more of these critical vessels.

As European commander Devers maintained a high profile and gained a measure of recognition. He met regularly with Prime Minister Winston Churchill, and King George VI and Queen Elizabeth entertained him; he made speeches and headlines and had direct access to General Marshall and President Roosevelt in Washington.[6] But his directness engendered strong animosities. He was not afraid to say no to anyone. He turned down a request from Eisenhower for the transfer of several squadrons of bombers to North Africa that soured their relationship and would have future consequences for Devers. He once so infuriated Churchill during a conversation about the timetable for the delivery of American tanks to North Africa that the prime minister angrily shook his cane at him.[7] Even worse, Devers refused to agree when the prime minister told him that the British deserved to be first into France.

Devers believed that General Marshall, his old friend and mentor, would be the man to lead the Allied forces into Europe, and Marshall's appointment would almost certainly ensure a major role for Devers as commander of an army or possibly even an army group. But Eisenhower's star was ascendant after his successes in North Africa, and Roosevelt felt Marshall's talents were best suited to his post as army chief of staff, where he could be available whenever the president wanted his advice. Ike's skills as an organizer and facilitator were best suited to forge a working coalition between the Americans and the British as he had done in North Africa. He had difficulties and setbacks in North Africa, but he led the Allies to victory in Tunis in May 1943, and his coalition-building skills were now well developed. He had also become something of a national hero and was well known and liked by the American public. In December 1943 Ike was named supreme commander in Europe.

The British also liked Ike and were dead set against Devers. "You know I was against you," Churchill told Devers months later when Devers commanded the 6th Army Group in France.[8] Churchill respected Devers, but like so many others, he found Ike to be more affable and approachable; and more important for Churchill, Ike was more easily persuaded than Devers to accept British military views and thinking. Above all, Eisenhower was the better politician. Devers may have been a hard charger who could get things done, but he found the responsibilities of maintaining a coalition with the British difficult to manage. Eisenhower did too, but he a master conciliator.

The difference between Devers' methods of leadership and Ike's were nowhere better reflected than in the lessons each took from their experiences serving as an assistant to Gen. Douglas MacArthur. Devers first served under MacArthur at West Point in 1919 when MacArthur was the academy's superintendent; Eisenhower served as MacArthur's aide in the mid-1930s in the Philippines when MacArthur commanded the Philippine army.

MacArthur was blunt and undiplomatic: "Truth—always tell it, always live it," he counseled. Devers recalled one incident that occurred when he was a young captain. MacArthur fired off a scathing letter to the president of the Eastern Inter-Collegiate Athletic League relating all that was wrong with the organization that regulated West Point's athletics.

"Well, General, I think it's pretty rough," Devers cautioned. "I think it's too direct and might do more harm than good."

"It's the truth, isn't it?" MacArthur said.

"Yes, sir," Devers replied.

"Well, remember this: Always tell the truth and from that time on you can always take the offensive, and that's what I propose to do in this case," MacArthur said.

Devers took MacArthur's dictum to heart. "That's the way I've been trying to operate ever since," he said, "and if I had been the smartest in my class, I'd have operated that way all along."[9] His frankness contributed to his troubles with Eisenhower on the western front.

Ike took a very different lesson from MacArthur's no-nonsense approach. When he served under MacArthur in the Philippines, he spent a lot of time calming waters MacArthur had roiled. Ike learned to be a diplomat and to get his way with a more conciliatory, softer touch.

Ike's new command in Europe meant a change for Devers. Marshall considered Devers qualified to command the 12th Army Group, with Generals Bradley and Courtney Hodges serving as army commanders under him. The new supreme commander in Europe had serious doubts about Devers' abilities, however, although he admitted to Marshall that his reservations were "based completely upon impressions and, to some extent, upon vague references in this theater."[10] Ike appointed old friends and associates to positions of authority for the cross-channel attack, code-named Operation Overlord. Devers and Eisenhower had never been friends; they had never even worked together, and Ike declined to give Devers a command. As much as he may have wanted Devers to command the 12th Army Group, Marshall refused to intercede on his friend's behalf. He allowed his generals to make their own decisions about commanders.[11] Marshall, however, still had confidence in Devers and saved him from obscurity by appointing him to command U.S. forces in the North African Theater of Operations (NATOUSA), the army's senior administrative post in the Mediterranean, based in Algiers. Devers also assumed the duties of deputy supreme Allied commander in the Mediterranean theater under British general Maitland Wilson, nicknamed "Jumbo" for his height and expansive girth. Wilson commanded Allied forces in northwest Africa, Italy, the Balkans, Turkey, many of the islands in the Mediterranean, and southern France.

Devers' new position was largely viewed as a demotion, but he threw himself into his work with his usual enthusiasm and energy, and labored at Wilson's side until early in 1944, when he was selected, again by Marshall, to lead the invasion of southern France, Operation Dragoon (formerly code-named Anvil). The planned invasion would test Devers' abilities as a combat commander to the limit.[12]

Dragoon was to be the "left hook" to the D-day invasion, forcing the Germans to deal with attacks in both the north and south of France. The military operations in Normandy were to be the main thrust against the Germans because it was closer to the Ruhr and to Berlin, and the enemy had more troops in northern France than in the south.

Dragoon was controversial from the start. Churchill, in particular, opposed the southern landings because it meant stripping combat troops from the Italian front, where the British and Americans were successfully, if slowly, fighting their way up the peninsula. The British Imperial General Staff held the view that once the Allies reached northern Italy, their armies could break out and fan across Austria and Yugoslavia and other parts of eastern Europe not only to defeat the Germans but to block Soviet armies from overrunning the region and creating a string of communist states. The British believed that reducing the number of Allied troops in Italy would simply enable the Germans to transfer divisions from the Italian front to France to oppose the Normandy invasion.[13]

Dragoon also worried the British because it would reduce Allied strength in the eastern Mediterranean, an area that had always held greater strategic significance for them than for the Americans. Their colonies in Egypt and Palestine bordered the Mediterranean Sea, which also provided a lifeline through the Suez Canal to British dominions in India and the Far East. Despite British resistance, the Americans prevailed, however, and Operation Dragoon took place on the French Mediterranean coast between Toulon and Cannes.

By midsummer 1944, the Allied invasion in Normandy had stalled. In six weeks of bitter fighting the Allies had been unable to break out of the narrow bridgehead that stretched from Caen to Cherbourg on the northern coast of France. After five years of war and more than 3 million casualties, the German army remained a formidable force. The Allies controlled the skies and the sea, and had vast matériel and manpower superiority. The individual German soldier proved almost invincible and Field Marshal Erwin Rommel's army held the Allies in check for nearly two months.[14]

Dragoon was not without great risks. The enemy maintained 250,000 men in southern France in the German 19th Army, which comprised ten divisions and ancillary units spread from Bordeaux on the Atlantic coast to the Alps along the Italian border. The Germans had constructed a continuous wall of defensive positions all along the Mediterranean coast to protect this vast area. Gen. Jean de Lattre de Tassigny described the fortifications as "continuous, close and solid."[15] The defenses enabled the German 19th Army's commander, General der Infantrie Frederich Wiese, to keep the bulk of his forces in reserve inland, where they could react instantly to an invasion threat anywhere along the coast.

Devers' 6th Army Group would eventually contain more than 450,000 men, but only three American divisions (in the Seventh Army's 6th Corps) and two French divisions made the initial Dragoon landings. General Patch commanded the U.S. Seventh Army, and General de Lattre commanded the French troops of Armee B, soon to be designated the French First Army.[16] Unless the French and American troops established firm beachheads, they risked being contained by the more numerous German forces or even thrown back into the sea. Devers pushed hard to have the 1st Armored Division attached to the 6th Corps to give the invasion forces more punch, but his request was rejected—an omission that would have consequences during the invasion. Devers and Patch had to make do with what they already had.[17]

The American Seventh was the first U.S. "army" to see combat in World War II. Born out of Patton's and Bradley's 2nd Corps, which fought in North Africa, it was officially formed at sea just prior to the invasion of Sicily (Operation Husky) in July 1943. General Patton took command of the Seventh Army aboard the USS *Monrovia*, Adm. H. Kent Hewitt's flagship; thus its motto became "Born at sea, baptized in blood, crowned with glory." Patton led the army through Sicily but was relieved of his command at the end of the campaign because of the notorious incident in which he struck a battle-fatigued soldier in an army field hospital. Patton remained in limbo in Sicily until he was transferred to Great Britain in 1944 to command the phantom FUSA army in southern England and later to lead the Third Army in France. Ironically, Ike had recommended to General Marshall that Patton be reinstated as commander of the Seventh Army when it made the landings in southern France.[18] Had Marshall taken Eisenhower's advice, the course of the war in Europe might have been different.

Lt. Gen. Alexander "Sandy" Patch was one of the few U.S. generals who came to Europe in 1944 combat tested in numerous wars and conflicts. Devers wanted him as his Seventh Army commander because Patch had been "blooded" in Pacific fighting on Guadalcanal. But Devers also knew and respected Patch from previous assignments.[19] "He had served under me as a colonel in the 9th Infantry Division," Devers recalled. "I knew him as a cadet. I knew most of his staff. Patch was a very fine commander, an excellent administrator, and he also was a good field commander because he knew tactics and strategy."[20]

Few of the highest-ranking commanders in the U.S. military slated to serve in France could equal Patch's credentials. A 1913 West Point graduate and the son of an army officer, Patch experienced his first combat in 1916 during the border skirmishes with the Mexican bandit Pancho Villa. The war diary of twenty-six-year-old Lieutenant Patch records an encounter during a skirmish as U.S. forces moved south into Mexico in pursuit of Villa: "One shell passes approximately ten yards over our heads in enfilade. . . . Men badly startled. . . . No necessity of ordering them to take cover."[21]

In World War I Patch saw action in France as a machine gunner. Early in World War II, while most of his comrades and West Point classmates, now colonels or generals, were chafing to get combat commands in Europe or the Pacific, Patch led U.S. forces on Guadalcanal in the South Pacific. He was credited with engineering the final defeat of the Japanese on the island.

On Guadalcanal, Patch was known as a strict disciplinarian with a temper "like the devil before dawn."[22] He was a hard driver who believed that his troops should be well conditioned and hardy, and he drove them mercilessly; but he was also revered for treating them well. After one lengthy forced march, his men staggered to the finish line to find kegs of beer awaiting them. Above all, Patch was known for his fanatical bravery. Col. Russell Reeder never forgot his first meeting with the general on a moonlit night at Patch's headquarters on Guadalcanal in 1943. Reeder had been sent to deliver a confidential message from General Marshall, and he arrived just as Japanese bombers attacked. Patch had issued standing orders that all his troops must move immediately to bomb shelters during air raids, but he himself refused to take shelter, considering it beneath his position as a general to do so. While thousands of his troops ran for cover, Patch went outside and stood at the rear of his headquarters building and calmly waited out the attack.

"I have often thought of this scene," Reeder recalled. "It would make a wonderful painting by a skillful artist. There in the brilliant tropical moonlight, under coconut trees . . . with the vivid shadows on the red hard-baked earth, stood the tall gaunt General. In this light his height seemed to be magnified. He stood there bare-headed with his shirt open at the throat—a striking figure."[23]

General de Lattre described the lean and ruggedly handsome Patch (in looks he was compared with movie actor Gary Cooper) as having "ascetic features," a "charming manner," and a "mystic turn of mind" that was coupled with a deep faith in God. De Lattre wrote years later:

> I recall a hot day in Algiers when he had thought that all our plans [for Dragoon] had been destroyed by the Adriatic alternative [a Mediterranean invasion through the Balkans]. He was disconsolate. With emotion he took from the drawer of his desk a box of sweets that had come from home that morning and offered them to me as if our mutual disappointment had opened his family circle to me, and said "Ah! General, there's not much more we can do." Then, after a silence: "We must pray." And in the evening, to drive away the blues, he organized a little dinner, at the end of which, as a surprise, he played Poet and Peasant on the accordion like a virtuoso. But this sensitive man who spoke tenderly of his wife and dearly loved his son . . . was a resolute commander, of high and clear intellect,

and exceptional steadfastness. The plans upon which he resolved were conceived with perfect wisdom.[24]

Several near-fatal bouts with pneumonia may have strengthened Patch's mysticism and faith. He also had a literary bent. He was fond of Kipling, and while commanding his troops in France took up a correspondence with the writer Gertrude Stein, who lived in the village of Culoz in southern France. In one letter to Stein, Patch wrote:

> I have regretted deeply that our rapid advance has prevented me from visiting the area of the Lac du Bourget and Aix les Bains of which I hold so many happy memories of a delightful, if short, vacation during the last war. The opportunity of meeting the lady whose literary works and humanitarian achievements I have long admired, together with the tempting offer of a chicken dinner, have convinced me that I cannot long postpone a trip to your delightful countryside. I shall make every effort, as soon as the military situation permits, to accept and thank you in person for your thoughtful invitation.[25]

By the fall of 1944 Patch showed the strains of war and sorrow more than most general officers on the western front. His faced was grooved and gaunt, and he sometimes appeared exhausted. He had other burdens beyond those of commanding the Seventh Army. In October 1944, his only son, Lt. Alexander M. Patch Jr., a 1943 West Point graduate whom the family called "Mac," was killed in action while leading his company in an attack with Patton's Third Army in France. General Patch preempted the heartless telegram that he knew his wife, Julia, would receive from the war department and sent her a radiogram, "Mac killed instantly yesterday assaulting enemy positions in France."[26]

The blow was devastating to the elder Patch, and only his determination, discipline, and iron will carried him through his personal tragedy. General Patch wrote to Julia of his sorrow, "I came close to the breaking point. I have recurring moments when it is hard for me to control my grief." Ironically, Patch had a soul mate in Kipling, who lost his son during World War I under similar circumstances. John Kipling, like Mac, had been a young lieutenant eager for combat; he was killed leading an attack against a German position in France, not far from where Mac would be killed twenty-eight years later.

Patch received a letter of condolence from Gertrude Stein. "I was very touched by your letter. The Colonel told me that your son was married and had left a boy, behind him. It is not much comfort, but it is some and will be more with the years. Thanksgiving is come. I wish you might come here to have it with us."[27] The fates would have it otherwise. Less than a year later, in September 1945, General Patch died of pneumonia in a San Antonio, Texas, military hospital. His grandson, "Little Mac," died in 1946 of the same affliction. General Patch; his father, Capt. A. M. Patch, a former cavalry officer on the American frontier; and Little Mac were all buried at West Point. Mac was buried in France.

Whatever his personal tragedies and physical weaknesses, Patch never let them interfere with his duties as a commanding general, but Devers was concerned for the well-being of his Seventh Army commander. Pneumonia had almost killed Patch several times before, and Devers assigned a medical officer to watch over him. Devers' order was explicit: "You stick with Patch . . . and keep him going."[28] Jake Devers was determined to ensure the success of the invasion of southern France.

# CHAPTER 5

# From Marseille to Alsace

★ ★ ★ ★

"D awn came at last," Lt. Gen. Lucian Truscott recalled as Operation Dragoon was launched on August 15, 1944.[1] The commander of the 6th Corps peered through binoculars into the distant gold and turquoise littoral mountains of the French Riviera from his perch in the invasion fleet that stretched to the distant horizons of the Golf du Leon and beyond into the Mediterranean Sea. The vast naval force, second in size only to the fleet that had assaulted Normandy on June 6, comprised 853 vessels: 505 ships from the U.S. Navy, 252 from Britain, 19 from France, and 63 merchant ships from various other countries. It included 5 battleships, 4 heavy cruisers, 18 light cruisers, 9 aircraft carriers, 85 destroyers, 20 large transports, and 370 large landing ships and craft. "Deck loaded" on various ships were 1,267 smaller landing craft.[2]

Truscott strained to see the invasion beaches through an early-morning haze that obscured the jagged escarpments, rutted vineyards, and rough-hewn farmhouses with their putty-colored walls and red-tiled roofs. The bucolic beauty of old Provence, so artfully depicted by Cézanne and Van Gogh, would soon be disfigured. Box formations of heavy bombers and swarms of fighters were appearing on the horizon from bases in Italy and Corsica "like birds flying shoreward," Truscott recalled.[3] Some 1,300 B-24s and B-17s droned over his post on the fleet flagship, *Catoctin*, and unleashed their sticks of bombs. The landscape exploded in brilliant flashes, and clouds of smoke and debris towered above the fabled beaches around the seaside village of Saint-Tropez. Seconds later the unearthly sounds of the bombardment rumbled out to sea to mingle with the roar of guns from warships that poured 5-, 8-, and 14-inch shells onto the shore. As the sun continued its slow rise in the east, German troops manning the defenses along the French Mediterranean coast east of Toulon were suddenly aroused from months of torpor by explosions bursting around their bunkers and communications centers. The invasion of southern France was under way, and the lead elements of three American infantry divisions were packed into bobbing, flat-bowed Higgins boats plodding toward the beaches along forty miles of coastline. The 3rd Infantry Division began landing at Cavalaire-sur-Mer, the 45th Infantry Division at Saint-Tropez, and the 36th Infantry Division at Saint-Raphael.

Sgt. Audie Murphy, a battle-hardened veteran of the 3rd Division's campaigns in North Africa and Italy, recalled the morning in his memoir. "We do not see the gigantic pattern of the offensives as we peer over the edge of the landing boats that are nearing the coast of France. We study the minute detail of the front that lies immediately before us." Murphy's unit was approaching a sandy stretch of coast code-named Yellow Beach. The early morning mist still hung low over the shore-line; inland, the hills rose to more rugged countryside.

> About us in the bay lying between St. Tropez and Cavalaire is the now-familiar design of an amphibious invasion. The battleships have given the beach a thorough pounding. Now their guns are quiet, but the huge gray ships steam slowly in the background. The rocket guns take over. As weapons, they are more intimate than the naval cannon. Fired in batches, their missiles sail hissing through the air like a school of weird fish. They hit the earth, detonating mines, blasting barbed-wire entanglements, and unnerving the waiting enemy.
>
> We jump from the landing craft and wade ashore through the swirling water. From the hills the German guns begin to crack. An occasional shell lands in our midst. The medics roll up their sleeves and get busy. An explosion sounds on my left; and when the smoke lifts I see the torn body of a man who stepped on a mine. A medic bends over him, rises, and signals four litter bearers that their services will not be needed.[4]

It was not just young GIs who faced the uncertainties of war and the fear of sudden death as the landings began. Maj. Gen. John Dahlquist, commanding the 36th Division, wrote his wife, Ruth, about his concerns the night before the invasion. A veteran of two world wars, Dahlquist had been deputy chief of staff to General Eisenhower in 1943 and had led his combat-hardened "Texas" Division into battle at Salerno and Cassino in the bitter Italian campaign. "You will know dear . . . that I am thinking of you because I always do. I have no particular fear for myself except that I may not do well. If anything should happen, be brave dear. We have had a wonderful life together. You have been the perfect wife for me and I only live for the time when I can have you again. Goodnight dear. I love you more than anything else in the world."[5]

The next day Dahlquist was in the thick of the fighting as he directed his men onto the beaches and into the countryside of occupied France. There were losses, but Dragoon was progressing well. All three divisions landed against light opposition, although the 36th Division ran into pockets of determined Germans in its landing zone just east of Saint-Raphael. French commando units, the British 2nd Independent Parachute Brigade, the U.S. 517th Parachute Regimental Combat Team, and an American glider regimental combat team had taken critical objectives while the U.S. 1st Special Service Force took two offshore islands to protect the beachhead.[6]

Within twenty-four hours, the 6th Corps had advanced inland farther and faster than the invasion's planners had anticipated, and by the end of the day on the sixteenth Truscott's forces were firmly in control of the invasion bridgehead. U.S. casualties were surprisingly light: only 95 soldiers killed and 385 wounded. In all, 94,000 troops and 11,000 vehicles had landed by nightfall on the first day. The Allies took some 2,300 prisoners, many of them low-caliber infantrymen, either overage Germans or members of "Ost" units—Russians, Poles, and other eastern European troops who had "volunteered" for service in the German army and were often unreliable soldiers.[7]

On the day after the invasion, two divisions of General de Lattre's French troops came ashore over the American-held beaches and turned westward to take the cities of Toulon and Marseille, which would provide critical supply ports for the remainder of the war. To gain experience for the Dragoon landings, some of de Lattre's forces had attacked the island of Elba, Napoleon's former prison a few miles off the Italian coast near Tuscany. The French took the island after a short battle in June 1944. By August 20, the French were fighting in the outskirts of Toulon and were closing a ring around Marseille. Hitler had ordered the garrisons in both cities to fight to the death to prevent the Allies from gaining the two ports, but German resistance was quickly broken and the enemy surrendered on August 28. Dragoon's planners had estimated that it might take more than a month to capture both cities, and the quick victories were a welcome break for the Allies.[8]

While the French were taking Toulon and Marseille, Truscott's three U.S. divisions began their drive against the German Nineteenth Army in the interior of France. The American plan called for the 3rd Division to strike west to outflank Toulon and advance to the Rhone while in the center the 45th Division attacked directly north toward the town of Barjols. To the east, the 36th Division and an armored group, TF Butler, were to move north-northwest from Le Muy in the direction of Grenoble to protect the 6th Corps' right flank.[9] TF Butler was a mobile mechanized force comprising a cavalry squadron, two tank companies, and a battalion of motorized infantry along with artillery and support forces. Butler's tanks and mechanized cavalrymen were ordered to probe as far to the north as possible to assess German strength on the Nineteenth Army's left flank. If the opposition was light, Butler was to keep on going either to Grenoble or to outflank the retreating German forces coming up the Rhone Valley.

Devers and Patch considered two avenues of advance inland from the Riviera, one northwest up the Rhone Valley, the other north through the Alps to Grenoble. Devers saw the northerly route as a way to exploit German weakness in the region along the Franco-Italian frontier; the other offered a more accessible route to the Belfort Gap in southern Alsace, which provided an unobstructed corridor into southern Germany. He chose to exploit the Rhone Valley.

As Truscott and Patch pushed aggressively forward, General Wiese's situation became desperate. The 6th Corps converged on the retreating Nineteenth Army from three angles, and Wiese had no alternative but to retreat and fight a rearguard action if he was to save his men to fight in the coming battles in Alsace. For once, Hitler, who seldom allowed his generals to retreat, saw the hopelessness of Wiese's situation and ordered him to withdraw northeast toward the German frontier.

Wiese had seen much combat in his military career. He looked like a farmer, with a slender, angular face, but his eyes gave away his intelligence. He had survived four years in the trenches during World War I, then left the army after the war to become a policeman. During Germany's rearmament, he rejoined the military and was given command of an infantry battalion in the Polish campaign of 1939. By 1942 he was leading a division. In 1943 he became a corps commander on the eastern front, and in June 1944 he took command of the Nineteenth Army, which was guarding the Mediterranean coast against a seaborne assault.

Wiese's service on the Russian front had given him extensive experience in the art of defense, and he began a careful withdrawal up the Rhone Valley using a succession of defensive lines to hold off the Americans as he extracted his men. But Devers knew from Ultra intelligence intercepts what Wiese was up to. The Germans did not have the troops and the tanks to attack the extended flanks of the American pursuit force, and Patch ordered Truscott to drive north up the east bank of the Rhone as fast as possible in pursuit of the enemy.[10] After the French took Toulon and Marseille, they were to follow.[11]

The geography of the Rhone Valley canalized Wiese's forces, making them vulnerable to encirclement and flank attack as they retreated northward in a narrow file into the interior of France. They also provided concentrated targets for air attacks by Allied bombers and fighter-bombers. "The terrain . . . was the worst possible for the ordered withdrawal—mountains on both sides, many defiles, increasing activity of the Resistance movement, excellent possibilities for the enemy to block the routes of retreat," Wiese later wrote.[12] His objective was to reach and hold the city of Montélimar. If this strategy failed, he intended to retreat north into

Alsace, where he could turn east and reach the safety of the Vosges Mountains and the Belfort Gap.

Wiese had reason to be thankful that the Americans were pursuing him up the Rhone and not taking advantage of his weak left flank by directing the main thrust of their advance north toward Grenoble. TF Butler reached the town of Sisteron and then turned northwest toward Montélimar and the Rhone. Wiese believed the Allied strategy saved his army, and he expressed amazement that U.S. forces did not press forward to cut the road to the Belfort Gap, Wiese's escape route into Germany. But Truscott was intent on catching and trapping the German Nineteenth Army before it could reach Montélimar and its ring of protective gorges and cliffs some seventy-five miles up the Rhone from Marseille.

There was no better American commander to pursue Wiese than Lucian King Truscott Jr.[13] Trained as a cavalryman, he had a horse soldier's instinct for speed and maneuver, and even in the twilight of the cavalry he was often seen in riding pants and boots. He was forged in the mold of George Patton, a polo-playing teammate with whom he had served during the interwar years. "Sentimental and uxorious, he was also brusque, profane and capable of hocking tobacco with the most unlettered private in the Army. 'Polo games and wars aren't won by gentlemen,' he asserted." Truscott had a weathered face, protruding eyes that were slightly askew, and a voice as "raspy as a wood file." His dress tended toward the eccentric, and he often sported an enameled helmet, silk scarf, jodhpurs, and a red leather jacket.[14]

Truscott had enlisted in the U.S. Army as a private on America's entry into World War I. He had spent the previous six years as a teacher in one-room schoolhouses. He received his commission as a second lieutenant in the cavalry in 1917 and later served with Eisenhower's staff at Fort Lewis, Washington, where Ike was sufficiently impressed by Truscott's abilities and bearing to help advance him through the ranks. Sent as a brigadier general to Britain in 1942 to study British commando units and tactics, he accompanied the British and Canadians on the ill-fated 1942 raid against Dieppe, France, carried out to test the feasibility of a cross-channel attack. Truscott later organized the first U.S. Ranger units and led them into Port Lyautey in the 1942 northwest Africa invasion. In 1942–43, he served as field deputy to Eisenhower, and then became commanding general of the 3rd Infantry Division. After fighting in Africa and Sicily, he commanded the 6th Corps in Italy and took it into southern France.[15]

Despite his reputation as a hard-driving, no-nonsense commander, Truscott was sensitive to the terrible cost of war. Bill Mauldin, the well-known World War II *Stars and Stripes* cartoonist, wrote that at Memorial Day ceremonies at Anzio in 1945, Truscott faced the graves of his fallen soldiers and apologized to them for his share of responsibility in their deaths. He tearfully promised them that he would never speak of the glorious dead because he did not see much glory in getting killed in one's late teens or early twenties.[16]

Nevertheless, Truscott was a born fighter, and he hoped to trap Wiese's troops in the narrow confines of the Rhone Valley. Truscott had developed what his men called the "Truscott trot." His infantrymen, carrying weapons and full packs, were expected to cover thirty miles in eight hours; they marched at a speed of five and a half miles per hour for the first hour, four for the next two, and three-and-a-half for the next four. At that pace they would certainly catch Wiese before he reached Montélimar.[17]

But Wiese was a wily and experienced opponent; he took control of the heights north of Montélimar and held the city, and his artillery was able to break up American attempts to drive the Germans from their positions. By the time U.S. forces gained the commanding terrain on August 28, the Nineteenth Army had slipped beyond their clutches and was continuing its retreat northward.

Wiese's forces paid dearly for their escape. They left behind in Montélimar some three thousand vehicles, more than eighty artillery pieces, and five big railway guns.[18] Sergeant Murphy remembered the piles of wreckage and German corpses as he and his men passed through the city.

> On the outskirts of Montelimar, a huge enemy convoy has been caught by our artillery fire. In their haste to escape, the doomed vehicles had been moving two and three abreast. Our artillery zeroed them in. The destruction surpasses belief.
>
> As far as we can see, the road is cluttered with shattered, twisted cars, trucks and wagons. Many are still burning. Often the bodies of men lie in the flames; and the smell of singed hair and burnt flesh is strong and horrible.
>
> Hundreds of horses, evidently stolen from the French farmers, have been caught in the barrage. They look at us with puzzled, unblaming eyes, whinnying softly as their torn flesh waits for life to drain from it. We are used to the sight of dead and wounded men, but these shuddering animals affect us strangely. Perhaps we have been in the field too long to remember that innocence is also caught in the carnage of war.[19]

Devers too was appalled by the destruction as he followed the action from his headquarters. He was a general known to stay close to the fighting. Once, in Italy, he reconnoitered the Monte Cassino battlefield in a flimsy L-5 courier plane with Lt. Gen. Ira Eaker, commander of the Fifteenth Air Force, at the controls. The two generals skimmed over the mountaintop to assess German strength and got so close they could almost look the enemy paratroopers in the eye. "I could have dropped my binoculars into machine-gun nests," Eaker reported.[20]

After Devers surveyed the carnage around Montélimar he wrote to Georgie: "We really destroyed the German 19th Army. Never have I seen such destruction of equipment of all kinds, horses and men." His note was in stark contrast to previous letters describing the beauty of the French countryside, which seemed untouched by the war. "France is beautiful. The fields are luxuriant. Cattle seem to be in numbers. Fresh butter and eggs are in abundance as well as all kinds of vegetables and fruit."[21] But not around Montélimar.

The remnants of the Nineteenth Army plodded northeastward in retreat, but Truscott was determined to win the next round. He and Patch immediately devised a plan to block Wiese's escape route into Germany farther to the north, but the enemy general again was elusive. "The man knew his job," General de Lattre said of Wiese, who was forced to use all his knowledge to save his army. "It was no longer only his Nineteenth Army which he had to save from disaster: the First German Army was also swinging back in the direction of Burgundy, retiring in great disorder from central and south-western France. From Bayonne [on the Atlantic coast] to Nantes, except for the sacrificed garrisons of the Atlantic ports, the whole Wehrmacht was in flight."[22] It fell to Wiese to hold open the gateway to the Reich as long as possible.

Devers credited the 6th Army Group's efficient command structure for maintaining the Allied drive up the Rhone Valley on the heels of Wiese's fleeing army. Intelligence agents dropped behind enemy lines fed information back to the advancing armies and to the engineers, who began repairing bridges the Germans destroyed as they fled. FFI (French Forces of the Interior) units were also helpful in delaying the enemy's retreat and capturing strategic objectives behind the lines. Experienced combat engineer groups tested in North Africa and Italy, among them the 540th and 40th combat engineer regiments, were on call, and the 6th Army Group employed an armada of transport aircraft to deliver supplies to the advancing Americans. Every plane available played a part, but C-47s, many of which had been sitting idly on the sidelines, were the real workhorses.

After fleeing from Montélimar, Wiese led his troops northward toward Belfort. The town of Belfort lies at the opening of the Belfort Gap, a fifteen-mile-wide natural passageway between the southern end of the Vosges Mountains and the Jura Mountains in Switzerland that has been of great strategic importance in past wars because its deep, wide valley joins with the valleys of the Rhone and the Rhine. The breach it forms in the wall of the mountain ranges forms a passageway into Germany.[23]

If the Allies could cut the Nineteenth Army's escape route through the Belfort Gap, Wiese would have no alternative but to continue retreating northward into the High Vosges. From there he would have to attempt to get through the mountain passes and reach the Alsace Plain on the west bank of the Rhine. Truscott knew that Patton's Third Army was racing from Paris eastward into Lorraine and might be able to advance into Alsace to head off the Nineteenth Army before it retreated through the Vosges. Wiese would then be trapped between the forces of the 6th Army Group advancing from the south and the Third Army advancing from the west. Devers was confident that his forces could block the gap. His diary records that he "urged Patch . . . and all the supply people that they must keep up this drive until they crossed the Rhine River and established bridgeheads at which time we would undoubtedly have to pick up our pieces before we could go on unless SHAEF could supply us with fresh troops."[24]

Truscott's attempts to entrap the Nineteenth Army had the support of de Lattre's Free French, who pushed northward up the Rhone Valley after taking Marseille and Toulon. "Armee B" grew daily in size, and after September 15, 1944, was designated the French First Army.[25] By war's end the army comprised some 290,000 men arranged in two army corps: the 1st Corps under Maj. Gen. Antoine Béthouart, and the 2nd Corps led by Gen. Joseph de Goiselard de Monsabert.

General Patch ordered de Lattre's divisions to advance together north toward Grenoble and guard the 6th Corps' right flank against possible enemy attacks coming from the Franco-Italian border. De Lattre's pride was hurt by Patch's command. He had come to liberate his homeland, and he knew quite well that his army would see little action on this flank. He appealed the new order to Devers, who was wise enough to recognize and understand the French general's frustration. Devers suggested that Patch send the French 2nd Corps up the west bank of the Rhone and then attack Lyon from the west. Devers also realized that the terrain on the west bank was a particularly good place for de Lattre to use his armored forces.[26]

With Patch's approval, the French 2nd Corps—comprising the French 1st Armored Division and the French 1st Infantry Division—were quickly deployed as a screening force west of the Rhone to protect the U.S. 6th Corps' left flank as it moved north toward Lyon and Dijon. The German forces remaining in western France constituted a threat to the Allied invasion forces; Allied intelligence estimates put the number of enemy troops in the Bordeaux region alone at 25,000.[27] The French 1st Corps thus advanced north toward Grenoble on the east bank of the Rhone to act as a right flank guard for U.S. forces. Once Truscott's U.S. troops reached Lyon, both French corps would unite as the French First Army, operating east of the U.S. 6th Corps along the French-Swiss border, and advance on the Belfort Gap.[28]

De Lattre was an experienced if excitable warrior who won the respect of the Americans as he moved his army toward the Rhine. Like Devers he had served as a cavalryman in World War I, but transferred to the infantry, where he rose to command a battalion and was wounded four times. After the war, he served in colonial Morocco, where he was wounded in 1925, and then returned to attend the prestigious French War College. When war broke out in 1939, he became the youngest general in French history. He commanded the French 14th Infantry Division until the French and Germans signed an armistice, then remained on active duty commanding Vichy French forces in Tunisia in 1941 and the French 16th Division in 1942. He began organizing an anti-German force and was arrested and sentenced to a ten-year jail sentence, but he escaped to Algiers and took command of Armee B.[29]

As the Americans and French approached the Belfort Gap, Wiese struggled to keep the passageway open, fighting a well-orchestrated rearguard delaying action. He made a brief stand at the ancient walled city of Besançon, about forty miles southwest of Belfort, as American troops closed in from the north, west, and south. Truscott continued to press. On September 8, he urged his forces to "make every effort to entrap enemy formations regardless of size. . . . Contact once gained must be maintained. The enemy must not be allowed to escape. Every attack must be pressed with the utmost vigor. Be vicious. Seek to kill and destroy."[30]

But once again Wiese was the better general. He maneuvered the Nineteenth Army into Belfort and slammed the door behind him by establishing a defensive line between the Doubs and Moselle Rivers. He knew that with a concerted effort the Americans and French could break through his meager forces and race toward the Rhine. "As long as the enemy did not turn up for a continuous general attack on a broad front," Wiese's chief of staff, Generalleutnant Walter Botch, later wrote, "the [Nineteenth] Army was still able . . . to fend off the enemy attacks in bitter fighting in defense, withdrawing and counter attacking."[31] Had an armored division been assigned to the Dragoon forces, Botch added, they could have taken Grenoble and cut off the German escape route to the Belfort Gap. He also noted: "It strikes a German military observer very forcibly that the American Army does not greatly believe in the formation of centers of gravity to the extent that the German Army has practiced in the past. It was as if the American still saw themselves fighting widely separated bands of Indians."[32]

Despite these deficiencies, the understrength, underpowered 6th Army Group had made a magnificent showing in its first month of operations. By September 20, as Devers took stock, he realized that he had come close to destroying an entire German army. In the first two weeks of combat after the landings on the Mediterranean coast, the 6th Army Group had captured 57,000 German prisoners while suffering only 6,700 casualties; ultimately, the American and French forces captured about 70,000 German troops in the first month of operations. Nor were the Germans' losses in manpower alone. As the Germans retreated from

Montélimar they abandoned thousands of vehicles that could never be replaced. The German Nineteenth Army had been whittled down to shattered battalions that now faced five American and French combat divisions.

Dragoon had been a major success. All of southern France was cleared of Germans, and Eisenhower had nothing but praise for the operation. "There was no development of that period which added more decisively to our advantages or aided us more in accomplishing the final and complete defeat of the German forces than did the secondary attack coming up the Rhone Valley," Ike later wrote.[33] *The Second World War: Europe and the Mediterranean*, a history published by West Point, praises Devers' leadership in directing Dragoon: "One of the most important considerations was the flexibility and aggressiveness of the high level leadership. In this regard Devers exercised considerable influence as the army group commander designate."[34]

The task that now fell to the 6th Army Group was to regroup and finish the job of driving the Nineteenth Army from Alsace and back into Germany.

# CHAPTER 6

# To the Siegfried Line

★ ★ ★ ★

As the 6th Army Group had prepared to invade southern France in July 1944, the Allied armies in Normandy were still engaged in a desperate struggle to break out of the narrow bridgehead they had established on the coast of Calvados. The heady first days after the successful D-day landings on June 6 had turned into weeks of frustration as Field Marshal Rommel's Seventh Army troops fought with typical German determination to prevent the Allies from advancing deeper into France. Field Marshal Montgomery's British and Canadian forces were held to limited gains in the open country around the city of Caen, and the Americans were bogged down in the Bocage, a region laced with swampy ground and miles of dense, towering hedgerows that framed every field and pasture. Advances came only a few yards at a time as soldiers on both sides of the hedgerows slugged it out in deadly games of cat and mouse. American lieutenant Jack Shea expressed the frustration of all when he noted, "Give me ten infantrymen in this terrain with the proper combination of small arms and we will hold up a battalion for 24 hours."[1]

All June and July, it seemed that the predictions of Allied planners prior to D-day were coming true and the Allies would fight protracted battles of attrition across France for at least a year before reaching the Siegfried Line in May 1945. Allied commanders had expected the German army to fall back through northern France and Belgium in a deliberate and painstaking retreat, making use of rivers, rugged ground, and fortifications to stop or stall the Allied advance. The hedgerows and the mud of the Norman spring negated the superior mobility of the Allied armies with their hordes of trucks, jeeps, and tanks; the tanks could not move among the hedgerows, and the battle lines were so close that even air support was limited. What the Germans lacked in armor and airpower they made up for in terrain and tenacity.[2]

In a desperate gamble to break out of Normandy and gain maneuver room for his highly mechanized and mobile army, General Bradley devised a plan to smash his way out of the bridgehead by employing raw air power. Hundreds of heavy and medium bombers were assigned to blast a hole in a narrow section of German front west of the ancient Norman city of Saint-Lô. Bradley expected the shock and destruction of the attack to be so devastating that the Germans would be unable to recover and the Americans could push several divisions through the breach.

The attack, code-named Cobra, came on the morning of July 25, 1944. The air above the battle lines throbbed from the motors of 1,500 B-24 Liberators and B-17 Flying Fortresses, each carrying fragmentation bombs to drop on the German infantry. Escorting the bombers were hundreds of fighter planes from airfields in Britain.[3]

"They came with a terrible slowness," Ernie Pyle wrote of the approaching planes. "They came in flights of twelve, three flights to a group, and in groups stretched out across the sky. They came in families of about seventy planes each. . . . I had a feeling that even had God appeared beseechingly before them in the sky with palms outstretched to persuade them back, they would not have within them the power to turn their irresistible course. . . . There is no description of the sound and fury of those bombs except to say it was chaos, and a waiting for darkness. The feeling of the blast was sensational. The air struck us in hundreds of continuing flutters. Our ears drummed and rang."[4] The German troops, only yards away from the American lines in their foxholes and trenches, could only watch in terror.

As the dust and debris rose in a giant cloud over Normandy, Gen. Fritz Bayerlein, commander of the elite Panzer Lehr Division, tried to maintain control of his forces. "After an hour I had no communication with anybody, even by radio. By noon nothing was visible but dust and smoke. My front lines looked like the face of the moon and at least 70 percent of my troops were knocked out—dead, wounded, crazed or numb."[5]

When the barrage finally ended, Maj. Gen. Lawton Collins' U.S. 7th Corps troops plunged through a moonscape of 60,000 craters, smashed artillery pieces, overturned tanks, and dazed and dead German troops. Progress was slow at first as the Americans struggled through the fractured landscape, but soon thousands of American troops began pouring through the breach. The German front was broken, and the Allies finally had the enemy on the run in northern France.

By August, fifteen American divisions were fighting in northern France, formed into two armies, the First and the Third, both pushing east toward Paris and the Seine. The reeling Germans attempted to regain the initiative and stem the Allied advance. Hitler ordered a ferocious counterattack toward the strategically positioned town of Avranches at the base of the Cotentin Peninsula. His objective was to split Bradley's First and Third armies and then to envelop and destroy the Third.

But intelligence intercepts had warned the Americans that the attack was coming, and the ensuing struggle, now referred to as the Battle of the Falaise Pocket, turned into a disaster for the Germans. The enemy's Seventh and Fifth panzer armies attacked head-on into the American front, but the Third Army, attacking from the south, and the U.S. First Army and British and Canadian armies, closing from the north, quickly enveloped their thrust.

The struggle developed into the largest tank battle fought on the western front in World War II. It ranged over eight hundred square miles of French countryside and lasted nearly two weeks. The Allies set a trap for the advancing Germans, drawing them forward like a spider waiting for prey to strike its web. Field Marshal Gunther von Kluge, Rommel's successor in France, saw the snare and urged Hitler to call off the ill-fated attack and withdraw to defensive positions on the east bank of the Seine. But the Führer refused and ordered his troops to drive forward.[6]

When the trap was sprung, the Allies nearly encircled two German armies. They took more than 200,000 prisoners and killed as many as 50,000 enemy troops, but failed to capture another 300,000 Germans who escaped over the Seine. These troops were little more than a disorganized rabble fleeing for their lives to the Siegfried Line. They had lost much of their equipment, including tanks, guns, and trucks, and their losses in human life shocked even Eisenhower.

"The battlefield at Falaise was unquestionably one of the greatest 'killing grounds' of any of the war areas," Eisenhower later wrote. "Roads, highways, and fields were so choked with destroyed equipment and with dead men and animals that passage through the area was extremely difficult. Forty-eight hours after the closing of the gap I was conducted through it on foot, to encounter scenes that could be described only by Dante. It was literally possible to walk for hundreds of yards at a time, stepping on nothing but dead and decaying flesh."[7] The Americans soon took Paris and kept advancing into the broad flatlands of eastern France on the heels of the Wehrmacht. By early September, some U.S. troops had crossed into Nazi Germany.

The collapse of the German armies in France in late July was so complete that Eisenhower authorized a rare change of plan from the pre-invasion Overlord strategy. The Allied armies would not halt at the Seine to regroup and resupply as originally planned; instead, Ike ordered his commanders to cross the river and continue in pursuit of the enemy.[8] The advance across France now became relentless as the Allied armies chased the Germans to the Siegfried Line, sometimes covering as many as sixty miles a day. Germans outrun by the rapidly advancing Allied armored divisions were surrounded and either killed or taken prisoner by the American and British infantry divisions plodding along behind. Historian Martin Blumenson describes the pursuit as resembling "a stampede of wild horses . . . fast and fluid, almost without control."[9]

Only in a few instances did the Germans try to make a stand, usually at river crossing sites. The inadequacy of the German forces, their lack of communications, their drastic shortages of equipment, and what seemed to be command confusion on the lower levels led to the abandonment of any pretense of establishing a line anywhere except at the West Wall. . . . For the soldiers, the countryside had become a monotonous blur of changing scenery. Their eyes bloodshot and tear-filled from sun, wind, dust and weariness, they followed the blinding road all day long and at night strained to keep the cat eyes of the vehicles ahead in sight.[10]

The enemy's situation was near catastrophic.

By the end of August, euphoria blinded the Allied camp. The northern armies were nearing the Siegfried Line, and Devers' forces had landed in southern France and were closing on the Reich from the south. A SHAEF intelligence summary declared: "The August battles have done it and the enemy in the West has had it. Two-and-a-half months of bitter fighting have brought the end of the war in Europe within sight, almost within reach." Another Allied intelligence estimate predicted that "organized resistance under the control of the German High Command is unlikely to continue beyond 1 December 1944, and [the war] may end even sooner."[11]

The Allied Control Commission, established to govern Germany following the war, was preparing to begin operations in Berlin by November 1.[12] The belief that the Germans were on their last legs persisted for weeks. General Marshall was so convinced of impending victory that he considered unleashing one of America's secret weapons, the proximity artillery fuse, to hasten the war's end. The proximity fuse was a radio device implanted in the tip of an artillery shell, designed to detonate electronically within yards or feet of an enemy target on the ground or in the air. The Americans had not yet used the fuse because they feared the Germans would retrieve one that failed to explode and copy the technology. In the hands of the enemy, the fuse could have caused havoc among American bombers.[13] Prime Minister Winston Churchill openly expressed his belief that the war in Europe would be over by Christmas. "Our Armies are racing to the Belgian frontier, faster by far than went the Panzers in 1940," Churchill wrote. "There is a feeling of elation, of expectancy and almost bewilderment, and it may well be that the end is now very close."[14]

The Germans' situation in the west was indeed critical. German generals knew that the Wehrmacht in northern France and Belgium had virtually ceased to exist as a cohesive force and could do nothing to stop the American and British armies from overrunning the Reich. In the last week of August 1944, the various Allied commanders began planning for a quick end to the war, possibly before Christmas, and they pushed forward as fast as they could to partake in the coming German defeat.

CHAPTER 7.

# Broad Front or Single Thrust?

★ ★ ★ ★

The Allies seemed unstoppable in August 1944. The Allied armies in northern France crossed the Seine on August 20 at the same time that Jacob Devers' 6th Army Group began its rapid advance up the Rhone on the heels of the German Nineteenth Army. Bernard Montgomery's 21st Army Group troops, comprising Lt. Gen. H. D. G. Crerar's First Canadian and Lt. Gen. Miles Dempsey's Second British armies, rolled along the English Channel coast, over the haunting British battlefields of World War I, through Rouen and Amiens, and across the Somme to Lille. They continued into Belgium and took Brussels on September 3, 1944.

In the center of the Allied line, Hodges' First Army advanced through Soissons to Mons and on to Namur in Belgium, where General Bradley would later establish his 12th Army Group headquarters, and continued its advance to the German border near Aachen. Patton's Third Army, on the First Army's southern flank, crossed the Marne River, drove over the American World War I battlefield at Château-Thierry, and continued on to Reims, while a second column of Patton's troops fought all the way to Nancy. The extreme right wing of the Allied line south of Paris would remain exposed and hanging until the 6th Army Group linked up with Patton's Third on September 14.

From the narrow bridgehead in Normandy—no more than 30 miles deep and 50 miles wide—the northern Allied armies had advanced some 300 miles to the German border in less than a month, fanning out to create a front that extended 275 miles from the North Sea coast in Belgium to Lorraine in eastern France.[1] The Allies advanced from Paris into Belgium in less than two weeks. On September 11, 1944, troops of the U.S. 5th Armored Division crossed the German frontier south of Aachen to claim credit for being the first Allied troops to set foot on enemy soil. Soon patrols from other American divisions were crossing into Germany. On the evening of the eleventh, a reinforced company of the 28th Division crossed the Our River into the German village of Sevenig while a patrol from the 4th Infantry Division crossed the Our into the village of Hemmeres. To prove that they had been in Germany, the patrol from the 4th brought back German currency, a German cap, and a packet of soil. But the Rhine was still 40 miles away.[2]

Devers' U.S. Seventh and French First armies had finally pushed General Wiese's Nineteenth Army back into the foothills of the Vosges Mountains by mid-September and were preparing to press on through the mountains to the Alsace Plain; after that, the Rhine and then Germany. Devers' 6th Army Group came under Eisenhower's command on September 15, 1944.

The unexpectedly rapid Allied advance across northern France and up the Rhone Valley raised questions about future Allied strategy. Prior to D-day, Overlord planners had targeted the Ruhr industrial area as the most important Allied objective, with the Saar industrial area in southern Germany being the secondary goal. There seemed little dispute about the importance of these objectives, although the British believed Allied forces should concentrate on the Ruhr.

The swift advance exposed the difference in British and American strategies on how best to achieve these objectives. The ensuing disagreements were an unwelcome burden and diversion for Eisenhower. They soured or complicated his relations with his top generals, and they affected the tactical and strategic decisions he would make in the conduct of the war in the west. Some historians have speculated that these concerns aggravated the supreme commander's already delicate relationship with Devers and distracted Ike from employing the 6th Army Group in more productive ways.

Eisenhower proposed a "broad front" approach of fighting the enemy. He wanted the British and American armies to advance abreast in two wide columns. Montgomery's 21st Army Group would attack through Belgium north of the Ardennes Forest with the objective of entering Germany north of Cologne to capture the Ruhr industrial area while Bradley's 12th Army Group attacked south of the Ardennes to take the Saar industrial region and then advanced into Germany to help Montgomery take the Ruhr.[3] Devers' 6th Army Group, which had been in action a little more than a month by mid-September, did not figure into SHAEF's plans except to protect Patton's right flank.[4]

The British, in contrast, favored a "single thrust" offensive. Montgomery in particular never tired of disputing Eisenhower's broad front strategy, arguing that wars are won by concentrating overwhelming power at the point of attack to break through enemy defenses, and not by dispersing those forces. Monty wanted the 21st and 12th army groups to advance side by side in one massive army to smash through the German line north of the Ardennes and capture the Ruhr. Afterward the two army groups would turn east and drive rapidly to take Berlin. Keeping the 21st and 12th army groups separated by the Ardennes Forest, Monty argued, would dilute Allied strength because two smaller armies attacking separately would not have the punch and momentum of one massive offensive. A broad front attack would grind to a halt in the Siegfried Line's defenses, and the delay would allow the enemy time to regroup. Monty believed his strategy would end the war by Christmas 1944.

Eisenhower argued that the Allies could not hope to destroy the German army in the west with a single, bold, powerful attack into Germany's industrial heart. The enemy, he said, would meet any Allied thrust head-on and would hurl counterattacks against its exposed flanks. Only by engaging the enemy all along the front and forcing German commanders to spread their defenses could the Allies win the war. The Allies' advantage in men and matériel would eventually wear the Germans down.[5]

Eisenhower's broad front strategy was in keeping with American military doctrine that drew on the U.S. experience in the Civil War. Gen. Ulysses S. Grant had used this strategy in his campaigns in Virginia, and the weight of the Union Army's numbers and firepower eventually overcame Confederate resistance. But this approach had distinct disadvantages. It was achieved only with heavy casualties, and it entailed the loss of surprise and maneuver.[6]

Overlord's planners had developed the broad front plan prior to the Normandy invasion. Monty offered no objection at the time because he was focusing on training his troops and getting them ashore into France. Strategies on how best to fight the Germans could wait until the Allies were well established in Normandy. He viewed the postinvasion strategy developed prior to Overlord merely as a guideline to be altered as circumstances required. The adage that few military plans survive contact with the enemy pertained here, Monty believed, and he assumed that the original plan would change as the Allies measured German capabilities and strength. He also expected to be named the Allied field commander, handling day-to-day tactical operations and controlling the strategy used to defeat the enemy.[7] Monty was not named field commander, however; Eisenhower was, and thus Ike's broad front concept won the day. Further, Eisenhower also remained supreme commander. He had the final say.[8]

Eisenhower's adherence to the broad front strategy was motivated as much by political factors as military ones. Nationalistic considerations had to be addressed to maintain the Anglo-American alliance. Implementing Montgomery's single thrust plan would place large numbers of American troops under British command or at least subservient to British direction, and Ike knew the American public would not stand for that. Additionally, if Monty's plan succeeded in defeating the Germans, he would be the general credited with defeating Hitler, also a politically unacceptable situation for the Americans. On the other hand, if an American general won all the accolades, the British public would be up in arms. Ike simply could not permit any one general, army, or nation to receive all the laurels for defeating Nazi Germany if he was to keep the coalition afloat, and the broad front strategy gave him better control over his generals.[9]

Serious differences between the British and Americans that could have destroyed or impaired the alliance were evident from the very beginning of the coalition in 1942 when American commanders, including Eisenhower, began arriving in Britain to coordinate the war effort. The two sides regarded each other with suspicion and condescension. The Americans found their British counterparts "insufferable" and arrogant. The British belittled the Yanks as newcomers with no idea how to fight a war, particularly against an enemy as formidable as the Germans. Even the diplomatic Ike remarked that he found the British "stiff-necked." On one of his first encounters with Montgomery as supreme commander Eisenhower casually lit a cigarette, only to be haughtily admonished by the clean-living Monty: "I don't permit smoking in my office."[10]

The British made no secret of their contempt for America's military leaders. Field Marshal Alan Brooke, chief of the Imperial General Staff, commented that Marshall was "rather overfilled with his own importance" and dismissed Eisenhower as a lightweight with no strategic sense and insufficient command experience.[11] To his credit, Ike never let on publicly how he felt about his British critics. A supreme commander with lesser diplomatic skills and less self-confidence than Eisenhower might have been unable to forge the British and Americans into an effective alliance.[12]

By 1944, the United States was providing the bulk of the troops and matériel for the war in Europe. The American public expected a lion's share of the credit for winning the conflict and was sensitive to any slights by the British. In the subsequent rapid advance across France in August 1944, the American people and President Roosevelt complained that Montgomery and the British were stealing the headlines because Monty received most of the acclaim for the breakout from Normandy. The Americans were advancing at a faster pace then the British, but their successes went unpublicized largely because the U.S. command imposed strict censorship on the American press, which could not publish the names of captured cities. British newspapers had greater liberty in that regard. Ike also kept Patton's name off the front page, hoping to continue the deception that Patton remained in command of the 1st U.S. Army Group, a phantom army based in southern England, designed to trick the Germans into believing that a second attack on the French coast would come through the Pas de Calais, the logical site—the Germans believed—for Allied invasion forces to land.[13] Located adjacent to the Belgian frontier, Pas de Calais was also closer to Germany. The enemy had been completely fooled by the ruse throughout the summer of 1944. The German

Fifteenth Army was kept around Calais awaiting a second invasion instead of sent to assist the German Seventh Army in Normandy, where the combined forces might have defeated the Allied invasion.

The British, for their part, had once confronted Hitler alone, and they believed they should share equally in victory even if their contribution to the war was diminishing. Tiny Britain could hardly compete with the United States in troop numbers or industrial output, but its spirit had saved Western civilization. In November 1944, the United States was fielding some 2,588,983 troops in Europe while the British could field only 807,028. By May 1945 the Americans had 3,021,483 troops in Europe while the British had 907,553.[14] British troops were fighting around the world to protect the interests of the empire, and Britain had few resources left to send into France. Ike had the nearly impossible task of ensuring that neither the British nor the Americans felt neglected.

Cultural differences played at least some role in the conflict between the American and British generals. The Americans had built their nation overnight, in the historical sense, and were apt to do things in a seat-of-the pants fashion with little forethought or preparation. They also had vast amounts of supplies and resources—including men—to squander. The British tended to think things through more carefully before acting, in part because their resources were limited. This difference manifested itself on the battlefield in the manner in which the two armies fought the enemy. The Germans often observed that the Americans were more flexible in combat and were quick to give ground. At the same time, they were equally quick to maneuver and attack, and to take advantage of the terrain. The Germans saw the British as more dogged in defense; they held their ground until overwhelmed. They were also more tenacious but less agile and imaginative in the attack.

The difference between the British and American methods of war was most evident in the ways in which Patton and Montgomery conducted operations. Nigel Hamilton, author of a biography of Monty, observes: "Patton believed that the exercise of command in battle was an art and 'he who tries to define it closely is a fool'— whereas it was Bernard Montgomery's great belief that command could be defined, and ought to be something so clear, so widely known among his subordinates, and so well rehearsed that victory over 'any enemy anywhere' was assured."[15]

The enmity between the two camps, particularly between Montgomery and the American generals, was always near the surface and ready to boil over. It began during the North African and Italian campaigns in 1942 and 1943, and now threatened the existence of the alliance.[16] In the later stages of the North African campaign Montgomery had proposed a decisive attack on Rommel's Afrika Corps in Tunisia that would have excluded full American participation. Eisenhower, at that time the supreme commander in North Africa, admonished Monty that such an act could alienate the American public and cause irreparable harm to the Allied cause. If the British believed the Americans were too inexperienced to fight the Germans, Ike warned, America would simply focus its attention and resources on the Japanese in the Pacific theater.[17]

The American officers, who were extremely sensitive about their lack of war experience, were angered by the low British opinion of American soldiers and generalship in North Africa. Temperatures reached the boiling point in 1942 and 1943 when the British referred to the Americans as "our Italians," a reference to the poor fighting qualities of the Italian troops fighting alongside the Germans.[18] The Americans dismissed these charges as unfair criticism of green U.S. troops and pointed in turn to the string of British defeats at the hands of the Germans in the early days of the war. The British Eighth Army, they were quick to point out, had fled in disarray before Rommel's Afrika Korps.[19]

During the invasion of Sicily, the ill will between the Allied commanders had serious consequences when Patton and Bradley decided that Monty intended to steal all the glory. Montgomery's Eighth Army was assigned to take the port city of Messina, the main objective of the campaign, while the U.S. 7th Army, commanded by Patton, was given the inglorious task of moving through the arid central part of the island to protect Monty's left flank as he moved up the east coast. Monty would certainly capture the headlines when he marched triumphantly into Messina, but Patton was damned if he would let Monty get there first. He raced up the center of the island and then across the northern rim of Sicily. He even ordered a risky amphibious landing by Truscott's 3rd Division troops behind enemy lines on Sicily's northern coast. Monty was incensed when, contrary to all expectations and preinvasion planning, Patton took Messina before the British. Bradley recorded the generals' conflict in Sicily in his memoirs. "Our slow progress was most disconcerting to Patton," he wrote, "because he had now become determined to 'beat Montgomery to Messina.' I was equally anxious to beat Monty to Messina. . . . For a long time our men had been ridiculed by the British media in Sicily. It seemed fitting revenge to rob Monty of the triumphant march into Messina."[20]

The animosity between the rival generals came to full bloom again in France in 1944. Who was to be the chosen one to strike the fatal blow against Germany: Patton, Montgomery, Bradley, or all of them? Patton's troops rode in a perpetual cloud of dust as though they were chasing marauding Indians in the American West. Patton often had little idea where his units were and was concerned mainly with their continued advance. Montgomery was deliberate to the point of inaction. He would attack only when every aspect of his plan had been set in place and was ready to go. He regarded the American commanders as inferior generals with untrained military minds, and the Americans saw him as a condescending, supercilious, silly little charlatan. He was so unmilitary in his strange habits and garb that the American generals loved to ridicule him. Major Hansen, Bradley's aide, recalled Monty appearing at a top command meeting dressed "in an old loose fitting gabardine hunting jacket with bellows pockets that seemed to accentuate its flappiness, a gray sweater, corduroy trousers and the well known beret" that gave him the appearance of "a poorly tailored bohemian painter."[21] Churchill wrote perhaps the best description of Montgomery: "In retreat indomitable; in advance invincible; in victory insufferable!"

But Montgomery was not just another general. He was a national hero. Monty stood as the symbol of Great Britain and the British Empire and had to be treated with greater deference than Eisenhower's American generals. Even Bradley recognized Monty's lofty stature. "The thin, bony, ascetic face that stared from an unmilitary turtle-neck sweater had, in little over a year, become the symbol of victory in the eyes of the Allied world."[22]

Once he was established in France with his 21st Army Group, Montgomery again made no secret of his disdain for Eisenhower's performance as a field commander. He told Alan Brooke that Eisenhower was "quite useless" as a ground commander and was even more derogatory in his diary, where he wrote that Eisenhower's "ignorance as to how to run a war is absolute and complete."[23] Monty would also write, "Eisenhower himself does not really know anything about the business of fighting the Germans; he has not got the right sort of chaps on his staff for the job, and no one there understands the matter."[24] Brooke shared Montgomery's opinion, believing Eisenhower to be at heart a staff officer with little knowledge of the realities of the battlefield; like many senior American generals (Brooke excepted Douglas MacArthur), he adhered to the classic Civil War doctrine of frontal assault in which "everybody attacks all the time."[25]

Eisenhower somehow kept the lid on the internal squabbling and ignored the professional insults, but these petty rivalries consumed his energies and obscured his military vision. Ironically, Monty liked Ike personally and called him "a very nice chap," while Eisenhower did not much care for Montgomery the person but greatly respected his military acuity and may have put up with Montgomery's impossible behavior because of this esteem. Nevertheless, Ike had to contend with this temperamental and difficult man, the vaunted victor at El Alamein, and his patience may well have preserved the U.S.-British alliance. Monty was not the only difficult personality Ike had to deal with, of course, but he proved to be the most persistent, self-centered, persuasive, and powerful of Eisenhower's generals—and the greatest thorn in his side. Patton's idiosyncrasies were just as disruptive as Monty's; some people even thought he was crazy. But Ike could control Patton with threats of dismissal.

Bernard Law Montgomery's behavior stemmed at least in part from a difficult childhood. He was the unplanned child of a tyrannical mother and a submissive, browbeaten father who became the Anglican bishop of Tasmania, where Montgomery spent his childhood from 1889 to 1902. "He was the bad boy . . . mischievous by nature and individualist by character," his brother Donald once said. His mother, Maud, dispensed no love and dealt him regular beatings. Montgomery himself later said: "My early life was a series of fierce battles from which my mother invariably emerged the victor." His struggles with Maud stunted Bernard's emotional development and turned him into a shy young man with "no charm at all," recalled a boyhood schoolmate, who described him as "a difficult, unattractive school companion." Maud Montgomery was so overbearing that she tried to rule her son even when he was not in her presence. If she did not know Bernard's whereabouts she would order one of his four other siblings to "go and find out what Bernard is doing and tell him to stop it." Montgomery responded by being wayward. Once when Maud assembled the children to give them instructions for an upcoming family party he displayed the outrageous feistiness that distinguished him as Eisenhower's unruly subordinate a half century later. Young Bernard yelled out: "Silence in the pig market, the old sow speaks first." Needless to say he was led away for severe punishment.

Although he was a good athlete, Montgomery performed poorly in academics at the prestigious St. Paul's School after the family returned to England. He was drawn to the military, an interest that only reinforced his parents' belief that he would amount to little in life. Montgomery won an appointment to Sandhurst, the British military academy, where he immediately took to army life and did well. He advanced to the rank of lance corporal but was assigned to a company known for its unruly ways. Always the rebel, Bernard was soon involved in scandal when he and fellow miscreants in his company set fire to another cadet, who suffered burns severe enough to land him in the hospital. Only Maud Montgomery's intercession on her son's behalf saved his army career; he lost his rank but was allowed to stay in the army. His biographer speculated that the behavior that so perplexed and vexed Eisenhower forty later was born of revolt, first against his mother and later against the English aristocracy. Monty's family lacked the wealth and status of many of the St. Paul's and Sandhurst students, and his antics were in part an attack on the class system.[26]

His first assignment was in India, and when World War I broke out in 1914, the young Lieutenant Montgomery was in the thick of the fighting in France; he was severely wounded in the chest in late 1914. After recuperating, Montgomery went back to the western front and gained a reputation as a talented division staff officer in a series of posts until the war ended. But while he was regarded as a superb officer, he was still something of a strange duck—celibate, argumentative, and often unpleasant. In the immediate postwar years Captain Montgomery was assigned to the British army's staff college at Camberly, which had returned to its prewar status as a gentleman's club where socializing, hunting, and networking trumped officer training. As a serious student of warfare, tactics, and strategy, Montgomery threw himself into the course, to the irritation of many of his colleagues. "I was critical and intolerant," he later admitted. His brother, Brian, recalled that Montgomery was regarded as a "bloody menace." So unpopular was Brevet-Major Montgomery that there was a story making the rounds that one student's punishment for a college infraction was to be sentenced to have breakfast beside the unpopular Montgomery for a week. Nevertheless, Montgomery was developing concepts from his experiences in World War I that he would carry into World War II. The young infantry lieutenant in 1914 had seen the effects of lack of training, planning, and leadership and the fog of war once men are engaged in combat. Later, as a staff officer, he saw the importance of coordinating the various branches of the military on the battlefield. Montgomery had learned that "if offenses are planned on a sound tactical understanding; if the troops are well-trained and have limited, realistic and identifiable objectives; and if the full weight of modern artillery is intelligently brought to bear on a concentrated front, there is almost nothing the enemy can do except withdraw." He later added, "All through history, from the days of the great phalanx of the Roman Legion, the master law of tactics remains unchanged: this Law is that to achieve success you must be superior at the point where you intend to strike the decisive blow." That, in a nutshell, was Monty's theory of war; it would run counter to that advocated by the Americans and was at the root of the conflict between Ike and Montgomery.

By 1939 Montgomery had risen to the rank of major general. In 1940 he commanded the 3rd Division and later the British 2nd Corps in France before falling back to Dunkirk in June 1940. He spent the next two years in relative obscurity in Great Britain, training troops and preparing for Armageddon with Nazi Germany until August 1942, when Lieutenant General Montgomery was summoned to Egypt to assume command of the British Eighth Army. His orders were clear: destroy Rommel's Afrika Korps and drive the Germans from North Africa. In November, he launched the attack at El Alamein that would lead to Rommel's eventual defeat and to Montgomery's rise to near sainthood among the British people.

But Alamein changed Montgomery. After that victory he underwent a transformation that startled family, friends, and colleagues. "The ambitious but essentially shy and—in all but military affairs—quite humble general became boastful, vain and anxious to gain the limelight—alone. Those who were fond of him . . . watched with shame the way Bernard cut his family, lorded it over his friends and abused those to whom he owed so much. To the end of his life he would mix Christian benevolence with acts of stunning condescension or even malevolence." This later version of Montgomery was the man that Dwight Eisenhower came to know and had to work with from late 1942 to the end of World War II in 1945.

The fact that Eisenhower managed to deal with the now vainglorious British field marshal attests to Ike's ability as a tactful politician. Nevertheless, there were times during the summer and fall campaigns in France and the Low Countries in 1944 when Monty's behavior toward Ike would have brought instant dismissal if he had been an American commander; but Eisenhower always pulled back from firing him. In one private session between the two, Montgomery lambasted Ike, asserting that the latter's broad front strategy would fail. He accused the supreme commander of double-crossing him, implied that Patton was running the war, and demanded that he be named field commander for all Allied forces in western Europe. Any other Eisenhower subordinate would have been fired on the spot, but Ike merely warned him, "Steady Monty! You can't speak to me like that. I'm your boss."[27] One British general remarked with condescension that Ike avoided direct criticism of Montgomery because Ike "knew jolly well that . . . Monty would run circles around him with a clear exposition of his strategy and tactics."[28] Ike's chief of staff, Gen. Walter Bedell Smith, became increasingly frustrated by Eisenhower's inability to deal with Montgomery. Smith "felt Eisenhower lacked the moral courage and 'firmness of will' to handle Montgomery."[29]

In deference to Montgomery's perceived military genius, Eisenhower altered his broad front plan as the ground war in France progressed. Although he stuck to his plan for smaller, parallel advances north and south of the Ardennes, Ike compromised and ordered Hodges' First Army to veer north of the Ardennes alongside Montgomery's 21st Army Group to cover Monty's right flank as he enveloped the Ruhr. Hodges, however, remained under Bradley's command to ensure that no U.S. troops fell under the command of a foreign general.

Montgomery was not mollified by this small change. He insisted to Ike that he needed the entire 12th Army Group to accomplish his mission. The 21st Army Group together with the entire 12th Army Group could advance north of the Ardennes in an unstoppable drive toward the Ruhr. The American generals were also aware that Monty could not take the Ruhr without their forces and did everything they could to forestall Ike's new directive. Patton felt that Eisenhower was attempting to satisfy every army commander in the ETO and consequently satisfied no one; he called it the "momentous error of the war."[30] Bradley disagreed with Eisenhower's changed strategy because it divided his own army group and reduced its effectiveness. Bradley was prepared to reach and cross the Rhine into Germany with the U.S. First and Third armies fighting abreast south of the Ardennes. In his plan, the Americans would advance through France and thrust into Germany to the Saar and beyond the Rhine to the vicinity of Frankfurt while Montgomery's British and Canadian armies would advance in a secondary thrust up the channel coast to Antwerp. But he needed both the First and the Third American armies to do it.[31] Without them, he had little chance of hurdling the Rhine. In this case, though, Ike held firm.

Patton's Third Army now formed the southern wing of Bradley's 12th Army Group south of the Ardennes, and he was determined to pursue the shattered enemy through the province of Lorraine all the way to the Saar and then to the Rhine. If Eisenhower gave all the available resources to Montgomery, however, as he seemed to be doing, Patton was certain to fail. Patton confided in his diary: "We have, at this time, the greatest chance to win the war ever presented. If they will let me move on with three corps . . . we can be in Germany in ten days. . . . It's such a sure thing that I fear these blind moles don't see it."[32]

CHAPTER 8.

# The Enemy Waits for the 6th Army Group

★ ★ ★ ★

The moles Patton saw in the supreme command were also blind to the 6th Army Group's progress as it advanced relentlessly against Wiese's Nineteenth Army in southern France throughout the waning summer of 1944. Nowhere on the western front was the Germans' situation more desperate than along the line that ran through Lorraine and Alsace in eastern France. By mid-September, Devers' troops were positioned along the western slopes of the Vosges Mountains in Alsace and had been so successful that Hitler ordered a change in command at German Army Group G.

Generaloberst Johannes Blaskowitz received no accolades for his attempts to stave off the 6th Army Group and the Third Army. He was a competent and experienced commander who had served in the 1939 Polish campaign until his criticism of SS excesses put him at odds with Hitler and Heinrich Himmler, the leader of the dreaded Gestapo. He held reserve commands until he was appointed commander of Army Group G in May 1944. He performed well and slowed the Allied advance up the Rhone Valley, but he lost the Führer's confidence.[1]

On September 20, 1944, General der Panzertruppen Hermann Balck and his chief of staff, Maj. Gen. F. W. von Mellenthin, motored through the thickly wooded crests of the northern Vosges to Army Group G headquarters in Molsheim, twelve miles southwest of Strasbourg.[2] On arrival, Balck had the unpleasant task of dismissing Blaskowitz for failing to halt the advances of Patton's Third Army through Lorraine and Devers' 6th Army Group from southern France into Alsace. Balck's new command comprised three battered armies—the First, the Nineteenth, and the Fifth Panzer—and he faced a severe challenge. His former command had been on the eastern front, and he performed very well there, but warfare on the western front was an entirely different matter.[3] Distances were much less in the west, and the Americans and British held an overwhelming superiority in air power and denied the Germans the ability to concentrate forces, particularly the panzers. Huge tank formations maneuvered and attacked across the broad Russian steppes, but in the west, a single tank could summon a swarm of rocket-firing and bomb-dropping "Jabos"—the Germans' nickname for enemy fighter-bombers— that could break up any attempted German offensive.

The new commander of Army Group G was particularly concerned about containing the advances of the U.S. Third Army. Of all the Allied generals, Patton was the one Balck feared most. If the Third Army broke through the Siegfried Line defenses, it could swing northward toward the Saar and the Ruhr, and then east toward Berlin. Despite the Germans' best efforts to stop him, by late September Patton was smashing his way toward the fortress complex in the city of Metz in eastern France.

Metz had been a fortified town as far back as Roman times, when it was called Mediomatrica. After the legions left, the city became the focal point in the continuing conflicts between the French and Germans over ownership of the province of Lorraine, providing pathways of attack for both countries' armies. Because of its strategic location Metz had been heavily fortified through the centuries: the medieval city was walled; more modern ramparts were constructed in 1550; and a citadel was built shortly thereafter. Additional fortifications were added in the nineteenth century, with an inner circle of fifteen forts completed in 1866 and an outer ring of fortifications constructed by the Germans when they annexed Lorraine and Metz after the Franco-Prussian War of 1870.

Patton believed that he had to take Metz; otherwise, its fortifications and garrison would constitute a dangerous pocket of resistance in his rear as he advanced into Germany. He began an attack on September 27, but the city's defenses proved formidable, and his troops quickly bogged down in bitter and costly fighting in and around the forts. No one since Attila the Hun in the fifth century had taken Metz by storm, and Patton would spend the next six weeks fighting to capture the complex before he could even contemplate an advance to the Rhine. In the meantime, the limelight he had gained on his advance through France shifted to Devers and his 6th Army Group just to the south.[4]

If Balck and Mellenthin feared Patton above all others, they also had no illusions about the danger posed by the 6th Army Group, new though it was to combat on the southern wing of the Allied line. The U.S. Seventh and French First armies together constituted the smallest of the Allied armies facing the Germans but they had thrown the Nineteenth Army back some 350 or more miles from the Mediterranean coast to Alsace. While General Wiese had so far managed to defend the Belfort Gap, Truscott's 6th Corps troops had sidestepped northward and were now advancing into the High Vosges and fighting to break out to the Alsace Plain. Unless the Germans mounted a defense in these mountains, Truscott would soon reach the Rhine. Had Balck and von Mellenthin known of Truscott's intent to break through the Belfort Gap with the 6th Corps the week before their arrival, they would have been even more concerned about the situation in Alsace. Truscott believed that the Nineteenth Army was near collapse, and the old cavalry-man positioned his three divisions to launch a final push through the gap.[5]

Fate intervened, however, as it would intervene again two months later in November. On September 15, the 6th Army Group fell under SHAEF's command, and SHAEF did not sanction a 6th Corps advance to the Rhine through the gap. Instead, Truscott was ordered northward into the Vosges, where his corps was to be tucked in tight next to the Third Army to protect Patton's right flank.[6] Truscott's objections were overruled, and he began slipping his 6th Corps northward toward the Remiremont-Épinal area in the High Vosges against relatively negligible enemy resistance and through undefended mountain passes. All the while, Wiese's army teetered on the brink of collapse. "Only with the aid of numerous battalions, formed by stragglers," he later wrote, "was it possible to build a continuous line of defense. . . . Thus the [Nineteenth] Army had yet succeeded to block and to defend the Belfort Gap."[7] But Wiese knew that the Nineteenth held the gap only because the Americans and French had failed to push their gains. He simply could not understand "why the enemy did not execute the decisive assault on Belfort between 8 and 15 September 1944 through a large scale attack."[8]

Truscott had wanted to execute this very assault. He and General Patch had worked up a plan to use Truscott's three veteran divisions to break through Wiese's flimsy defenses, move through the gap, and reach Mulhouse near the Rhine. From this pivotal position Truscott could advance up the Rhine Valley to cut off the Nineteenth Army from the rear. When he was denied the opportunity, he angrily suggested to General Patch that he be allowed to take his 6th Corps back to Italy, where it could be used in an attack against Genoa. His troops would meet little resistance there and could come in behind the German forces resisting the Allied army moving up the Italian peninsula.[9] "As you stated the other day," Truscott wrote angrily to Patch, "the Belfort Gap is the Gateway to Germany. . . . Every consideration points to the fact that that time available to him should be reduced to the minimum. Consequently, the assault on the Belfort Gap should begin at the earliest moment that sufficient troops can be made available and sufficient sup-plies can be built up." Truscott further complained:

> The axis prescribed in FO 5 [the 6th Corps' new orders to move north] leads through the Vosges Mountains, where roads are limited, terrain rugged and easily defended. With the approach of weather in which rain and snow are to be expected, operations will be most difficult. As demonstrated in Italy during last winter, the Boches can limit progress to a snail's pace and even stop it entirely, even against superior strength.

With the SHAEF main effort in the direction Aachen–Bonn–Berlin, this mountainous area has little value if the Belfort Gap is breached and operations therein can contribute little to the success of SHAEF's main effort. It would seem wasteful to employ the three most veteran divisions in the American Army in an operation where they can be contained by a fraction of their strength and where their demonstrated ability to maneuver is so strictly limited. The greatest assistance to the SHAEF main effort by troops in this area is through the Belfort Gap.[10]

Truscott's aide recorded the general's reaction to the change of plans in his journal. "Plan sacrifices valuable time in Belfort attack, relegates Army [Truscott's 6th Corps] to minor role with possibility of complete bogging down in Vosges during the winter. CG [commanding general, Truscott] spends entire morning stewing about it."[11] Truscott may have known that no modern army had successfully fought through the Vosges. French Revolutionary troops bypassed the mountains in the late eighteenth century, as did the Germans during the Franco-Prussian War of 1870. The French declined to dislodge the Germans who took the High Vosges in World War I, and during the Battle of France in 1940 the Germans went around the region.[12]

SHAEF's refusal to allow Truscott to advance through the Belfort Gap is testimony to the rigidity and shortsightedness of Eisenhower's strategy. If the broad front plan was to be effective, the supreme command should have been ready in an instant to reinforce any breakthrough along the western front, particularly one that promised to entrap an entire German army or drive it back across the Rhine. That would have fulfilled SHAEF's stated near-term objective of clearing enemy forces west of the Rhine.

This was not the only time SHAEF failed to exploit an unexpected gain. American troops actually broke through the Siegfried Line at Wallendorf in September 1944 and could potentially have advanced to the Rhine, but SHAEF did not give the necessary orders. The supreme command may not even have known about the breach until later.[13] And in November of that year Devers was on the Rhine at Strasbourg and could have breached German defenses on the east bank, but the supreme command failed again to seize the opportunity.

As Truscott began moving his forces to the north, the two corps of the French First Army took over the southern end of the line around Belfort. De Lattre attempted a breakthrough but lacked the necessary men, guns, and tanks to punch through.[14] The French had to regroup and resupply before resuming the attack. Nevertheless, the French positions around Belfort were now within thirty-five miles of the Rhine and the German homeland.

Hitler's unequivocal order to Balck had been "hold Alsace-Lorraine in all circumstances," but Balck's chief of staff, von Mellenthin, was far from certain that the order could be carried out.[15] He was much less convinced than the Führer that Devers' army group in Alsace would soon outrun its supplies and be forced to stop and regroup. Winter would enhance the Wehrmacht's ability to defend the forested slopes of the Vosges, which in some places rise to heights of four thousand feet, but Balck was expected to block the American and Free French forces at least until spring.

Balck had risen through the ranks by leading a reconnaissance battalion that spearheaded Gen. Heinz Guderian's army across the Meuse in France in 1940.[16] As a brigade commander he defeated the Allies in Greece by leading a tank column through the "impassable" Tempe Gorge. As the commander of an armored division Balck successfully defeated the offensive thrusts of at least two Russian tank armies during the Germans' futile struggle to relieve their encircled Sixth Army at Stalingrad in December 1942. When Field Marshal von Manstein, one of the finest German commanders of the war, appointed Balck to command the 48th Panzer Corps on the Russian southern front in 1943, he told Balck, "I need the best commander of armor." Balck lived up to his reputation by becoming Germany's most highly decorated general officer.

Despite his brilliance, Balck faced nearly insurmountable odds. Army Group G was a withered force. The First German Army, under General der Panzertruppen Otto von Knobelsdorff, held a seventy-five-mile front, most of it opposite Patton's Third Army in Lorraine, and was retreating while fending off punishing attacks. Knobelsdorff's NCOs and men, he reported, were "with very few exceptions only fit for assignment in the homeland and the average was over forty years of age or seriously war disabled. All personnel fit for battle duties had already been combed out prior to the commencement of the offensive for the benefit of the east front." As for his combat divisions, "most of these formations had suffered great losses in men and matériel during the retreat. They were therefore very weak in fighting power when [he] took command."[17]

The Fifth Panzer Army, commanded by the highly decorated veteran tank commander General der Panzertruppen Hasso von Manteuffel, held a thirty-mile stretch of Army Group G's center. The Fifth also had been battered by Patton's troops and was a tank army in name only. Von Manteuffel had honed his skills on the Russian front under Guderian and as a subordinate to another celebrated panzer commander, Gen. Herman Hoth. At his next post in North Africa, he became a division commander in Rommel's Afrika Corps. In December 1943, von Manteuffel took command of the elite Panzer "Grossdeutschland" Division, and in May 1944 he was credited with stopping Soviet Marshal Konev's drive into

Romania. Six months later, in September 1944, he was given command of the Fifth Panzer Army in Alsace-Lorraine and promoted to the rank of general of panzer troops. He was only the twenty-fourth man to be awarded Diamonds for his Knight's Cross with Oak Leaves and Swords.

The Nineteenth Army under General Wiese held a ninety-mile stretch of front from Rambervillers in Alsace to the Swiss border. Wiese showed rare talent as a defensive tactician during his retreat up the Rhone, but by late September 1944 his army was, in von Mellenthin's analysis, "barely battle worthy." Von Mellenthin was equally pessimistic about the status of the entire army group, whose "striking power," he thought, "was exhausted."[18]

The situation was considerably better on the Allied side. While tired and in need of rest, the Americans had access to nearly unlimited supplies now that the port of Marseille had been opened. Devers' forces also held a manpower advantage over the Germans that was growing daily as the French tapped into the pool of civilians and former soldiers eager to avenge France's defeat in 1940. In numbers of tanks, guns, and transport and combat aircraft the Americans were far superior to the enemy. The Allied juggernaut was moving inexorably forward through France.

Devers' objective was nothing less than the destruction of Wiese's Nineteenth Army in Alsace and an advance across the Rhine somewhere in the vicinity of Strasbourg. His plan of attack at the end of September was to send Patch's U.S. Seventh Army in a strike north through the Vosges Mountains toward Strasbourg and the Rhine while de Lattre's French First Army to the south would simultaneously attack to the Rhine through the Belfort Gap. The twin offensives would form pincers to envelop the Nineteenth Army on the eastern side of the Vosges on the Alsace Plain. If the attack were successful, the enemy's only recourse would be to fall back across the Rhine into Germany, leaving the Americans and French in control of all of eastern France west of the Rhine from Karlsruhe to the Swiss frontier.[19]

CHAPTER 9.

# Into the Vosges

★ ★ ★ ★

The beauty of the Vosges Mountains is subtle and inviting. They are more like the Appalachians of western North Carolina and West Virginia than the majestic and spectacular Alps. The corrugated formations of the High Vosges extend some seventy miles through Alsace, from the town of Saverne in the north to Belfort near the Swiss frontier. Their greatest elevations are in the southern portion of the range around Belfort. The Low Vosges are in upper Alsace north of Saverne. The Vosges region mirrors the rugged Black Forest on the German side of the Rhine. Both mountain chains have the same geological makeup and are characterized by forests on their lower slopes and open pastures and rounded summits at higher altitudes, and both fall steeply toward the Rhine.

In peacetime, the Vosges is a destination for tourists. The hills and valleys are dotted with vineyards, ancient castles, and medieval villages, and the region is known for its health-giving waters. In 1944, however, the Vosges held immense strategic value for the Germans. The mountains formed the last barrier blocking an Allied advance into Germany on the southern flank of the western front.[1] The forested foothills and dominating heights gave the Germans an excellent defensive advantage, and the fall and winter weather would also work to their benefit. Rain and fog in the fall would slow any American advance, and the thick overcast would hamper air support. Winter snowfalls would make combat operations even more difficult if not impossible. The roads were narrow and in poor condition, making it difficult to get tanks and infantry support vehicles through the mountains.

Devers established his headquarters at the Heritage Hotel in Vittel, a town noted for its mineral water. He described the forested beauty of the surrounding Vosges in a letter to Georgie: "If you were to tour through any of our eastern mountains now you would see the same country with . . . much green grass, vigorous flowing mountain streams, lots of cattle and fowl."[2] Paul Fussell, a young lieutenant in the 103rd Infantry Division who later became a noted writer, thought the terrain and its cover resembled the Civil War Wilderness battlefields of Virginia.[3]

The Americans had to fight through dark thickets of dense underbrush that detonated artillery and mortar shells before they hit the ground. The ensuing shower of shrapnel was much more lethal than if the projectiles had hit the earth and blasted fragments of superheated metal upward.

Combat in the Vosges also was similar to that experienced by Union and Confederate forces in the American Civil War. The fighting was close in, man to man, and often conducted with fixed bayonets. The Americans' overwhelming air power was useless, and the forests prevented all but the smallest artillery in the forward area. But the Americans proved their ability to fight even when deprived of their heavy weapons. "Our troops were very good," Fussell remembered, "particularly when their orders were good and clear."[4]

German commanders finally gained a measure of respect for the "Amis" during the battle for the Vosges, a judgment not always afforded to American infantry. In general they rated American infantry as poor, but in the Vosges, "The fighting methods of the American infantry were very clever and very well adapted to the terrain," recalled General Botch.[5] "Whenever they found they were not making sufficient headway in one place they [would] simply have a try somewhere else. They would just make a detour and come up again from behind. . . . This was . . . very sound tactics . . . in the wooded terrain of the Vosges Mountains. . . . [T]he Americans would always find a way through—keeping away from the roads all the time." Botch also applauded the American tank crews. "They appeared to be everywhere at once. There was hardly any type of terrain where the tanks did not turn up in support of the infantry. It was perfectly astonishing the way they kept appearing in the thickest woodland and on the most impossible bypaths."[6]

Devers and Patch had tried to avoid the rugged slopes of the Vosges; they knew the many obstacles. The best route to the Rhine was through the Saverne Gap, a narrow defile in northern Alsace that separates the High Vosges from the Low Vosges, which extend farther to the north and angle into Germany to become the Hardt Mountains. But the Saverne Gap was in the Third Army's zone of operations. The Belfort Gap offered another avenue to the Rhine, but Wiese was hastily building new defenses in the area, and the French First Army was not yet up to the task. De Lattre's forces were still arriving from North Africa and Corsica, and he would need all of them to punch through the German line. Devers' only alternative was to push through the Vosges and attack aggressively to deny Wiese the time he needed to prepare strong defensive positions.[7]

If any Allied troops were experienced in tackling the Germans in mountainous terrain it was the men of Truscott's 6th Corps.[8] They were veterans of the Italian campaign, where the ground was similar to the Vosges and where they had learned to deal with bad weather and masterful German defenses. In Italy, they had fought from foxhole to foxhole and from ridge to ridge. The Germans always had fallback positions and counterattacked to regain lost territory. The fighting was deadly and time-consuming. Yards were gained in days, a mile or two in weeks. At Monte Cassino, German paratroopers blocked the road to Rome for five months and forced the Allies into the near disastrous amphibious landings at Anzio in a bid to come in behind the prepared German defenses of the Gothic Line. Truscott certainly remembered Anzio; he had commanded the troops in the bridgehead. The enemy nearly drove the invasion force into the sea and then sealed it off and reduced it to near impotence. The Allies took more than six months to advance from Naples to Rome, a distance of about one hundred miles.

The Americans could claim one advantage in the Vosges. They had not managed to surround Wiese's army, but they had arrived before the Germans had constructed adequate defenses. The Germans found themselves constantly outmaneuvered on rugged ground that should have been ideally suited to defense. An operations report from the 3rd Division's 30th Infantry Regiment noted: "The enemy was apparently unable to correctly evaluate our threats against him. When we first entered the sector his troops sometimes walked right into our lines. . . . As we continued our attack, the enemy's defensive main line was seldom placed to meet our threat effectively."[9]

Patch and Truscott believed that if the Seventh Army could take advantage of the Germans' lack of preparedness, the 6th Corps could smash through the Vosges to the Alsace Plain and drive to the Rhine. The Germans worked feverishly to erect defenses, however, and constructed a series of well-positioned strong points in elevated spots and in open terrain along the line. All roads were blocked, and minefields were strategically located.

Devers ordered the drive to the Rhine to begin on September 20, 1944, and Truscott's three divisions moved out toward the Moselle River and advanced into the Vosges foothills.[10] The attack began along a forty-mile front west of the Moselle from Chatel in the north to Faucogney in the south. The 45th Division held the northern end of the line; the 36th, the center; and the 3rd, the "Rock of the Marne" Division, was on the southern end.

Audie Murphy's present-tense narration of his memories evokes the season and the infantrymen's determination as the 3rd Division began its advance.

The leaves of the trees are turning color. The gold and red contrast sharply with the evergreens; and the camouflage men must start mixing new paints to conform with the changes in nature. It is a prelude to another long, grim winter. We plod up the wet roads doggedly, wondering vaguely which of us will still be alive when the new leaves will return to the trees. The Germans fall back stubbornly, but steadily. Each day, however, their resistance grows stronger, their retreats shorter. As they approach strongly prepared positions in the Vosges mountain area, they lash back at us with counterattacks. My regiment is on the verge of some of the hardest fighting of the entire war.[11]

By September 25, the 3rd Division had managed to establish bridgeheads on the east bank of the Moselle. The 45th Division crossed the river at Chatel and at Igney.[12] The division's 157th Regiment became heavily engaged in the Bois de la Foresterie north of Épinal; and the 180th Regiment encountered roadblocks, minefields, barbed-wire entanglements, and booby traps as it advanced toward the town. The 36th Division moved out toward Remiremont, with the 141st Regiment crossing the Moselle near Noir Gueux and the 3rd Regiment soon following. All three regiments of the 36th Division were advancing into the Vosges.

"If breaching the German Moselle River line seemed difficult, it soon became dwarfed in our minds by the imposing barrier of the forested Vosges Mountains that lay ahead," wrote one veteran of the 141st's campaign.

Distance measured in miles in our drive up through southern France was now to be measured in yards. St. Jean du Marche, Lepanges, Herpelmont, Lavaline du Houx, and other French villages at the Vosges foothills soon became familiar landmarks; not merely spots on a map that were sped by on the top of tanks and in trucks and jeeps, but places that were approached on foot, liberated only after overcoming stubborn resistance. . . .

For some of us it was a new experience battling it out with the enemy and the terrain yard by yard, but for others it recalled bitter memories of the Italian campaign. The mountains, the mud, and the minefields were in front of us once again, but, unlike Italy, there was no Rome glittering on the horizon. After one mountain was gained there was nothing ahead but another, always another mountain, higher and more heavily defended than the last. Seldom did our thoughts reach out beyond these confining barriers. Only occasionally did we talk of the Alsace Plain and the Rhine beyond. Even less did the armchair strategists among us discuss the war in broad outlines. Our horizon was a limited one, extending only to the particular valley or forested hill immediately in front of us. More often it stretched only a few hundred yards ahead through a maze of pine trees or to a farmhouse at the edge of a woodline. Ours was an outlook as provincial as the isolated peasants around us, but we were too occupied to be concerned with more than our immediate surroundings. A small strip of land became our sole interest, our life.[13]

General Wiese had to stop the advancing Americans or fail in his mission. He ordered a series of counterattacks. The Germans were aided by mist, rain, and intermittent fog that enabled them to infiltrate through the mountains unobserved. They struck suddenly and without warning, taking the various American units by surprise and making small inroads into their lines. But the Americans were learning that the way to defeat the Nineteenth Army in the Vosges was by sidestepping. If they attacked head-on over the limited road network, even with the support of tanks, the Germans could fend them off. So they began advancing overland, avoiding the roads where the enemy strong points were concentrated. These altered tactics discouraged General Wiese. "When later the enemy [Americans] made his attacks diagonally though the mountain area," he noted, "then the lack of [German] forces became alarmingly clear to the defense." Reluctantly the German commander was forced to pull his troops back lest they be outflanked by continued U.S. advances.[14]

By September 26, all of the 6th Corps was across the Moselle. Truscott's penchant for rapid advance had paid off; he had caught the Germans off guard west of the river, and U.S. troops were pushing toward the summits to the east. The Germans could only hope that the American advance would grind to a halt in the winter snows.

The 6th Army Group's situation changed dramatically on September 29 when SHAEF, at Devers' request, authorized the transfer of Gen. Wade Haislip's 15th Corps from the Third Army to the Seventh Army to give the 6th Army Group more muscle and flexibility and to enhance the drive to the Rhine.[15] The transfer made strategic sense to SHAEF. The Allied armies to the north, including Patton's vaunted Third, had been stopped. Only the U.S. Seventh and French First armies were making progress, and Devers needed more troops to sustain his advance. With the 15th Corps on his northern flank, he could now coordinate attacks north and south through the Vosges to keep the Germans off balance. More important, Devers could push through the Saverne Gap, which was now in his zone of operations.

Patton objected strenuously to losing two top divisions, but his ranting fell on deaf ears. "If Jake Devers gets the XV Corps, I hope his plan goes sour," Patton railed. "May God rot his guts."[16] Patton had good reason to complain about losing Haislip, a well-respected and well-liked corps commander. Eisenhower characterized Haislip as "calm and cool in action but a determined and resourceful leader. He possesses a high tactical skill and experience."[17]

SHAEF also committed three newly arriving infantry divisions to the 6th Army Group. They were not immediately available but would be in the line sometime in late October or early November. SHAEF gave them to Devers because it had no means to supply them if they arrived over the Normandy beaches and became part of the 12th Army Group.

The supply system from Normandy for the 12th and 21st army group fronts was already strained to the breaking point.[18] Ammunition stocks for many divisions were low, and all the divisions were suffering from severe shortages of gasoline. Winter was approaching, but many soldiers lacked even adequate warm-weather gear. Foster Gould, an infantryman in the 28th Division, was just one of thousands of U.S. troops inadequately supplied and clothed in late 1944. Gould slept on the ground without a sleeping bag or even an overcoat the night before his unit attacked in the Hürtgen Forest in November 1944.[19] The 6th Army Group was being supplied through the port of Marseille, however, and had a more efficient delivery system through southern France. Devers also had many fewer divisions to supply than Bradley and Montgomery did.

Haislip's 15th Corps, comprising the U.S. 79th Division and the French 2nd Armored Division, now held the 6th Army Group's northern wing and would push east while Truscott's 6th Corps continued its drive northeast into the High Vosges, with its ultimate objective being Strasbourg on the Rhine. The French First Army would open an offensive in the south to break through the Belfort Gap and reach the Rhine farther to the south.

The combat-tested 15th Corps had won laurels during the Battle of the Falaise Pocket in northern France in August 1944.[20] When Field Marshal von Kluge, the German commander in chief in the west, mounted a massive counterattack toward Avranches to blunt Patton's eastward drive and cut his lifeline to the Normandy beaches, Haislip's forces were in the thick of the fight on the Third Army's right flank. Reflecting Haislip's aggressive leadership, the 15th Corps slipped to the right of the German advance and came in behind the enemy forces near Falaise. In the ensuing battle, the 15th Corps was instrumental in defeating the Germans, who nearly lost two armies.

A 1912 graduate of West Point, "Ham" Haislip was a career infantryman and a longtime friend of Eisenhower. The two served together at Fort Sam Houston, Texas, and Ham was present when Ike met his future wife, Mamie Dowd.[21] Short, pudgy Ham did not fit the description of a fighting general, but he was known for his enthusiasm and aggressiveness. Haislip first saw action as a young lieutenant with the U.S. Expeditionary Force to Vera Cruz, Mexico, in 1916. During World War I, Major Haislip was assigned to the 5th Corps in France as secretary to its general staff, and participated in operations in the Vosges and in the Saint-Mihiel and Meuse-Argonne offensives in 1918. Ham knew the French well and spoke their language, having spent 1925 and 1926 studying at the French École Superieur de Guerre, the equivalent of the U.S. Army's War College, which Haislip attended in

1931. Ham got his first star in January 1941 and his second the following year when he assumed command of the 85th Infantry Division. He was given command of the 15th Corps in 1943 and took it into France in July 1944.

The 50,500-man-strong 15th Corps included the 106th Cavalry Group and the 813th Tank Destroyer Battalion. While the corps' orders remained much the same as they had been under Patton—to protect the left flank of the Third Army—Devers also directed Haislip to support Truscott's 6th Corps and to seize Sarrebourg, which lay about ten miles west of the Saverne Gap. Once through the gap, the 15th Corps could roll onward to Strasbourg and the Rhine.

# CHAPTER 10.

# Logistics

★ ★ ★ ★

General Devers' great advantage throughout the campaign in southern France and in Alsace—one that SHAEF was quick to acknowledge—was an efficient and effective supply system that fed his two armies. Supply shortages affected the entire western front, but they were more pronounced in the northern army groups. The 6th Army Group faced constant and often critical matériel shortages that slowed Devers' forces as they raced to seize the Belfort Gap in mid-September 1944. The supply deficits lingered into the fall, when General Patch's troops struggled to break through the Vosges Mountains to the Alsace Plain. But the 6th Army Group's logistical problems were never as debilitating as those that shackled Bradley, Patton, and Montgomery.[1]

Unlike the situation in Normandy, where Allied troops were bottled up for nearly two months, Patch's Seventh Army troops hit the ground running and immediately advanced out of the southern landing zones. Four days after the invasion, forward elements of the U.S. force pushed past Sisteron, more than one hundred miles from the beaches. By D-26 Seventh Army troops had advanced three hundred miles beyond the invasion beaches, a distance it had taken SHAEF forces in northern France three months to cover. The southern armies needed gasoline and vehicles to continue the pursuit, and logistics personnel quickly responded to deliver as much gas as possible to the rapidly advancing American and French forces.[2] As in the north, the biggest problem was getting supplies from the coast to the combat zones.

As Bradley's forces in northern France had done, the Seventh Army rounded up deuce-and-a-half (two-and-a-half-ton) trucks from newly arriving units and took vehicles from existing units to transport gasoline and critical supplies northward to the fighting forces. The 6th Corps created ammunition truck trains to haul artillery shells some two hundred miles to the front on the Rhone.[3] The French First Army commandeered civilian automobiles, boats, horse-drawn carts—anything with wheels that would move troops and supplies.[4]

A number of factors were behind the shortages the Seventh Army endured. The delivery of supplies to the front was slowed early in the Dragoon campaign as American and French engineers labored to clear the ports of Toulon and Marseille of the debris left by German demolition crews. The enemy sank ships at strategic points in channels and alongside quays to prevent Allied cargo vessels from unloading and destroyed everything that might be of value to the Allied effort.

Dragoon planners had also miscalculated on the types of supplies that would be needed in the opening days of the campaign. Devers' commanders expected more of a fight from the Germans on the beachhead than they got. Previous landings at Salerno, Anzio, and Normandy, where the first waves of infantry encountered stiff resistance, gave Devers and his staff reason to believe they would have a fierce struggle to break out of a tightly held German ring of fire. Thus the equipment and supplies designated for delivery in the first days and weeks of the Dragoon campaign were "combat-heavy." Topping the list of supplies to be offloaded on the beachhead were artillery shells, small arms ammunition, medical supplies, tanks, guns, halftracks, and tank destroyers. Large numbers of trucks and large quantities of gasoline for rapid advances inland were designated for later delivery.[5]

When Patch's troops began to advance out of the bridgeheads of southern France, they faced immediate shortages of two-and-a-half-ton trucks and gasoline. The damage inflicted by Allied bombings on the railways north along the Rhone also slowed the delivery of supplies. Railway and highway bridges had been destroyed either by Allied bombing or by German demolition crews.[6] Resistance groups also blew bridges to slow the Germans' retreat in hopes that French and American forces could catch up to and encircle them.

After Marseille fell in late August, the 6th Army Group had one of the biggest ports in Europe as its supply depot and the largest port held by Allied forces until Antwerp was fully operational in late November 1944.[7] Six weeks after D-day in southern France, Devers' two armies were being supplied through Marseille and its satellite ports. In October 1944, for example, Marseille and its satellite ports took in 524,894 long tons of supplies, while all of the northern ports combined received only 784,290 long tons.[8] The southern ports soon received more than a quarter of all Allied supplies delivered to the Continent. By November 1944, these ports handled more than one-third of all the supplies arriving in France.[9] As the war progressed, Marseille lived up to expectations and discharged more cargo than any other European port.[10] By the war's end, the southern French ports, mostly Marseille, had discharged 4,123,794 long tons of cargo; the next most productive ports were Cherbourg, which processed 2,697,341 long tons; and Antwerp, which unloaded 2,658,000 long tons. The southern ports debarked 905,512 troops, second only to Le Havre, where 1,014,036 service personnel came ashore.[11] Devers believed that clearing the port of Marseille and rendering it usable so quickly "was one of the outstanding accomplishments of the war."[12]

Until Antwerp was opened in late November 1944, the small northern French ports of Cherbourg, Le Havre, Rouen, and the Normandy beaches supplied the entire 12th Army Group—thirty-plus divisions—as well as hundreds of thousands of auxiliary and service troops, the Services of Supply (SOS) command, and the entire staff of SHAEF, which by February 1945 totaled 16,312 service personnel.[13] In October, the 6th Army Group was responsible for the supply needs of some twelve combat divisions and many fewer service troops. According to the official Army history, *Logistical Support of the Armies*, "discharges of this magnitude" from the southern French ports virtually ensured the support of the 6th Army Group.[14] General Marshall noted the advantage Marseille and Toulon gave to the southern armies: "Port capacities and transportation facilities were sufficient to meet the requirements of the entire Southern Group of Armies and also to assist in the supply of the Central Group of Armies until the stubborn defense of the water entrance to Antwerp was reduced."[15] For the most part, however, the southern ports could not provide the surplus capacity to help support the 12th Army Group until late in the fall.[16] Although there were shortages, the 6th Army Group commanders squeaked through the lean periods and stockpiled supplies when the situation improved. Inadequate supplies sometimes slowed the advance, but Devers never had to halt an entire corps or army because of logistical concerns.[17]

Devers had other advantages besides two ports dedicated strictly to supplying his forces. In its initial phase, the 6th Army Group's drive northward in France was confined to the narrow Rhone Valley, at least until it reached Lyon. And even beyond this regional capital the width of the 6th Army Group's front was relatively narrow until it reached Alsace, where the battle line became static for some time. The British and American front in northern France, in contrast, was spread over some 275 miles. Truck convoys and rail transport delivering supplies to the 12th Army Group had to fan out from the Normandy beaches—where prior to October most of the supplies were unloaded—over a large area from a point near Luneville in the south to a point north of Aachen in the north.[18] In the 6th Army Group's sector, supplies were rushed up the Rhone on only one line of communication—roads and railroads—from Marseille. Eisenhower seemed to envy Devers' access to "the magnificent railway lines running up the valley of the Rhone." With these lines, Ike wrote, "we should have no great difficulty with the logistic support of any of our lines south of the Luxembourg region."[19]

But more than "magnificent railway" lines and a large port enhanced the 6th Army Group's supply situation. Devers was an able and hands-on administrator who oversaw many details of the Services of Supply for Dragoon's forces. As Commanding

General, NATOUSA (North African Theater of Operations, U.S. Army), he was responsible for planning the assault in southern France, and he chose "imaginative and improvisatory leaders" to design the logistics of this Herculean operation.[20]

In contrast to Eisenhower, whose energies were consumed by political and territorial disputes between his commanders in the 12th and 21st army groups, Devers could focus on the immediate military situation on his front. No detail of the supply pipeline was too small for his attention. He was on the beach shortly after the invasion began and experienced an attack by German JU-88 bombers that targeted ships in the invasion fleet. Ike, in contrast, did not make it to the Normandy beaches until six days after the invasion, and even then he was on a secure inspection tour with three of the American Joint Chiefs of Staff.[21]

Because he was present on the Dragoon beaches, Devers could spot problems and fix them right away. "I was one of the first ones in there," he later said. "I observed certain landings that didn't go according to schedule and I was in the headquarters of the corps commander, Truscott, . . . and smoothed out some things that needed to be smoothed out and [saw] . . . that they got the proper supplies." Devers inspected the invasion beaches closely to ensure that the cargo ships were speedily unloaded and that the matériel was shipped to supply dumps and on to the frontline soldiers. "We just didn't waste a ship. We didn't waste an hour and we didn't waste a man." If Devers saw that additional men were needed to expedite the supply system, he took them from other units, even hospitals. "When I say we went into the hospital, we had a lot of men that wanted to get back into the war. They . . . couldn't have walked anywhere, but they could sure drive a truck. They were easy to train because they were already disciplined. They were hard workers; they knew what they had to do."[22]

The "trucks" unloading the ships were DUKWs, amphibious four-by-four vehicles that fascinated Devers. He remembered that the DUKW was developed at Fort Knox "by a young scientist down there by the name of Putnam who said he could take a two-and-a-half-ton truck and make a boat out of it. . . . He did just that."[23] In Marseille, DUKWs were critical to efforts to supply the invasion forces because the Germans had destroyed the Marseille docks. They chugged out to waiting cargo ships to take their supplies ashore. "We could run three of these ducks up on one side of a Liberty Ship, three up the other side," Devers remembered. The cargo was unloaded in huge nets, and it often arrived already wrapped in nets. "So we'd just lift them out. . . . We could pick those nets right off those ducks, drop it on the ground, and the German prisoners would throw an empty net back into the truck and it would just keep going. It didn't take us three minutes to unload that truck and get (it) back on the road. . . . We worked those ducks right around the clock."[24]

As the invasion forces moved inland, Devers continued watching to make sure there were no delays. He kept an eye on his front from an airplane or jeep. "I was flying around a lot in a light plane with some very good aviators," he remembered. "We kept things moving. If we saw any congestion anywhere, we went down and got it cleaned up. If we found anybody that was in trouble, we had a method of getting information to them pretty fast." When supplies ran low, Devers was out there goading his commanders to get more guns, ammunition, and gasoline to the troops. He told his supply people to dip into closely guarded reserves that were not to be used except in extreme emergencies; if the troops were running short of needed supplies, it was an emergency! Devers' supply chief, Maj. Gen. Thomas B. Larkin, once warned him that they were using up critical reserves. Devers replied, "What are they for anyhow?"[25]

The reserves had to be replaced, of course, but Larkin had already planned for that contingency. When Devers asked Larkin how he intended to replenish his reserve stocks, Larkin told him not to worry. He would send teletype messages to New York to load the supplies on the next convoy sailing to southern France. "We have a convoy just waiting to be told what to load. They got it there, they'll load it and in fourteen days it'll be here."

"Well," Devers replied, "then I'm gambling on fourteen days. I've got enough to live fourteen days. . . . Just be sure you don't bring me over a lot of concrete and barbed wire that we don't need."[26]

In contrast, the lines of authority controlling the Services of Supply organizations in the northern armies were muddled. Army historian James Huston notes that SHAEF acted as both theater command in charge of American forces in France and as the supreme Allied command in charge of American and British forces, and "ill-defined lines of authority and responsibility bred chronic problems of coordination throughout the war in Europe."[27] The 6th Army Group escaped much of this confusion as long as its supply organizations remained somewhat independent of SHAEF. Even after Devers fell under Ike's command, his supply groups retained some autonomy.

Speaking years later about some of the elements that made the southern campaign successful, Devers stressed that "foremost . . . were the logistics. . . . I got the best man in logistics that existed in the whole world at that time, Larkin. We had a wonderful logistic plan." Devers also boasted of another logistics wizard. "We got the best railroad man, . . . Gray [Brig. Gen. Carl R. Gray Jr.], and got him working on the bridges."[28] General Gray had been director general of the North African military railroads, and before the war was the executive vice president of the Chicago, St. Paul, Minneapolis and Omaha Railway. His father had been president of the Union Pacific Railroad. Gray was known as "hearty and joke-loving," but he was also "a red-tape-hating general" who won respect for "his ability to push rail lines into one side of a European town almost before German forces could retreat out the other." Devers also liked him because Larkin loved football. "He was a football fiend and we used to talk about 'three deep' and he was about three deep in men that were capable."[29] Devers was well aware of Gray's exploits. "He had a great organization because he knew every section hand in the United States and he had them all over there in Italy. He brought them over to southern France and knew where to get their own crews so we had a trained group."[30]

The railroads in southern France had been badly damaged by Allied air forces to prevent the enemy from transporting reinforcements to the invasion area, but now the Allies needed the railroads. Seventh Army engineers worked feverishly to repair the damage and keep the supplies moving forward. In one case, the Seventh Army's chief engineer, Brig. Gen. Garrison Davidson, armed photographers with Speed Graphic cameras and sent them in L-5 Cub airplanes to make low-level passes over blown bridges, many of which were behind German lines. With these photographs in hand, the construction troops could compute their needs long before they reached the bridges.[31]

The engineers became masters at improvisation. They had to be because much of the equipment and supplies needed to maintain the advance were still onboard ships coming from the United States. Construction regiments used whatever materials they could find along the way to repair bridges and other transportation facilities. The 343rd Engineer General Service Regiment restored a bridge on the rail line to the city of Aix by using the frame of an enemy 270-mm railway gun as a new span in place of one that had been destroyed.[32]

General Gray was the man who made much of that happen. Devers recalled the night that Gray arrived at his headquarters. "We sat down at midnight on my cot, with a map in front of us, and we outlined the whole railroad system for the Rhone valley, and for Nancy, and where I thought I had to go. I said, 'How long is it going to take you to get that bridge in?'

'We'll have it in the next twenty days,' Gray replied.

'How are you going to do it?' Devers asked.

'I know the foreman I'm going to put on that job. He knows who he's going to get to do the work. All I got to do is call him and tell him to get [him] on the job,' Gray replied. 'We know where the supplies are . . . and what we haven't got we'll get by ship from Italy. You needn't worry anymore about this, General,' Gray added.

'That's it!' Devers said. 'That's the kind of man you need.'

'We got those bridges up—not in three months—but in one month, and sometimes in fifteen days,' Devers said. 'So we had the logistics and we moved up the [Rhone] valley very promptly.'"[33]

The Seventh Army also made effective use of its trucks, and truck transport eventually became the principal means of getting matériel to the front. Where rail lines had been severed, deuce-and-a-half trucks were brought in to carry supplies between the two ends of the wrecked tracks. Trucks carried some 222,000 tons of supply forward in September versus the 63,000 tons carried by rail. By November, the 6th Army Group had acquired an additional 1,100 vehicles for port discharge and to transport supplies to the front.[34]

Devers also touted his army's use of aerial transport. "We used every transport plane we could get, which were lying idle, to fly in a lot of this stuff. Those C-47s could land on most anything. They'd come in and throw the stuff out the door. We'd pull this stuff with jeeps and ropes off the runways so that others could come in behind them. We did this in every critical stage."[35]

In mid-October 1944, General Eisenhower, concerned about logistical problems in the northern armies, asked Devers when the 6th Army Group command could begin passing supplies to Patton's Third Army. Devers estimated that he could begin offering a thousand tons a day to the Third after November 15.[36] Eisenhower wrote Marshall on October 26 to say that he expected Devers to supply Patton with three thousand tons from Marseille by December 1.

During October and the first part of November, the Seventh Army stockpiled supplies to support Devers' planned drive to the Rhine.[37] Patton, always looking for a fight, was outraged that Devers' command was much better supplied than was the 12th Army Group in which Patton served. Historian Martin Blumenson attributes that advantage to Marseille, "through which a steady stream of supply items and replacement soldiers flowed. The Twelfth Army Group, as well as the [21st] Army Group, had no comparable port."[38] At least some of the Seventh Army's logistical success should be attributed to the competence of Jacob Devers.

The noted military historian Martin Van Creveld suggests that the supply crisis of the northern armies in the late summer and early fall of 1944 was of Eisenhower's and SHAEF's own making. Historians have painted a logistics crisis in northern France of monumental proportions, but Van Creveld argues that the situation for Montgomery's 21st Army Group was never as dire as it was for Bradley's 12th Army Group. In fact, Gen. Miles Dempsey, commander of Montgomery's Second Army, said that his supply situation was "very favorable." Monty's troops were always close to a channel port as they advanced along the coasts of France and Belgium. In fact, notes Van Creveld, SHAEF logisticians had been consistently wrong in anticipating the needs of the northern Allied armies in the push across France. They had argued that the advance from Normandy to the Seine would require much more time and matériel than it actually took. Preinvasion plans called for a halt on the Seine to regroup and resupply, but the logisticians were forced to revise those plans in mid-August when Allied troops reached the river and commanders were eager to cross and pursue the fleeing enemy. SHAEF planners recalculated and suggested that the Allies might be able to support four divisions across the Seine, but only by September 7; that is, after a delay of two weeks. Further, the study stated that to continue the pursuit, operations south of the Seine would have to be suspended, the channel ports would have to be opened, and the liberation of Paris postponed until late October. As it was, the Allies were supporting sixteen U.S. divisions across the Seine by early September, and lead elements were some two hundred miles past the river. "Seldom can calculations by staff officers have proved so utterly wrong," Van Creveld asserts. Van Creveld also suggests that Eisenhower probably could have continued the rapid advance to the Ruhr had he heeded Montgomery's advice and halted part of his army. Ike could have committed some eighteen Allied divisions from the British Second Army and the U.S. First Army to break through to the Ruhr. There would have been ample supplies for such an undertaking provided other forces were halted. Eighteen divisions represented a small force, but it was probably large enough "to break through the weak German opposition at this time."[39]

Such a thrust to encircle the Ruhr in September would have encountered fewer obstacles than were met during Operation Market Garden. To reach the Rhine at Arnhem Montgomery's forces had to ford four rivers, while only two rivers barred the way to an encirclement of the Ruhr. Van Creveld also notes that the road network serving the Ruhr was superior to that leading north into Holland. Field Marshal Montgomery may have heightened and complicated the logistics crisis in the minds of SHAEF planners. Monty never fully articulated his plan. He vacillated about the number of divisions he would need to take the Ruhr and what form his attack would take. He spoke of a "solid mass" of troops involving all of the 12th and 21st army groups. He called for a "full-blooded" thrust toward Berlin," and a few days later called for a "knife-like thrust . . . into the centre of Germany."[40] Eisenhower was well aware that an attack on the German capital would have required many more troops than would be needed to capture the Ruhr and was obviously fraught with danger. Van Creveld concludes that had Eisenhower stuck with a limited plan of taking the Ruhr, halting the rest of the armies on the western front, and pushing through the weak point in the German lines, the Allies had the logistical resources to succeed. After all, they found the resources to supply Market Garden.

By mid-November the logistics crisis along the western front had eased. A depot system was established, and critical supplies were being stockpiled. Years after the war, General Devers was asked if the logistics would have supported a major drive across the Rhine at Rastatt. "Yes!" was Devers' unequivocal reply. "We had our OP [oil and gas] pipelines up into Strasbourg and we had our supply systems working; we had railroads running, we had the Nancy Yards fixed up. By the time of the Battle of the Bulge we were all fixed up on our end of the fence."[41]

CHAPTER 11.

# On to Strasbourg

★ ★ ★ ★

To reach Strasbourg and the Rhine, Haislip's 15th Corps would first have to fight through the Forest of Parroy—a six-by-four-mile patch of dense woods—and then somehow bull its way through the Saverne Gap, which bristled with enemy defenses.[1] As long as the Germans controlled the Parroy, they controlled the main highway leading to Saarebourg, the Saverne Gap, and Strasbourg. General Balck realized the significance of this heavily wooded ground and ordered his commanders not to yield an inch and to regain all lost ground by mounting immediate counterattacks. Behind Balck's order was Hitler's determination to blunt the American advance and buy time to strengthen the fortifications of the Siegfried Line protecting the German border.

The fighting in the Parroy was vicious and was not unlike the battles farther north in the Hürtgen and the Ardennes. The Germans maintained a thin screening line through the woods and concentrated their defenses in strong points. Forward observers called down artillery strikes on the advancing Americans, and the barrages were often followed by local infantry-armored counterattacks. At night, small bands of Germans infiltrated the American lines to disrupt resupply efforts. The enemy's efforts paid off; they drove the Americans back and forced them to reorganize and launch their own counterattacks. The struggle seesawed back and forth for a week until October 9, when the enemy, too depleted to continue, withdrew to a line several miles east of the forest. In so doing, they had lost their main defensive position on the approaches to the Saverne Gap.

While the 15th Corps was engaged in the Parroy, farther south the 6th Corps pushed on toward Saint-Dié, a principal road, rail, and communications center on the western edge of the Vosges vital for the Americans' advance to the Rhine. Audie Murphy's memoir describes the fighting around Saint-Dié.

> As we sneak up the slopes, we hear only the creaking of our boots and the patter of water from the trees. The Germans remain silent. But we have

seen them pull this trick before, and will not be fooled by it. We advance from point to point, using trees and huge rocks for cover and examining every possible foot of the ground that lies before us. . . .

We are driving into the Vosges mountain chain, which is the chief obstacle lying between us and the Rhine. Speed is most important. The rain still falls; the coldness increases. Soon snow and ice will take over the rugged hills, increasing the difficulty of our advance immeasurably.

The terrain is perfect for defense. The thick forests, hiding innumerable snipers and machine gun emplacements, must often be cleared by tree-to-tree fighting. The enemy has dug in high upon the steep craggy slopes, from which they pour artillery and mortar fire into our ranks. At night the fog closes in. Under its cover, the Germans infiltrate our lines; and hand-to-hand fighting becomes commonplace. I whet my bayonet until it is razor sharp and keep it always handy.[2]

Men lost their sense of direction in the dense underbrush of the Vosges, and bands of enemy troops easily infiltrated American lines. "Sometimes the enemy deliberately lets us get as close as seventy-five or one hundred yards to him before disclosing his presence with fire, and on occasion lets the leading elements pass by. This reduced the fights to small arms fights with the enemy enjoying the advantage of good cover. . . . Holding the top of a hill or even what is ordinarily termed the military crest of a wooded hill does not necessarily give us control of the surrounding terrain," wrote a regimental commander with the 36th Division.[3]

Troops in the 36th gave similar accounts of the action. One wrote:

We weren't in the Vosges Mountains long before we realized that the Germans were not our only enemy. Jerry had made an ally of the forested hills and rugged terrain. The high mountain peaks gave him OP's [observation posts]; the dense forest growth, concealment. Practically every natural advantage was his. It was a terrain friendly to the defender, hostile to the attacker. What defenses nature failed to furnish, Jerry provided for himself. With characteristic efficiency he constructed well dug-in positions. Every rifleman and machine gunner had deep, heavily covered foxholes that looked down on the only lanes of approach open to us. Jerry had always been a master of camouflage, and his dug in positions in the Vosges forests, which made use of every available leaf and pine needle, showed that he had lost none of his technique. Many of us never saw his positions until we were right on top of them, and then it was usually too late. Minefields, which had been such a curse to us in Italy, became a part of the Vosges landscape as the dreaded foot-shearing Schu mines were sprinkled over the ground before us. Planted under the forest floor, their trip wires camouflaged by the maze of twigs and underbrush, they were an unseen, but ever-present enemy. Every step was a probed one as a misstep meant a foot, a leg, or sometimes even a life. Then there was the artillery.[4]

On October 25, Truscott turned over command of the 6th Corps to Maj. Gen. Edward Brooks, who continued the drive to the northeast.[5] Truscott had been reassigned to take command of the Fifth Army in Italy, and while he would be sorely missed for his tactical savvy and aggressiveness, Brooks would prove to be a competent replacement. The taciturn New Englander had commanded an armored division in Bradley's 12th Army Group prior to his new assignment with the 6th Corps, but his experience went back much further than that. Brooks served in five major engagements with the 3rd Division artillery in World War I, when he was a battery commander and assistant G-3 of the 3rd Field Artillery Brigade. He was awarded the Distinguished Service Cross for bravery for driving an ammunition truck, whose driver had been killed, to safety during an artillery barrage. He was also a standout on the 3rd Division football team, and in 1919 he was assigned to the American army of occupation in Germany. More than two decades later, he took command of the 11th Armored Division at Fort Knox in 1941 before taking over the 2nd Armored Division in 1944.

Devers and Brooks were old friends. Brooks had been an instructor at West Point while Devers was director of athletics, and their wives were good friends as well. The two officers worked together again at Fort Sill, Oklahoma, where Brooks was an instructor when Devers was head of the department of gunnery. Devers considered Brooks a "brilliant" artilleryman, "very quick, sharp, knew his business."[6] Devers also liked Brooks because he organized the Fort Sill Headquarters Detachment football team and proved to be a winning coach.

As war approached and Devers was given command of the army's armored forces, he wanted "a topnotch, aggressive, imaginative artilleryman." Ted Brooks, who was in the G-3 section of the General Staff under General Marshall at that time, was his first choice.[7] Devers recalled:

> I had orders from General Marshall when I wanted to see him to just walk into his office and sit down. When he was ready to talk he would raise his head and ask me a question. Well, that's what happened. I said, "Sir, I need an aggressive artilleryman to get this Armored Force Artillery straightened out."
>
> He said, "Have you got anybody in mind?"
>
> "Yes, I'd like to have Major Brooks."

"Does he want to go?"

"Yes."

He said, "You can have him."

I got up, saluted, walked out there, and told Bedell Smith, "Give orders to Ted Brooks to report to Fort Knox, Kentucky, just as soon as he can."

Brooks was on the train for Fort Knox that night and was in Devers' office the next morning. Devers and Brooks would work well together in the 6th Army Group.

Devers liked to finish the story of his "stealing" Ted Brooks from General Marshall, who apparently had not been paying close attention to what Devers was saying. "The next morning the Chief of Staff had some papers on his desk, he pushed the bell, and said, 'Send Major Brooks in here,' and Bedell said, 'Well, General, you gave Major Brooks to General Devers yesterday.' 'Where is he?' 'He's at Fort Knox, Kentucky.' I don't think General Marshall ever got over that one."[8]

The 6th Corps' advance toward Saint-Dié and the Meurthe River continued in mid-October. The 3rd and 45th divisions made steady headway initially. The 30th Regiment of the 45th Division advanced all the way to the Magdeleine woods to take the high ground overlooking Saint-Dié. But German resistance stiffened as Wiese once again played a desperate game of chess to stop the Americans.

To the south, the 442nd Regimental Combat Team—the famed "Go for Broke" Japanese American Regiment—made its appearance on the western front. Together with the 36th Division, the 442nd penetrated the forbidding Domaniale de Champ forest, a thickly wooded area southwest of Saint-Dié.[9] The regiment added to its long list of laurels when it went to the relief of a battalion of infantry from the 141st Regiment.

The Japanese Americans who made up the 442nd had already fought a war just to be there. Thousands of Japanese Americans who lived on the West Coast had been forcibly interned after Pearl Harbor and deprived of their rights as citizens, including the right to fight for their country. When a group of second-generation Japanese Americans, or Nisei, were forced to retire from the Hawaii National Guard, they demanded their right to fight and were put to work as laborers. Having demonstrated their loyalty to the United States, they were formed into an infantry battalion and sent to the mainland United States for training. The 442nd was formed out of this group and grew to include Nisei from the mainland, many from the internment camps. The men of the 442nd RCT were not sent to the Pacific; instead they went to North Africa and later to Italy, where their unit established a reputation as one of the fiercest fighting outfits in the army.

In late September, the 442nd was shipped from Italy to southern France and attached to the 36th Division. The unit's first action came on October 14 in the battle for Bruyères, a small town some fifteen miles east of Saint-Dié, where they encountered conditions typical of the fighting in the Vosges. Bruyères was in a valley surrounded by broken terrain and mountains that rose several hundred meters and were covered by tall pines and thick underbrush. The sky was overcast, the day was cold, and the men advanced through penetrating rain. "Sometimes low hanging fog rolled in to lend the whole picture an atmosphere of unreality, as if the men were fighting in a cold, alien dream world." German artillery exploded in the treetops and showered the men below with jagged steel fragments. There was no place to take cover. The fighting raged back and forth. The enemy troops were well entrenched in prepared defenses and counterattacked regularly at dusk and dawn. The fighting was often hand to hand, with guns fired at point-blank range. By October 23 the 442nd, operating on the 36th Division's left, had penetrated several miles toward the center of the Domaniale forest. Thus began the saga of the "the Lost Battalion" of World War II.[10]

For a week, worldwide attention focused on efforts to relieve the 1st Battalion of the 141st Regiment, which was trapped on Hill 645. The struggle to save the unit became a contest of wills, with Hitler reportedly issuing orders to destroy the battalion at all costs while the Americans fought desperately to save their comrades. All three of the 442nd's battalions attacked in the relief effort on October 27. The "Buddhaheads" were held up by tank-supported enemy infantry, artillery, and snipers. Roadblocks slowed the rescuers, as did the rugged terrain.

Finally, they attacked. In groups of ones and twos, the men in Companies I and K advanced toward the enemy positions on top of the hill as shells fell around them and machine-gun fire took its toll. The attackers moved slowly from tree to tree and from cover to cover; men fired from the hip and then rushed in with hand grenades. Some of them died in the advance, but the enemy was overwhelmed. When the Lost Battalion was finally relieved, both defenders and saviors were too exhausted to celebrate.

Despite these successes, the American advance into the Vosges had stalled by the end of October. Bad weather coupled with ammunition shortages and battle fatigue among the troops conspired to slow the drive. The relief of the Lost Battalion had also diverted energy and resources from the main objective of reaching the Alsace Plain.

With the approach of November and winter coming on in the Vosges, the Americans now faced the prospect of stalemate as fatigue sapped the aggressiveness of the troops. When the 103rd Division relieved the 3rd Division around Saint-Dié, Pfc. Robert Elsner, who was with an intelligence and reconnaissance platoon, was appalled by the condition of the men his division was relieving. "I thought, my God, these guys are really beaten. They looked like Zombies, they were dirty, unshaven and absolutely without emotion. They looked old enough to be our fathers. Within two weeks we looked the same."[11]

Exhaustion gripped the men of the 3rd Division at all levels and grades. To his wife, Ruth, General Dahlquist wrote: "The fatigue of the officers and men is so great. . . . The fatigue on regimental and battalion commanders almost passes comprehension. The soldier finally falls asleep but the commander cannot. I'm sometimes afraid some are getting a little punch drunk."[12]

But the Germans were equally exhausted and in no condition to fight the well-supplied and numerically superior Americans. Little by little the Americans ground down the defenders, giving them no rest and no chance to resupply. Had the battle continued, write U.S. Army historians Jeffrey J. Clarke and Robert Ross Smith, "Wiese would have no troops to man and defend the Vosges foothills positions or any other winter defensive line. The fighting . . . thus seemed to be coming down to a matter of will and stamina—a war of attrition that, without assistance from the outside, only the more determined opponent would win."[13]

If the fight through the Vosges seemed interminable, the progress of the 6th Army Group was no less than that of 21st and 12th army groups to the north. Efforts to breach the Siegfried Line all along the western front had failed. But Devers had one advantage over his immediate opponent, General Wiese, that other Allied commanders lacked. Wiese's Nineteenth Army was probably the weakest of the German formations on the western front. In the fall of 1944 Balck's Army Group G, which included the Nineteenth, was being depleted of some of its best units as they were withdrawn from the line and sent to plug gaps farther north or were reassigned to train for the planned German attack through the Ardennes. But the Allies were oblivious to the Germans' intention to mount the massive counterattack that came to be known as the Battle of the Bulge. In mid-October Army Group G lost the bulk of the 15th Panzer Grenadier Division, which was sent to bolster Army Group B that held the German front north of the Ardennes.[14] The 553rd Volks Grenadier Division, which had been whittled down to a few battalions, replaced it. Balck also lost von Manteuffel's Fifth Panzer Army, which also was reassigned to Army Group B, leaving Balck with only the First and Nineteenth armies. On October 28, Wiese lost the 89th Corps to the German First Army. The Nineteenth was being stripped more than the others because Balck saw Patton's Third Army as a greater threat than Devers' 6th Army Group.[15] The Americans' plan was no secret to anyone; the principal objectives were the Ruhr and the Saar, not the south from Karlsruhe to Mulhouse on the Swiss frontier. Balck also calculated that even if Devers broke through the Nineteenth Army's defenses and reached the Rhine, he would not cross.

On October 31, Devers was preparing to renew what he hoped would be the final drive to break through the Vosges. Leclerc's 2nd Armored Division attacked in the north in the vicinity of Baccarat; the 6th Corps pressed forward toward the Meurthe River in the center; and the French 2nd Corps launched a diversionary attack in the south to freeze the Germans in place and prevent them from sending reinforcements to contain the attacks by the 15th and 6th corps. By the first week in November, the 15th Corps was poised to attack toward the Saverne Gap, the 6th Corps was in a strong position on the west bank of the Meurthe, and the French were preparing an offensive to break through the Belfort Gap.

Two fresh American divisions came on the line in early November to reinforce the 6th Army Group. The 100th Infantry Division took over the zone covered by the 45th Division, and the 103rd relieved the 3rd Division. These new divisions were two of the three that Eisenhower had redirected to Marseille from their previously scheduled landing area of Normandy. Devers' 6th Army Group would soon have an overwhelming manpower advantage over the rapidly diminishing Nineteenth Army.

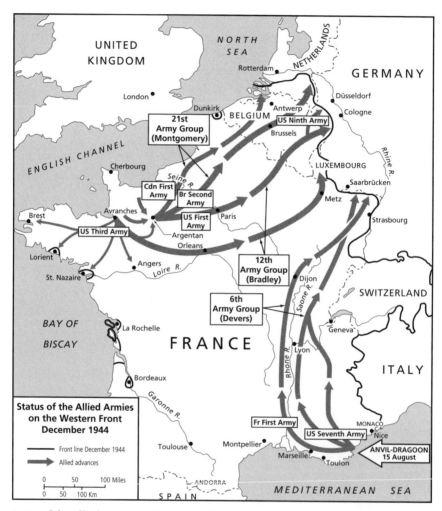

Status of the Allied armies on the western front, December 1944.

# CHAPTER 12

# Whither the 6th Army Group?

★ ★ ★ ★

Despite successes that rivaled or surpassed those of the 12th and 21st army groups, the 6th Army Group fought on without clear strategic direction from SHAEF or General Eisenhower.[1] This army of Frenchmen and Americans, which eventually exceeded 400,000 men, was relegated to a secondary and passive role on the western front. Devers' forces held the southern end of the line some 170 miles south of the Ruhr, but the 6th was not designated to assist in taking this critical objective. SHAEF limited Devers' role to tying up enemy troops on the southern end of the western front and to guarding the Third Army's right flank as Patton pushed to the Rhine. The Germans knew of Devers' role in Allied plans and considered his upper Rhine front a low risk for a major offensive into Germany. Thus, they assigned mediocre and depleted units to Alsace and withdrew more effective ones, such as the Fifth Panzer Army, to fight elsewhere or to prepare for the Ardennes offensive.

The supreme command's refusal to consider Devers and the 6th Army Group as a genuine fighting force throughout the war was directly related to a clash of personalities between Ike and Devers. Eisenhower disliked and mistrusted his three-star subordinate and seemed determined to exclude him from major operations on the western front. He also ensured that the northern army commanders would bask in glory before Devers did.

"Ike's unwonted coolness toward the 6th Army Group commander went beyond the usual and immediate explanation that Devers, unlike Bradley and Patton, was not an old friend," historian Russell Weigley asserts; indeed, there was a touch of "irrationality" in Ike's aversion to Devers.[2] Patton confirmed the supreme commander's sentiments when he wrote in his diary that Ike "hated" Devers.

Historian Carlo D'Este agrees that "Eisenhower's low regard for Devers was based too much on personal dislike and too little on his effective performance as 6th Army Group commander. Had Devers not been an outsider and an unwelcome protégé of Marshall whose mere presence in the Allied lineup led to criticism of virtually everything he ever did, Eisenhower's attitude might have been quite different."[3] Likewise, had the 6th Army Group been under the command of a general chosen by Ike, its role might have been very different and the strategy employed to defeat the enemy more flexible.

Ike's disrespect and dislike flared in 1943 when Devers, the U.S. commander of Allied forces in Europe, refused Ike's request to transfer several bomber squadrons from the Eighth Air Force in Britain to the North African theater.[4] Despite the fact that General Marshall and the Eighth's top general, Ira Eaker, supported Devers' decision, Eisenhower never forgave Devers.

There were other contentious encounters between the two men prior to D-day in 1944. After Ike was appointed supreme commander in Europe in December 1943, he snubbed Devers by not personally informing him that he had been reassigned.[5] Devers heard of his new posting through the grapevine and later read about it in *Stars and Stripes*. Shortly thereafter, when Devers was in Algiers as commander of U.S. forces in the Mediterranean under Gen. Maitland Wilson of the British army, Ike asked him to release a number of generals serving in the North African command for field positions in the upcoming Normandy invasion. Devers demurred, complaining that Eisenhower wanted to strip his headquarters bare. He eventually gave Ike all the men he had asked for but the one he wanted most, Lucian Truscott. Devers had selected Truscott to command the 6th Corps in the invasion of southern France and refused to release him for Operation Overlord. "We have tried to meet your requests for personnel to the utmost possible limit," Devers wired to Ike. "Sorry we could not do it 100 percent. . . . You may count on me to be in there pitching with one idea, to assist you." Eisenhower called Devers "obstinate" and complained to Marshall that Devers was standing in the way of the Normandy invasion. But once again Marshall concurred in Devers' decision. Bedell Smith sneered at the communiqué in which Devers declined to release Truscott and penned a sarcastic note at the bottom of the page, "This is just swell. I love this. 'One idea to assist you.'"[6] Smith's and Eisenhower's lack of confidence in Devers continued to grow as the war progressed. Kay Summersby, Eisenhower's driver and confidant, summed up in her diary what was undoubtedly the supreme commander's opinion of Devers: "Bedell Smith announced that he frankly had not 'much confidence in our friend Jakey.'"[7]

Adding to the Devers-Eisenhower split after the Allies had established themselves in France in 1944 was the fact that Devers had not been part of Eisenhower's coterie of generals who planned and executed the Normandy invasion. Ike's commanders had worked together for months and formed a coordinated team. Devers was an outsider, and Eisenhower was at a loss about what to do with him and the 6th Army Group when SHAEF took command of them on September 15, 1944.

From the moment the 6th landed in France, Devers sought a defined mission for his troops. On August 20 he requested permission from General Wilson—his boss until SHAEF took control of the 6th Army Group—to visit SHAEF headquarters "with a view of learning at first hand how [Eisenhower] proposed to use . . . the 6th Army Group coming up from southern France."[8] But a well-thought-out mission statement from the supreme command had not been and never would be developed. SHAEF had already determined that the main effort of the war in the ETO would be in the northern sector of the Allied line against the Ruhr and the Saar.[9] SHAEF planners saw the southern end of the Allied line as without strategic importance. Regardless of what the 6th Army Group did, its actions would in no way materially enhance Allied plans to capture the Ruhr. Devers' forces would have to cross the High Vosges to reach the Rhine and then fight through the expanse of the Black Forest once across the river to reach Nuremberg or Munich, cities SHAEF did not consider strategic objectives. The southernmost army before Devers' troops arrived was Patton's Third Army. Patton's objective was the Saar, but he was also responsible for holding the right flank of the First Army in the drive to take the Ruhr. Now the 6th Army Group would take over the flanking role.[10]

Commenting on Devers' breakout in Alsace at a November 1944 press conference, Ike told reporters, "I would say the Germans won't regard it as seriously as one farther north. The position we now occupy [in Alsace] is far from the Ruhr, and that section of the Rhine does not lead as quickly to the definitely decisive areas as some of the other avenues."[11] As Ike saw it, a 6th Army Group attack across the Rhine offered little threat to the enemy's rear. While Devers was planning to cross the river and unhinge the German front, the supreme commander concluded that the 6th Army Group's best role would be to support the Third Army's right flank as Patton pushed to take the Saar.

Ike would have preferred to disband the 6th Army Group altogether and attach Patch's Seventh Army to Bradley's 12th Army Group. The Seventh Army could then operate in conjunction with Patton's Third Army to cross the Rhine and approach the Ruhr south of the Ardennes through the rolling hills of Hesse.[12] Bradley believed that the two armies working together could deliver a powerful blow to the Germans.

Much as Ike wanted the Seventh Army for Bradley, however, General Marshall was still his boss, and Devers was Marshall's protégé. Dismantling the 6th Army Group and depriving Devers of a job would be construed as a slap at the army chief of staff.[13] A more logical step for Eisenhower in dealing with his southern front would have been to assign the Third Army to the 6th Army Group. Devers endorsed that move, but Ike was not inclined to help Devers at the expense of his old friend Omar Bradley.

Regardless of what Eisenhower thought, Devers and his commanders saw great advantages for the Allied cause in using his two armies to drive the Germans from Alsace and continue the offensive across the Rhine. Historians Clarke and Smith suggest several possibilities for Devers' forces. Eisenhower could, for example, have sent

> a reinforced 6th Army Group north through the Rhenish plains in a vast enveloping maneuver against the flank or rear of the German forces defending the Saar and Ruhr regions; or . . . north as far as Frankfurt and then northeast, following the famous Napoleonic route towards Berlin. Instead, both Eisenhower and his major subordinates remained preoccupied with their existing plans, which called for a drive into Germany by two army groups, one operating north of the Ardennes forest, and the other to the south. . . . But SHAEF planners had never taken into consideration a major force coming up from the south, and SHAEF concepts had not changed after CCS [Combined Chiefs of Staff] approved Dragoon, or even after the Seventh Army had landed and sped northward faster than anyone expected.[14]

Believing the 6th Army Group's role in the ETO to be peripheral, SHAEF gave it a quasi-independent status as long as it covered the Third Army's right flank, and Devers was allowed to develop his own strategy with little interference and oversight. Nevertheless, he sought direction from SHAEF on several occasions. An entry in the Seventh Army diary for September 19, 1944, reflects the frustration of Devers and his commanders as they sought a course of action from the supreme command, at least on the tactical side. The entry notes that they wanted (1) "a definite zone of action"; (2) "a definite objective"; (3) "a broad scheme of maneuver"; and (4) "means to accomplish their mission."[15] Devers believed that his orders and priorities were identical with those for the 12th and 21st army groups: to destroy the opposing enemy forces, capture crossings over the Rhine and establish bridgeheads on the opposite bank, and breach the Siegfried Line. But SHAEF never considered what to do if the 6th Army Group actually succeeded in achieving these goals before the 12th and 21st army groups, and it ignored many of the communications issued by the 6th Army Group headquarters, including those spelling out in detail Devers' plans to cross the Rhine.[16]

Devers had sympathetic subordinates. Truscott was champing at the bit to finish off the enemy, and he believed that the 6th Army Group's role was anything but peripheral. SHAEF and Eisenhower might be more interested in adhering to old plans and in capturing real estate in the Ruhr and Saar than in destroying the German army, but Devers intended to push on aggressively and accomplish his objectives nevertheless.

CHAPTER 13.

# The Prickly French

★ ★ ★ ★

Ike's dislike for Jacob Devers was not the only reason he was reluctant to make better strategic use of the 6th Army Group. Ike did not care much for the French army under Devers' command either. In general, the Americans perceived the French as haughty, excitable, sometimes insubordinate, and mediocre in performance. The French defeat in the month-long Battle for France in May and June 1940 had lowered the French army's esteem in American eyes. In 1944, the Americans and British still questioned French resolve and regarded the *poilus* as inferior soldiers who had to be pushed to fight.

"Eisenhower never really believed in them," Devers remarked in a 1966 interview. "He didn't think the French were doing the best they could."[1] Devers thought the English and Americans were often wrong in their assessment of the French and that with leadership and adequate supplies they made excellent and proud soldiers. Many Americans who fought alongside the French regarded them favorably. "We resented them because they wore American uniforms, but we thought they were very good," recalled Paul Fussell. "They had something to fight for, namely to restore the honor of France."[2]

Friction between the Americans in the Seventh Army and the French in the French First Army became severe enough that army group headquarters initiated an investigation to uncover the sources of the conflicts. Among the problems identified were the language barrier and the Americans' failure to explain military decisions, rudeness toward French officers, and unwillingness to credit the French with any military prowess.[3]

Ike's low opinion of the French as soldiers may have been influenced by his year-long assignment in France in 1929, when he was stationed in Paris to write a history of the American military cemeteries established in France after World War I. Major Hansen, General Bradley's aide, remarked on certain of Eisenhower's prejudices: "Ike spoke volubly of Paris and the Parisiennes whom he described as unpleasant people with uncommon percentage of rude and filthy folk and spoke of his experience with Frenchmen whom he observed making advances towards French women in the Metro and the Dome. Also spoke of filthy peep shows so prevalent in prewar Paris and insisted that his command would avoid this sort of thing if they were interested in remaining in his headquarters."[4]

A far greater problem for Ike was Gen. Charles de Gaulle, the self-appointed leader of the Free French, to whom the French First Army owed political allegiance. Major Hansen described de Gaulle as "tall, stern, dour and unsmiling; he looked like Heathcliff from the moors." De Gaulle had reason to be dour. He was a proud man in a difficult situation, and he knew the Allies perceived him as an unreliable ally. When he proclaimed, "I am France," in Great Britain in 1941 after France surrendered to Germany, he in essence established a government and a rallying point for the French army.[5] Initially, few in the Allied camp were willing to deal with him as the country's new leader. De Gaulle stood alone for a free France after its surrender, however, and refused to yield his country's power and glory to the British and Americans.

Regardless of the Americans' opinion, De Gaulle was a well-educated and well-trained soldier who had learned his craft at the École spéciale militaire de Saint-Cyr, the foremost military academy in France. In 1913, as a young second lieutenant, he joined an infantry regiment commanded by Col. Philippe Pétain, who would become the German puppet leader of Vichy France during World War II. In World War I de Gaulle fought at Verdun, was three times wounded, and spent two years and eight months as a prisoner of war (he made five unsuccessful attempts to escape). At the outbreak of World War II de Gaulle commanded a tank brigade attached to the French Fifth Army. In May 1940, he was made a temporary brigadier general in the 4th Armored Division. Here he applied his theories on tank warfare and was one of the few French officers to force a German retreat. On June 6, 1940, he entered the government of Paul Reynaud as undersecretary of state for defense and war, and undertook several missions to England to explore the possibility of continuing the war after France's inevitable defeat. When Marshal Pétain took power and sought an armistice with the Germans, de Gaulle fled to England. On June 18, he broadcast from London his first appeal to his countrymen to continue the war under his leadership.

Although perhaps not as obstinate and sensitive to insult as de Gaulle, General de Lattre too was a difficult man to deal with. "He hears only what he wants to hear and retains only what he believes," Devers wrote about his French First Army commander.[6] De Lattre was prone to tirades, particularly about his forces not receiving adequate equipment from the Americans, who supplied all the French troops. He once complained so stridently to General Marshall that the taciturn chief of staff barely kept his temper and never trusted de Lattre afterward. Among the items required by the French army were wine and brandy, and the U.S. Quartermaster Corps did its best to keep up the French troops' spirits.

The new French army of 1944 barely resembled its predecessors of 1914–18 or 1940. How far the French had fallen! A little more than a quarter of a century earlier, during World War I, the French had maintained one of the largest and finest armies the world had ever seen—some 8,317,000 men were called to duty— and one of the best dressed. French soldiers charged into battle wearing *ciel* (sky blue) uniforms with matching blue helmets; 1.3 million of them died.

At the outset of World War II, the French army comprised 101 divisions and more than six million men, many of them veterans. Its top officers, like General de Gaulle, had been trained in the maelstrom of World War I. No one imagined that Hitler's legions could defeat this army protected by the impregnable defenses of the Maginot Line. But the Germans did not assault the Maginot Line's defenses. They attacked through the Ardennes, whose terrain the French judged to be too rugged for an offensive. German armor followed by infantry punched through the French front and swung north and south in a sweeping envelopment. The French army suddenly found the Germans in their rear; within a month, in June 1940, the French Army met disastrous defeat on all fronts. A few remnants fled south and established a zigzagging front line stretching from the Bordeaux area to Switzerland near Geneva.[7] This once-proud force, the envy of the world, was disbanded, its men sent home in disgrace or to labor camps in the Reich. A skeleton army under Pétain's Vichy government was maintained in southern France and in colonial North Africa.

The French army invading Alsace was a conglomeration of disparate groups, some at odds—and sometimes at war—with each other. The bulk of de Lattre's units came from various parts of the Mediterranean. One hundred thousand French troops—a corps of four Moroccan and Algerian infantry, motorized, and mountain divisions—were drawn from Italy, where they had fought alongside British and American troops. Another 150,000 French troops had been stationed in Tunisia, Algeria, and Morocco, where they had joined with the British and Americans after the Allies conquered North Africa.[8] De Lattre also began absorbing resistance fighters and new recruits on French soil. He later remarked that "never before had there been such a melting pot as this . . . the flower of our youth was assembled . . . [w]ell-officered and superbly trained. Never in our past had a French army been given such a task; it was not a matter only of winning battles, but of bringing freedom to the homeland and restoring it to its place in the world."[9]

The ranks of the new army were heavy with colonial Moroccans, Algerians, Senegalese, and Tunisians. The 2nd Moroccan Division was composed of *saphis* (cavalry) and *tirailleurs* (infantry) units. Not many years before, these troops were the stuff of Beau Geste. The saphis, who raced into battle on Arabian horses, wore flowing capes of dark blue and wide pantaloons that bloused down to leather boots. The infantry, which attacked with long-barreled rifles, wore light blue jackets and pantaloons; on their heads they wore chochias, a cross between a Turkish fez and a Tyrolean fedora. In France in 1944, however, these dark-skinned men wore field brown; their steeds had given way to tanks, and the long rifles to American M-1 semiautomatic Garands or Carbines.[10] The Moroccans were naturals in a fight, remarkable on patrol, and especially talented in night infiltration. A Seventh Army press release praised them: "They glide along in the dark with a stealth that would startle a Sioux. They delight in slipping up to German outpost guards and leaving them breathless—literally! They relish hand-to-hand combat."[11] But the native North Africans were unused to the European winter, and their effectiveness declined as the weather became colder. They were slowly reassigned to duty closer to the Mediterranean along the Italian frontier, where winter is milder, but the ranks of French First Army were depleted in the process.[12]

Men also came to de Lattre from French units that had guarded the French colonies in Africa and the Middle East. There were officers and men who had joined de Gaulle's Free French forces in Great Britain and officers, like de Lattre himself, who had commanded Vichy units in North Africa.[13] Also included in the new army were thousands of FFI (French Forces of the Interior) fighters who had stayed behind after the fall of France and joined the resistance movement. Many of the FFI fighters were avowed Communists who detested the men who had served Pétain and the Vichy Nazi puppets. "A certain number [of FFI], especially among the leaders, showed a coolness which with some went as far as hostility. . . . Some thought themselves qualified—and alone qualified—to give France its new army, made in the image of the maquis [resistance fighters]," de Lattre recalled.[14]

The differences between the various factions comprising the French First Army sometimes erupted into such serious conflict that General Patch had to consider withdrawing the army from the line. The bad blood in the new French army was perhaps nowhere more evident than in the relationship between General de Lattre and Gen. Philippe Leclerc. Leclerc refused to serve under de Lattre because he believed the French First Army was "corrupted and spoiled"; he made no secret of his preference to fight with the Americans, who were unencumbered by age-old military traditions that interfered with military efficiency. A French liaison officer serving with Leclerc's division described the difference between life in the French First Army and in Leclerc's Americanized 2nd Armored Division. Meeting with de Lattre and his staff "was like walking into another world," remembered Capt. Jean Chatel. "It was so elegant. But after they had dined and wined me and been very kind I could soon see there was so much there still of the bad old ways of the French Army, the love of elaborate routine and paper-work and written orders. By contrast Leclerc was a realist."[15] Leclerc may also have bridled at de Lattre's former ties to Vichy and believed that his own amalgamated 2nd Armored Division, which had fought in the Saharan sands of North Africa and through Normandy to regain the honor and glory of France, more truly represented France.

The animosity between the two French generals seriously affected the Allied cause in November 1944 when, after the capture of Strasbourg, Leclerc was half-hearted in carrying out Devers' order to advance south along the Rhine to link his 2nd Armored Division with de Lattre's French First Army in southern Alsace. Had Leclerc moved aggressively, Wiese's Nineteenth Army would have been surrounded and its destruction almost assured. Instead, the Nineteenth survived in its bridgehead in Alsace, the Colmar Pocket, until February 1945.[16]

Eisenhower reportedly told Bradley that only his reluctance to allow the French to fight on their own prevented him from assigning the Seventh Army to the 12th Army Group, and Ike assured Bradley that the Seventh Army would "always be maneuvered to support your operations."[17] Had Ike transferred the Seventh to Bradley, the French First Army would probably have gone under independent French command, with serious political and military repercussions. The prickly French might have decided to fight their own war against the Germans.

Ike may not have considered Devers a competent commander, but he could at least be expected to obey an order, whereas the French had already shown a proclivity to disregard directives from the supreme command. General Leclerc was prepared to disobey SHAEF orders not to advance into Paris as the Germans retreated from northern France in August 1944. He wanted his French armored division to be the first Allied unit into the capital, and he began sending in troops and tanks without SHAEF's approval.[18]

De Gaulle likewise was prepared to defy Eisenhower in Alsace in January 1945 when he refused the supreme commander's orders to evacuate Strasbourg during the German counterattack code-named Operation Northwind.[19] Eisenhower wanted to pull back from Strasbourg to defensive lines in the eastern foothills of the Vosges Mountains to shorten the 6th Army Group's front in Alsace. De Gaulle would have none of it. He deemed Strasbourg so politically important to the French cause that he threatened to remove the French First Army from SHAEF command and defend Strasbourg to the last man with his own forces.

The glue that held this makeshift army together was a common hatred of the Germans, and the only thing that kept it going were American supplies and equipment and the promise of a vast, untapped manpower reserve in a liberated France. In the fall of 1944, however, the proud French could muster only some 256,000 troops, many of them natives of North and Central Africa, to fight the hated Boches.

# CHAPTER 14

# The Greatest Obstacle

★ ★ ★ ★

The Rhine flows swift and deep more than seven hundred miles from Switzerland to the North Sea. It is a river of magnificent beauty with precipitous gorges and lush green banks studded with vineyards. Tugboats and barges chug up and down its length from Basel, Switzerland, to the Netherlands, gliding past storybook villages and ancient castles. From the earliest times, the Rhine has protected the German heartland from invasion from the west, and only the greatest of armies could breach its wide expanse and rapid waters. Caesar's legions erected a bridge over the river near the present-day city of Neuwied in 55 BC to pursue Germanic tribesmen who threatened Roman rule. Caesar needed to demonstrate that the Rhine was not the limit of the Roman Empire and "that a Roman army could and would cross the Rhine and terrify Germany."[1]

It took Caesar's engineers ten days to span the Rhine. "The construction of a bridge presented great difficulties by reason of the width, rapidity and depth of the river," Caesar wrote.[2] The same considerations would face American and British engineers as they attempted to span the Rhine in 1944 and 1945. Even with modern tools and equipment, bridging the river would be a formidable task. Caesar accomplished the job by erecting a structure formed of beams laid on a foundation of piles driven diagonally into the riverbed to withstand the force of the current. His engineers erected another structure of diagonal piles a few yards upstream to act as a buttress to protect the bridge against tree trunks and barges the barbarians might launch downriver in hope of destroying it. The German army of 1944 could be expected to use similar methods of destruction along with aerial bombs and artillery shells.

Nearly two thousand years after Caesar, Napoleon's armies crossed the Rhine on their way to the Battle of Austerlitz in 1805. Napoleon was acquainted with the difficulties of the river, as was Field Marshal Alan Brooke, chief of the British Imperial General Staff a century and a half later. Brooke described the Rhine during World War II as "the greatest water obstacle in western Europe."[3]

Indeed, the Rhine loomed as a major obstacle from the time the Allies landed in Normandy in June 1944 and all through their advance through France during August 1944 in pursuit of the defeated and demoralized Wehrmacht. So daunting was the river that American engineers in both the Third and Seventh armies drew up plans to span it as early as September 1944 and established river-crossing schools on various waterways in France to train engineers for the rough conditions they would encounter.[4] The Germans had an almost mystical belief in the Rhine as an impenetrable barrier. As they retreated through France to the defenses of the Siegfried Line, they always knew that behind them lay the Rhine, the perfect fallback position and the most effective defensive line of all.

Even with Germany's resources stretched to the limit in late 1944 and enemies approaching in the east from Russia and from the south in Italy, many Germans viewed the Rhine as both a real and a symbolic barrier to invasion; if the Rhine should be breached, all would be lost. Hitler agreed with the teachings of Count Alfred von Schlieffen, chief of the German General Staff in the late nineteenth century, who viewed any enemy on or across the Rhine as more dangerous than an impending invasion from the east. Behind the Rhine in northwestern Germany lay the Ruhr industrial area, the heart of Germany's war-making machine.[5]

Seven months before the Allied invasion of France in June 1944, while the Russian armies still presented the greatest threat to the Reich, Hitler reiterated his fears that Germany could not survive long if the Ruhr fell to the western Allies. He warned his generals that the danger posed by the Russians approaching from the east "was outweighed by the threat from the West where enemy success would strike immediately at the heart of the German war economy."[6] Several German generals spoke of the Rhine's importance as a military obstacle in postwar interviews with American military historian Brig. Gen. S. L. A. Marshall. Their remarks related to the American capture of the Remagen bridge on March 7, 1945, but they could have pertained to a Rhine crossing at any place and at any time during the last year of the war.

"How could it have happened? We are a military people. We are not that careless," Marshall reported several German generals lamenting during interrogations after the war.[7] Marshall added:

> Their reverses at Avranches [in Normandy], Utah Beach and in the Ardennes they could understand and even accept with no feeling that the results were other than mathematically inevitable. But toward Remagen they had the demoralized view of men who feel [that] . . . black magic fights on the other side. When the first Rhine bridge [Remagen] was lost, the Hitler Army reeled and its combat leaders became gutted of hope. . . . Until Remagen occurred there was always another barrier behind which

this fraying army could dream of collecting itself and holding until some terms could be made. Thereafter the dream died. . . . "Remagen killed us" the German generals said over and over.[8]

Gen. Siegfried Westphal, a highly rated staff officer who served under Rommel in North Africa and with Field Marshal von Rundstedt in Europe, said of the Americans' capture of the Remagen bridge, "Just as an elastic band under excessive tension no longer extends but snaps, the thin line which now represented the German front was torn asunder. As there were no reserves in the rear the enemy was able to push forward to the bridge unhindered."[9]

The Americans understood this concept very well. Col. William W. Quinn, the Seventh Army's chief intelligence officer, wrote to General Patch: "So long as the Rhine river is not crossed, . . . the German nation would probably hold out in its present status in the political grip of Nazism . . . and German troops will continue to fight until the threat against the lives of their relatives has been eliminated."[10]

The Allies had given little thought to reaching the Rhine when they drew up plans for the Normandy invasion; Overlord's planners did not expect Allied troops to reach the river until mid-1945, too far in the future to be of immediate concern. But as the Allies approached Germany, Eisenhower and SHAEF were fixated on capturing the Ruhr and the Saar, and were planning to cross the Rhine in the vicinity of these objectives. No amount of arguing about crossing the Rhine farther to the south would change their minds.

# CHAPTER 15.

# Cross the Rhine!

★ ★ ★ ★

Jacob Devers issued the following instructions to his armies in November 1944: "Sixth Army Group . . . continues the offensive, destroys the enemy in its zone of action west of the Rhine, seizes bridgeheads across the Rhine and breaches the Siegfried Line."[1] His plan was not a half-baked scheme hatched by field commanders on the fly. On the contrary, it was a well-prepared and detailed proposal and a well-rehearsed plan of action produced over a period of nearly three months, discussed with corps and army commanders, disseminated in its various parts to SHAEF, and essentially in keeping with the broad scope of Allied military thinking in the ETO. It conformed to directives from Eisenhower and SHAEF for the Seventh Army to protect the Third Army's right flank, drive the Germans from the west bank of the Rhine, and establish bridgeheads across the river for an advance into Germany's heartland.[2]

Devers and his 6th Army Group officers saw the Rhine crossing as a legitimate interpretation of SHAEF's orders. Historians Clarke and Smith agreed years later when they wrote that Supreme Command, Allied Forces, "directed Devers to clear the Germans from the Sixth Army Group's sector west of the Rhine and ultimately seize crossings over the river in the vicinity of Karlsruhe and Mannheim."[3] The 6th Army Group's plan was no different from those of the other Allied armies engaged on the western front in the late summer and early fall of 1944.[4] The objective of every operation along the line—from Aachen and the Hürtgen Forest north of the Ardennes to Metz in Lorraine and Strasbourg in Alsace—was to breach the Siegfried Line, drive the Germans back, cross the Rhine, and deliver the fatal blow to Germany.

Typical of the zeal of all commanders to cross this important water obstacle are orders drafted in mid-September 1944 by Patton's 20th Corps commander, Maj. Gen. Walton Walker. He called for his corps to cross the Rhine near Mainz and strike toward Frankfurt, 50 miles distant, in one uninterrupted attack. Patton noted in his diary on September 12, 1944, "It was decided today that we had

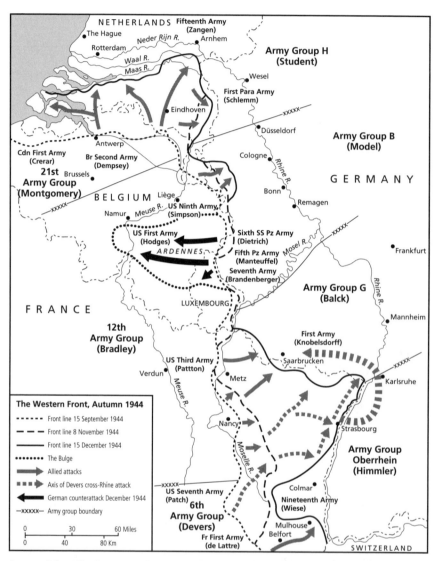

The Western Front, Autumn 1944

- - - - - - - Front line 15 September 1944
- - - - Front line 8 November 1944
——— Front line 15 December 1944
•••••••• The Bulge
➡ Allied attacks
▶▶▶▶ Axis of Devers cross-Rhine attack
◀ German counterattack December 1944
—xxxxx— Army group boundary

0       30        60 Miles
0     40      80 Km

Status of the Allied armies in late November 1944. The axis of the German Ardennes offensive that began December 16, 1944, is shown with the black arrows. Farther south, Devers' Sixth Army Group (solid gray arrows) is poised along the Rhine in Alsace with the axis of his proposed cross-Rhine attack shown in segmented gray as it cuts across the Rhine near Rastatt and swings back against the German First Army facing Gen. George Patton's Third Army in Lorraine, France.

enough supplies to get to the Rhine and force a crossing."[5] His cross-Rhine attack was not contingent on his army clearing every German from the west bank of the Rhine in his zone of operations. Patton was the master of lightning strikes deep into enemy territory that left large groups of enemy troops marooned in his rear to be rounded up later.

In September, many Allied generals were so confident of reaching the Rhine that they began betting among themselves on the date they would reach the river and when the German Reich would collapse. Major Hansen noted in his diary in mid-September that "Brad and Patton agree neither will be surprised if we are on the Rhine in a week."[6] Montgomery predicted the war would end by November 1, 1944; Bradley thought it would be a little later, but still before Christmas. Hansen chose November 25, 1944, as the date that he believed the First Army would reach the Rhine. His prediction was precise by date, but he had the wrong army. It was the Seventh Army that reached the objective first.

Devers' orders to division and corps commanders about preparing for a Rhine crossing dated to September 1944 and stated clearly that the river was the ultimate objective of Operation Dragoon. He never hid his intention to breach the Rhine. It was, he noted in his diary on October 27, 1944, "the main play." He intended to "destroy the German Army west of the Rhine," drive up along the Rhine with the 6th Corps, and then cross the river "and go up and cut in behind the [German] defensive lines and loosen up that whole front so Patton's Army . . . could move."[7]

Ike had encouraged his commanders to plan for Rhine crossings in their respective zones and had recently written Devers a letter to clarify the role of the 6th Army Group along the southern front. "Twelfth Army Group will strike with two armies astride the Ruhr," he instructed, "while the Third Army will secure the SAAR, cross the RHINE near FRANKFURT and advance probably towards Kassel." Ike then spelled out the responsibilities and objectives of Devers' forces:

> In these circumstances your role would be to protect the Southern flank of the Third Army throughout its operations. This, as I see it, will entail your advance into GERMANY in the direction of NURENBURG. It may be that the logistical situation will not permit your advance as deep as NURENBURG. Nevertheless to fulfill your protective role, your main operations in GERMANY are likely to be in the general area of MANNHEIM, COBURG, NURENBURG, KARLSRUHE. An advance to MUNICH and the clearing of the southern portion of your Army Group area I look on as a subsidiary role to be carried out as and when resources permit.
>
> The above should be sufficient guidance as to the general direction of the main weight of your attack and as to the area in which you will make

your main crossing of the Rhine. *This will presumably be in the general area KARLSRUHE–MANNHEIM.*[8]

Ike's assumption that the 6th Army Group would force a Rhine crossing around Karlsruhe conformed to Devers' own planning. But Eisenhower offered him no timeline for a cross-river assault; nor did he tell Devers not to jump the river until Patton had crossed or until the action was approved by SHAEF.

Eisenhower's directive, which Devers took as authorization to cross the Rhine, was supported by various other instructions from Eisenhower and SHAEF. The history of the headquarters of 6th Army Group states: "The attacks launched by Seventh Army on 13 November and by First French Army on 14 November were governed by the directive in SCAF [Supreme Command, Allied Forces] Message 114, amended as quoted in paragraph 111. This directive, in paragraph 7, called for taking advantage of any opportunities to 'seize' bridgeheads East of the RHINE during the first phase of the action while operations leading to their 'capture' were reserved for the Second Phase. The term 'seize' implied sudden action against little or no resistance."[9]

The history notes that the French First Army was not in a position at that moment to grab a bridgehead across the Rhine near Mulhouse, but adds: "The situation with respect to the Seventh Army was somewhat different. Its mission included 'protection of the southern flank of the Central Group of Armies' [the 12th Army Group], which was considered to include assistance on that flank in such form, as the Twelfth Army Group Commander, General Bradley, considered most effective. Which would be most helpful? Continued operations West of the RHINE or a crossing and advance to the North? This was essentially a choice between emphasis on close-in support on the one hand and indirect support by wide envelopment on the other."[10] Devers chose to accomplish both. The Seventh Army would attack north into the Siegfried Line defenses in eastern Lorraine and the Palatinate, and it would also cross the Rhine to come in behind German forces blocking the Third Army's path.

Clearly, SHAEF's directive to "seize" a bridgehead had to be interpreted as the immediate dispatch of forces across the Rhine, not an order advising restraint and waiting for some propitious moment in the future. By November 23, 1944, Devers was prepared and ready to carry out Ike's orders. He would cross.

Devers considered crossing the Rhine into Germany as the first step toward Berlin. He confided in his diary in early October 1944 that after a Rhine crossing, a drive "on to Berlin should be easy."[11] The 6th Army Group had virtually destroyed the German Nineteenth Army west of the Rhine, as Eisenhower had directed, and Devers' forces had surrounded its remnants around the city of Colmar in south-central Alsace. He did not believe the enemy in the Colmar Pocket constituted much of a threat, and he looked across the Rhine and into Germany for his next important objective.

While Devers reluctantly accepted Eisenhower's thinking that the Ruhr and the Saar were the primary focus of the Allied forces in bringing down Nazi Germany, he took issue with what he saw as Ike's fixation on these two objectives. "I shall emphasize in all my orders that we must capture the German army or what exists of it and take our minds off terrain; terrain to be considered of course in our efforts to capture or kill the maximum number of Germans."[12] Devers believed in November 1944 that his forces were in a position to play a critical role in helping to achieve Ike's goals. By crossing the Rhine he would draw enemy troops away from the Ruhr and the Saar, protect Patton's flank by attacking the Siegfried Line defenses in northern Alsace and in Lorraine from positions on both the east and west banks of the river, and force the Germans to shift critical reserves of men and matériel into southern Germany.

His independent supply line from Marseille into Alsace enhanced Devers' ability to contemplate a cross-Rhine assault. The 6th Army Group absorbed three combat divisions newly arrived from the United States in October—the 100th and 103rd infantry divisions, and the 14th Armored Division—to give the Seventh Army additional fighting power.[13] Devers' forces were ready to cross.

# CHAPTER 16.

# Planning the Crossing

★ ★ ★ ★

Planning for the Seventh Army to cross the Rhine began in September 1944—even before Devers' forces linked up with Patton's Third Army near Dijon—when General Patch's staff decided to use airborne forces to seize key bridges across the Rhine. A September 14 entry in the Seventh Army diary notes two options:

> Plan "A"—a parachute drop in the MULHOUSE area not earlier than 18 September for the purpose of blocking roads in the vicinity and exploiting toward MULHOUSE and the RHINE within capabilities.

> Plan "B"—a parachute drop in the MULHOUSE–FREIBERG area after 23 September for the purpose of seizing and holding existing bridges across the Rhine or blocking important roads in the FREIBURG–BASLE area to assist a crossing of the Rhine in the MULHOUSE–COLMAR area.[1]

When Truscott's 6th Corps was ordered north into the Vosges, however, a crossing in September in southern Alsace had to be postponed. The Seventh Army planners continued the process nevertheless. On September 24, a special board of officers was created "for the purpose of coordinating the planning of the crossing of the Rhine and operations subsequent thereto." The board was instructed to "submit plans in broad outline for crossing the RHINE river at the most feasible points within the present SEVENTH ARMY zone of action. Plans will be submitted to the Chief of Staff, through A.C. of S., G-3 by 1800A, 28th September. Upon acceptance, the plan will be developed to include details of crossing."[2]

The planning board evaluated each possible crossing site and produced a document titled "The Assault Crossing of the Rhine River from Basle to Manheim" that included briefs on such topics as "Terrain Appreciation," "Appreciation of the Communications Network," climate and flood conditions, and "Considerations Affecting River Crossings and Evaluation of Possible Zones of Action." Other aspects of the study considered such issues as the "Meteorological Considerations Affecting the Crossing of the Rhine."[3]

The Seventh Army intended to make extensive use of the French railway system to supply its advance into Germany.[4] An October 6 directive from the 6th Army Group called on the headquarters staff "to consider and formulate a railway plan to include the rehabilitation and use of railways in forward areas extending to and including the crossings of the Rhine." The 6th Army Group also requested a study "to formulate plans as pertains to Military Government, Counter-intelligence, and Provost Marshal activities in conformance with existing SHAEF policies for entry into Germany."[5]

The final report considered all of these aspects, as the extracts quoted below show.

Obstacles to Military Operations

a. On the west side of the Rhine north–south movements will be fairly easy, especially along the terraced land at the foot of the Vosges and along the ridge between the Rhine and the Ill [River]. East–west movement along existing roadways should not present any problems. . . . Free movement of mechanized units along the many roads of the floor of the Rhine valley is anticipated although narrow bridges might be encountered. Towns are local bottlenecks for vehicular traffic and are not readily bypassed. In general, areas for the deployment of mechanized units are limited due to marshes and lakes of the flood plains of the Ill and Rhine. . . .

b. For cross country movement the flood plain of the Ill . . . would present some difficulties, as would swamps, backwaters, and drainage ditches of the Rhine. Thickly wooded areas are readily avoided. All points are accessible to foot troops and light artillery.

c. On the east side of the River Rhine similar ground and road conditions are anticipated in the plains and lowlands rising eastward to the foot of the Black Forest mountains.

Observation, Cover, and Concealment

a. Observation from the floor of the Rhine is generally obscured by vegetation and buildings. Church towers and tall buildings in towns will afford good lookouts. Groups of hills in the Rhine Plain between Mulhouse and Strasbourg afford excellent observation up and down the valley. Areas of good cover alternate with those where there is practically none. . . .

The Existing Road Net, Climate Conditions. . . .

a. There are two excellent, paved highways running the entire length of the corridor; on the east side along the foot of the Black Forest Mountains and the Odenwald; on the west side along the terrace land at the foot of the Vosges and the Hardt. There also exists a good accessory net of surfaced secondary roads running in general east–west and north–south directions.

b. On the east side, the principal highway starting at Basel passes through Freiburg and thence to Mannheim. From Kehl, secondary roads run in a southeast, east and northeast direction connecting to the main highway near Lahr, Offenburg and Rastatt. To the north of Karlsruhe, a secondary road running north parallels the river to Manheim.

c. The principal highways are surfaced and well drained, wide enough for two (2) lanes of traffic and follow low grades and open curves on the plains. The secondary roads are also surfaced and are suitable for two (2) lanes of traffic. Due to the nature of the terrain thru which the roads pass numerous bridges and culverts are necessary.

d. In general the north–south and east–west main and secondary roads are connected with numerous metaled roads which will provide alternate routes and detours although narrow and light load bridges will be found. The unsurfaced roads are apt to be narrow, poorly drained and muddy in winter. In the lowlands, ditches adjacent to the road might be encountered.

[Anticipated Weather Conditions]

a. Along the Rhine valley winter will be dry and cold. . . . During the months of December thru March snow falls on an average of 3 to 5 days a month. The snow might remain on the ground for a few weeks. In the spring alternate periods of cold with frost and sudden warm weather will be experienced. The summer is made up of hot and sultry days although the nights are relatively cool. Heavy early morning fogs cover the valley bottom in autumn, clearing to bright hot days.[6]

The assault crossing study also considered the best locations for a Rhine crossing. Nine "zones" were selected as "most desirable" for a river crossing.

ZONE A (Huningue–Niffer)
- —Enemy defenses of average density. Commanding ground on east bank will increase strength of defenses, but is unfavorable for counter attack.
- —Commanding ground on east bank when seized will provide a strong bridge-head. . . .
- —Good communications in zone.
- —Cover and concealment not very good except in the Fôret de la Harth in the northern portion of the zone.
- —Control of Kembs dam and canal locks secured, eliminating possibility of damage to our crossing by artificial flood action. . . .
- —Most vulnerable of all sectors to artificial flood conditions. . . .
- —Piers of former bridge at Huningue may be of assistance in construction of ferries and floating bridges.
- —River is shallowest in this zone.
- —Control of the river up to the Swiss border will prevent launching of debris and obstacles by enemy in an attempt to damage our stream crossing installations.
- —Zone A has fair tactical and technical characteristics for making an assault crossing. If at the time of the crossing the enemy were incapable of interfering by creating artificial flood waves, this zone would be considered to have excellent characteristics.

ZONE B (Hamburg–Blodelsheim)
- —Enemy has commanding ground of the Black Forest escarpment at distance of from 2 to 5 miles from the river.
- —Enemy's maneuver room is restricted by the narrow plain between the river and the Black Forest.
- —Fôret de la Harth on the west bank will furnish excellent cover and concealment for large troop and matériel concentrations, and for artillery position areas well forward.
- —River depths are among the lowest on the river.
- —River velocities reach the higher figures of 8 to 10 miles per hour.
- —Zone B has fair characteristics for the assault crossing.

ZONE C (Geisswesser–Mackenheim)
- —Enemy fixed defenses of average strength.
- —Enemy has the commanding ground . . . fronting immediately on the river and superior observation.
- —Good cover and concealment exists on the west bank. . . .
- —Adequate communications nets on both banks of the river.
- —Permanent railroad bridge debris will be useful for crossing on foot . . . for anchoring ferries or a floating bridge. . . .

—Several good sites for the development of approach road exist.

—Zone C has good characteristics for an assault river crossing.

Zone D (Schonau–Gerstheim)

—Enemy prepared defenses of average density.

—Enemy has commanding ground at 8 miles distance from the river, and will have better observation up to and at this commanding ground.

—Width of plain at this point gives enemy sufficient maneuver for counter attack.

—Cover is sporadic on west bank.

—Communications net not highly developed.

—No particular advantage offered excepting that depths will be shallowest of those zones in Seventh Army sector.

—Stream velocities highest here in Seventh Army sector.

—Low flood plains early flooded by rising water.

—This zone offers no tactical or technical advantage in affecting a river crossing.

Zone E (Plobsheim–Watzenan)

—Greatest density of fixed defenses.

—Excellent communications net. . . .

—Enemy has superior cover. . . .

—Black Forest scarp gives enemy commanding ground. . . . The terrain favors his maneuver.

—Adequate cover and concealed approaches to the river. . . .

—Numerous extensive protected water bodies . . . to assist the assault crossing.

—Three permanent bridges or their remains. . . .

—Zone E offers no particular advantage. . . .

Zone F

—Considerations are the same as in Zone D excepting for a greater density of fixed defenses.

—Zone F offers no particular advantage. . . .

Zone G (Newhausen–Lautenbourg)

—Greatest density of enemy defenses. . . .

—Enemy has high commanding ground at approximately 10 miles from the river, with maneuver room on the intervening slopes for counter attack.

—Low hill mass gives some commanding ground on west bank near the river.

—Cover on this hill mass is poor. . . .

—Communications in this zone not sufficiently developed.

—Tributary near Munchhouse can be used to assist assault crossing.

—Debris of fixed bridge at Wintersdorf can be of assistance in crossing personnel . . . in anchoring ferries and bridges, and in protecting obstacles floated downstream.

—No road crossing of primary or secondary development.

—Depths probably too great for fording water-proofed vehicles. . . .

—This zone offers some advantages. A crossing here however would require a penetration of the enemy's deepest and strongest defenses.

Zone H (Leimersheim)

—The crossing in this zone separates into two operations the two very difficult operations of breaching the Siegfried line and forcing the Rhine River. By breaching the Siegfried line west of the river, the river crossing is then made against a lightly organized switch position.

—Good cover and concealment. . . .

—Good communications systems on both banks. . . .

—The commanding ground on the east bank escarpment becomes considerably lower and more distant from the river here, less of an obstacle to our advance, and less of an advantage to the enemy.

—Enemy is favored by his communications net and maneuver room for counter attack.

—Siegfried line defenses on the west bank are deep and well organized.

—Fixed bridge crossing. . . .

—River, although deeper and wider, becomes slower.

—Zone H has the definite advantage that it breaks a major task into two parts, permitting each part to be accomplished separately with a greater concentration of ability and means.

Zone I (Sonderheim–Speyer)

—Tactical considerations are generally as for Zone H.

—River line less strongly organized, with no deliberate defenses in the northern half of the zone.

—Existing highway and railroad crossings at Speyer and Germersheim highly developed.

—Two large fixed bridge crossings. . . .

—Large tributaries available for protected preparations for the assault crossing.

—Current velocities lowest in the Army Group sector, although the river width and depth are greatest.

—Several present and former ferry sites furnish additional potential crossing points. . . .

—Damage by artificial or natural flood action to bridge installations virtually impossible in this site.

—Zone I possesses the maximum number of technical advantages and greatest promise of successful crossing and bridging operations.

The assault study also listed for commanders the available engineering and bridging units needed for conducting a river crossing. For the 7th Army it included:

a. Three divisional combat engineer battalions (one per division)
b. Four corps combat engineer battalions
c. Five army engineer battalions, combat
d. Four army general service engineer battalions
e. Two heavy ponton bridge battalions
f. One Treadway bridge company
g. One Bailey bridge company
h. Four DUKW companies (50 DUKWs each)

For the French First Army the list included:

a. Five divisional combat engineer battalions (one per division)
b. Four corps combat engineer battalions
c. Five army general service engineer battalions
d. One heavy ponton bridge company
e. One Treadway bridge company

Engineering matériel required for the crossing included:

a. 440 M2 Assault Boats with 22 hp outboard motors
b. 100 10-man pneumatic boats
c. 350 Storm Boats with 55 hp outboard motors
d. 2,800, 100-foot Heavy Ponton Bridge units
e. 72 infantry support rafts
f. 3,440, 360-foot Treadway Floating Bridge units
g. 350 DUKWs
h. 117 130-foot Bailey Bridge sections
i. 44, 320-foot Bailey Bridge Ponton units
j. 4,000 2-way Fixed Bridge sets

The above matériel will be sufficient to equip suitably for the assault crossing a total of nine infantry battalions. All personnel and equipment of these battalions will be assigned places in storm or assault boats making a first trip, and will move forward to the near river bank with the proper boat. First waves will be loaded in storm boats, succeeding waves in assault boats; and each wave will consist of the same type of boats, i.e. of boats having the same speed and other characteristics. The number of divisions which can make the assault crossing is then a function of the organization for the crossing and of the number of battalions in a divisions making the assault.[7]

CHAPTER 17.

# The River-Crossing Schools

★ ★ ★ ★

No detail of the Rhine crossing went unexamined. On September 26, the Seventh Army established two river-crossing schools, one at Dole on the Doubs River and the other twelve miles from Lyon on the Valbonne River. The school at Camp de Valbonne was operated by the 85th Heavy Pontoon Battalion. Company F, 40th Engineer Combat Regiment, was assigned to train on the Doubs. Training at both locations was to last up to two weeks.[1] Elements of two other engineer combat regiments, the 36th and the 540th, also began training. The assignment that brought these engineers to Dole and to Camp de Valbonne might be their toughest yet.

Military concerns were paramount, but commanders worried about the condition of their weary troops as well. The weather conditions were terrible in late September. It rained almost every day in eastern France. "Sometimes the sun would shine for an hour or two, then it would rain and then it would be foggy and drizzle on an off." And despite SHAEF's buoyant predictions that the war would soon be over, the troops believed it might never end. "I'm beginning to think we'll be lucky to get home in two more years," said one soldier who belonged to a regiment that had followed the Seventh Army from the Mediterranean beachheads into Alsace.[2] Nevertheless, the men had to be strong and alert for the crossing.

The Germans would be sure to oppose any Rhine crossing with small arms, artillery, floating mines, and aerial attack. The Rhine itself presented significant problems. DUKW drivers and boat handlers had to be taught to maneuver the amphibious trucks and assault and storm boats in the swift current, which approached ten miles per hour in some places on the Rhine. One false move and the current could carry away a small craft. The engineers built pontoon bridges and learned how to operate barges and ferries and to protect them from floating mines. Infantrymen, guns, tanks, and equipment would have to be transported across as quickly as possible. One boat handler recalled practicing cross-river trips with assigned infantry teams until it all became second nature.[3]

General Patton also saw the value of training engineer groups to master the Rhine. He set up crossing schools for his Third Army at Toul, France, in August 1944 in case an opportunity to cross should arise in the Palatinate region. Toul also became the assembly point for all the equipment the Third army would need to cross the Rhine.[4]

The Seventh Army training sites on the Doubs and the Valbonne were chosen because they best approximated the conditions the army was likely to encounter in a Rhine crossing. The upper Rhine in the Seventh's sector was seven hundred to eight hundred feet wide with a current velocity of six to ten miles per hour. The Doubs was eight hundred feet wide at some locations, but the current ran only three to four miles per hour. The engineers and infantry would get their preliminary training on the Doubs and then move to the Valbonne, which was seven hundred feet across at its widest point, and where the current could reach speeds of six miles per hour.[5]

Tests on the Doubs found a problem with the DUKWs. A DUKW that tried to traverse the Rhine under its own power would quickly be carried downstream in the current. Conversely, if the driver angled into the current to maintain position, the vehicle lacked the power to keep moving in a straight line and would again drift downstream. If lines were attached to the front and rear of the DUKW, it could capsize. The solution the engineers devised was to install heavy cables across the river that attached to and guided the DUKWs. To get heavy equipment across, the engineers tied four or five assault boats together and placed bridging sections on top, creating a miniature pontoon bridge that, like the DUKWs, could be guided across the river by the cables.[6]

Transporting troops to the opposite bank would require a fleet of small, fast boats with outboard motors. Ten-foot-long plywood "storm boats" with low gunnels and rounded bottoms, each powered by a fifty-five-horsepower Evinrude outboard motor, could plane the river's surface and deliver eight to ten infantrymen to the far shore in about a minute. Larger "assault boats," squared-off skiffs with two-foot-high sides, could make the crossing in several minutes and could carry up to twenty men. Each boat carried a motor operator and a "bowman" who looked out for mines and directed the boat to shore. The bowman was equipped with a luminous "button" that he wore on his middle finger like a ring. If crossing in the dark, the bowman could direct the motor man left or right by waving his hand. At least one bowman discovered that the luminous dial made him a perfect target for Germans dug in on the opposite bank.

Storm boat operators would sometimes fill their Evinrudes with the highest-test gasoline they could find, ignoring instructions to mix the gas with oil in the two-cycle engines. The high-test boosted the power so much that some operators could not turn off the engine and the boat went shooting up the opposite bank. The more potent gas burned out the engine in short order, but that was not important; the storm boats were to be used primarily in the first wave to get infantry across quickly to establish a bridgehead. The following waves would come in the larger craft.[7]

Engineers solved the bridging problems in several ways. Assault boats could be used as pontoons for floating bridges. Many of the bridging companies were designated ponton companies rather than pontoon companies.[8] On October 4, the Seventh Army asked SHAEF to make available specialized bridging equipment "to obviate the unnecessary delay when need of them should arise."[9]

The engineers at Dole and Camp de Valbonne were joined by the 69th and 78th Smoke Generating Companies, which determined that smoke generators would have to be positioned on both banks of the Rhine to create an effective smokescreen. "ESSO" smoke generators came on two-and-a-half-ton prime mover trucks and accompanying trailers, which together were too heavy and cumbersome to transport across the river in the first wave. Instead, arrangements were made for light, portable smoke units to be carried across in infantry assault boats and set up on the far shore.

Gen. Garrison Davidson, the Seventh Army's chief engineer, drove his staff to anticipate every eventuality that might occur from enemy action before, during, and after a Rhine assault. For example, experiments were conducted on creating barriers to protect the pontoon bridges from mines that the Germans could be expected to float downstream. "I doubt if any other army crossing plans included floating trip wires upstream of its bridges to detonate possible floating mines launched . . . before they reached the bridges, or had dummy bridges to dilute the effect of any bombing attack," Davidson later wrote. He and his engineers were taking a page from Caesar's legions.[10]

One major concern facing the assault planners was the possibility that the dams on the upper Rhine between Germany and Switzerland might be blown. If that happened, the resulting floodwaters would swamp the American pontoon bridges at downriver crossing sites. Seventh Army representatives sent word through diplomatic channels to alert the Swiss to this danger. The Swiss were not worried, replying that any German action to destroy the dams would be counterproductive because the dams provided hydroelectric power to many areas along the German border with Switzerland. The Swiss had greater concerns at that moment. The U.S. Twelfth Tactical Air Force had bombed targets on the Swiss-German border between Lake Constance and Basel, aiming to disrupt enemy military operations on the German side. But some of the bombs had fallen on Swiss territory, and these air assaults did threaten the dams. The Swiss government warned the Americans that it would "take necessary action to guard the Weirs [dams]" if the bombings continued.[11] Not wishing to provoke Switzerland into taking military action in conjunction with the Germans, the 6th Army Group notified the Twelfth TAC to stop the bombing. The Twelfth Air Force's job would be to provide air support for a forthcoming cross-Rhine assault.

When all the Seventh Army's preparations and communications are considered, it is surprising that Eisenhower was unprepared when Devers announced his intention to cross the Rhine on November 24. Sixth Army Group planners had alerted the supreme command on numerous occasions that Devers' forces intended to cross the Rhine at the first opportunity. Devers sent a daily report of 6th Army Group activities and progress to SHAEF headquarters.[12] On September 28, 6th Army Group headquarters dispatched a message to SHAEF and Eisenhower outlining future operations that were also to include directives for the 15th Corps, newly assigned to Devers.

The 6th Army Group had also asked SHAEF to provide two heavy ponton (bridging) battalions to supplement the three ponton battalions already assigned to the army group and thirteen additional truck companies to carry supplies across the Rhine into Germany.[13] As the cross-river attack plans took shape, 6th Army Group headquarters sent another request to SHAEF asking for duplex drive–equipped tanks ("DD" tanks were modified M-4 Shermans with special flotation and propellers that allowed them to operate in the water) to be used in the assault. SHAEF responded that the DD tanks were "presently available in the UK and have not, as yet, been allocated to British or U.S. forces."[14]

In late November, as Seventh Army troops approached the Rhine, Devers asked SHAEF to allocate a number of airborne units for use in seizing a bridgehead over the river. The Seventh Army diary noted: "In a message to SHAEF (BX-20053) SIXTH Army Group notified SHAEF that plans for crossing the RHINE indicate that Airborne Troops will be needed to seize critical terrain features. Accordingly, SIXTH Army Group has requested that a minimum of two Airborne Regimental Combat Teams be made available to Seventh Army for this purpose. . . . It was further requested that planning officers from the First Airborne Army and the supporting troop carrier command be sent to this headquarters in order that joint planning may be affected."[15]

On November 21 Devers' headquarters issued clear orders that on reaching the Rhine, the 15th Corps was to "reconnoiter the Rhine between Strasbourg and Soufflenheim [a town of about four thousand people located some twenty miles north of Strasbourg], and take advantage of any opportunity for a quick crossing of the Rhine River."[16] Brooks' 6th Corps was instructed to "seize and guard all bridges, barges, pontoon equipment, cranes, pile-drivers, etc. discovered on the Rhine and tributaries."

On November 18, 1944, a week before the planned crossing, the Seventh Army issued orders to its engineering groups: "In order that your Corps may take advantage of an unexpected opportunity to make a hasty crossing of the Rhine, river-crossing equipment is being assembled and segregated into sets in the Luneville area as fast as it arrives from Marseilles. Each river-crossing set provides assault lift for one R.C.T. [regimental combat team]. Two R.C.T. sets provide the lift required to cross a reinforced division on a two R.C.T. front. Attached are the loading diagrams for an infantry assault battalion and for a reinforced division on which the composition of the sets is based."

The men and combat units were in place, and General Davidson was ordered to assemble all the stream-crossing equipment he could gather for assault crossings for "a corps on a two division, eight battalion front in accordance with loading plans already prepared."[17] All equipment was to be assembled and available on six-hour alert after 6:00 AM on November 23, 1944. The assault into Germany was on. The Seventh Army awaited the order from General Patch and General Devers to move out and cross the Rhine.

CHAPTER 18.

# Moving Up

★ ★ ★ ★

Allll through the night of November 24, 1944, the men of the Seventh Army's 2nd Battalion, 40th Engineer Combat Regiment, readied themselves for the assault crossing of the Rhine.[1] DUKWs were given their final inspection; bridging equipment and storm and assault boats were assembled for the short trip from the forested base near Haguenau to the banks of the Rhine. The wheeled DUKWs were to travel to the river under their own power while the bridging equipment and the boats had to be loaded on two-and-a-half-ton trucks for the trip.

Crossing the Rhine would be nothing new for the combat engineers of the 40th ECR.[2] They had won battle stars for crossing waterways in earlier campaigns in North Africa, Sicily, and mainland Italy. They had also rebuilt port facilities, erected supply dumps, and hauled supplies from Tunis to Naples before joining the Seventh Army in southern France. Along with the 540th combat engineers, they were among the most experienced and battle-tested engineer groups in the U.S. Army.

On this night in November 1944, all hands anxiously anticipated the order to move out. They waited into the next day, when word came down to head back to the bivouac area; there would be a short delay in getting the artillery and infantry units into position for the cross-Rhine attack. Nevertheless, spirits were high.

The same buoyant attitude was reflected at Devers' and Patch's headquarters, where the excitement was electric. Brig. Gen. Morris W. Gilland, in the Seventh Army's logistics command, pulled aside a subordinate, Col. Edward D. Comm, and told him of the forthcoming Rhine crossing. "Ed, I've got fantastic news. . . . We are on the Rhine, we are all prepared and we are going to cross tonight."

"I could hardly believe my ears," Comm remembered, "although I knew that the [Seventh Army's] advance had gone extremely well."[3]

The high spirits among the 6th Army Group units were in marked contrast to the glum mood at SHAEF.[4] As November progressed, Eisenhower all but concluded that none of his generals would force the hoped-for breakthrough to the Rhine and end the war in Europe before 1945. He particularly discounted the likelihood that the U.S. Seventh and French First armies would contribute much to defeating the Germans on the western front. The 6th Army Group had made little progress in the Vosges during the last weeks of October; the fighting had been bitter and advances limited. Success on the western front seemed so unlikely that Ike briefly considered halting all offensive operations along the front line until the port of Antwerp became fully operational. Fresh infantry and armored divisions from Great Britain and America could come in through Antwerp and beef up the Allied front lines.[5] The Germans had somehow mustered new divisions in August and September 1944, and the Allies no longer had overwhelming numerical superiority. Except for the American penetration at Aachen, the enemy tenaciously held the Siegfried Line and had the Allies stopped cold.

In the end, Eisenhower opted for a series of limited attacks all along the front in hopes that the German defenses might somewhere collapse and leave a gaping hole through which the Allies could gain the Rhine. He knew any respite would give the Wehrmacht even more time to refit and restock, and the enemy would be stronger in the spring than it was in November. The political damage to Anglo-American and Soviet relations could also be severe if the Russians interpreted a cessation of combat operations in western Europe as treachery. A halt to Allied operations along the Siegfried Line also might tempt the Soviets to stretch their territorial conquests deeper into western Europe.

Eisenhower met with his top commanders to plot strategy for the coming attacks, but SHAEF's original plans remained largely unchanged.[6] The main Allied objective remained the Ruhr, and the Third Army's objective south of the Ardennes was still the Saar Basin. Patton's forces would then advance northeast through the German Palatinate to the Rhine and secure bridgeheads across the river. Eisenhower remained largely indifferent to the 6th Army Group's role in the November offensives as long as it protected the Third Army's right flank. The timing and objectives of the army group's upcoming attacks were left entirely to Devers.[7]

But Eisenhower did alter the missions of two of his army commanders. He restrained Montgomery's 21st Army Group from further northward advances aimed at capturing the critical Ruhr region, directing Monty instead to clear German troops from the Schelde Estuary in Belgium and open up the port of Antwerp. Monty's British and Canadian armies had taken the city in late September, but the Germans continued to hold the riverbanks and deprive the Allies of the use of the port. Any Allied cargo vessel coming upriver would have to run a gauntlet through withering enemy fire. Antwerp was less than fifty miles from the front in Belgium, and its port facilities were considered essential to the future progress of the Allied armies.[8]

Much to Monty's dismay, the main role of breaching the Siegfried Line, crossing the Rhine, and invading Germany now fell to Bradley's 12th Army Group. One of Eisenhower's aides described the new plan as the strategy of stretching out the enemy defenses, and confirmed in the minds of British generals Ike's deficiencies as a military commander in chief.[9] Eisenhower appeared to be moving even further away from Montgomery's plan for a bold, concentrated thrust through the northern sector of the Allied front.

Bradley, of course, was pleased with the supreme commander's new directive because the main task of breaking through the Siegfried Line now fell to his army group.[10] He had long thought that Montgomery should cease advancing northward toward the Ruhr and focus instead on clearing German troops from the Schelde Estuary. Like Ike, he believed that the Allies should move en masse and occupy the entire west bank of the Rhine before contemplating any advance over the river into Germany, believing that a simultaneous advance by all the armies could end the war. And now that Monty was turning west, Bradley and Patton had a better chance of being first over the Rhine.

Eisenhower called his generals together in Brussels on October 18. He held the meeting near Monty's 21st Army Group Headquarters to ensure that the fickle field marshal would attend. Ike wanted no misunderstandings about Montgomery's new responsibilities, as had happened in the past when Monty failed to show up at meetings and instead sent a subordinate, leaving him free to misinterpret or disregard Ike's orders. Miffed at being ordered to attend, Monty complained that such meetings might not be necessary if Eisenhower visited 21st Army Group headquarters more frequently. He grumbled that the supreme commander/field commander was out of touch with his armies because his headquarters was miles away in Versailles. The old animosities flared as soon as Monty appeared. One American attendee described him "as a little monarch with a fantastic scarf wrapped around his battle jacket and hanging halfway to his knees."[11]

Over Montgomery's objections, Eisenhower ordered Hodges' First Army to establish a bridgehead across the Rhine near Cologne and then to swing north to capture the Ruhr.[12] Gen. William H. Simpson's Ninth Army was ordered to protect the First Army's left flank, while Patton's Third Army was to advance northeast from Lorraine to protect the First Army's right flank.

Devers, left to his own devices, decided to begin his November offensive on the thirteenth, three days after Patton began his drive.[13] The delay was designed to catch the enemy just as General Balck began shifting his meager reserves to reinforce the German First Army front opposite Patton's Third Army. Wiese and Balck would then have to decide whether to send reserves to counter Patton and leave the Nineteenth Army front stretched dangerously thin, or keep them in place to face a renewed Seventh Army offensive. The three-day delay would also give Patch's 3rd, 36th, and 45th divisions a much-needed respite from combat. Devers was confident that his men would be ready.

The weather before the attack was abominable. "It was raining cats and dogs and the mud is awful but we have the stuff," Devers wrote Georgie. "The Germans are fighting hard in spots but we are too powerful for them and throw them off balance. . . . I have two breakthroughs, one getting strong and past the difficult mountains [the Saverne Gap] the other just as strong and at the gateway [Belfort]. With the blessing of God we shall do it and bag this terrible world of men called Germans."[14]

In a November 13 letter to Vice Adm. Alan G. Kirk, commander of naval forces in France, Devers expressed confidence that he would reach the Rhine, cross it into Germany, and smash the Siegfried Line. "Our chief problem is to overcome weather," Devers wrote to Kirk. "If we can do this, we shall break through to the Rhine, clean up, and can then start thinking about how we are going to get across that river. However, always a gambler, I have hopes that we may approach the Rhine so fast that we will be able to get a bridgehead over it before the Germans can stop us."[15] Eisenhower had ordered Kirk to assist the ground armies in any area the Combined Chiefs of Staff designated. This included helping with river crossings, although Ike did not specify the Rhine.

Devers had visited many of his units on the line to determine the effects of the weather on his men. "Some of the troops suffer severely but most of them get a relief to dry out and clean up," he wrote to Georgie.[16] Not all the men were so lucky. In his diary, Hallet K. Brown, a member of Company D, 410th Infantry Regiment, 103rd Division, described the weather as his unit moved up to relieve the 3rd Division: "Up early to build fires to dry, or attempt to dry our woolen blankets and clothes. I had no beanie [woolen knit cap]. Dry wood was scarce so we spent most of the time looking for something that would burn. It was no use. . . . So, another night in a damp bed (damp clothes on damp leaves on the damp ground wrapped in damp blankets)."[17]

On these visits Devers also saw firsthand the aftermath of the Germans' devastating scorched-earth policy. The retreating enemy troops had pillaged and burned all the way across Alsace. Saint-Dié, which had a prewar population of twenty thousand, was now packed with more than forty thousand civilian refugees. "I was all over the front on the north and traveled through lots of German dead," he wrote to Georgie. "Every village is a mass of rubble and burning. The defenses were well built, he [the Germans] thought he was going to stay through the winter."[18]

General Dahlquist was also moved by the destruction wrought by the retreating enemy. To his wife, Ruth, he wrote: "The Germans are burning all villages and farms, I imagine in order to deny us shelter but it is raising hell with the French. I saw dozens today coming into the town in which we are located pushing their goods on baby carriages, wagons, or any other sort of conveyance. It is a tragic sight and of course will not do the Germans any good when we finally finish them off."[19]

J. Glenn Gray, an intelligence officer with the Seventh Army, recalled the horror and dislocation of the war in Alsace. "We had just come into this area from the Vosges Mountains, from which the Germans withdrew only after they had set fire to everything. . . . Almost worse were the recriminations and persecutions among the unfortunate Alsatians of those thought to be pro-German. Shopkeepers were changing their signs as well as their language from German to French after having done the reverse in 1939; political opinions were not so easily reversed in a vengeful atmosphere where nearly everyone was suspect."[20]

Devers was more determined than ever to succeed in driving the Germans from Alsace. He ordered elements of the Seventh Army to drive south along the west bank of the Rhine from the Strasbourg area while elements of the French First Army advanced north along the river. The German Nineteenth Army would either have to retreat over the Rhine or face annihilation in Alsace. Simultaneously, Devers planned to leapfrog the Rhine and establish a bridgehead near Rastatt. The time and the signs were good. The troops would be rested, their morale was high, and the Americans held every advantage over their enemy. Furthermore, West Point had just beaten arch-rival Notre Dame in football for the first time in years. To Devers it was "a good omen for the offensive on this front."[21]

Haislip's 15th Corps, on the 6th Army Group's left wing, would lead the November attack northeast toward Saarbourg to break through the Saverne Gap. Brooks' 6th Corps, in the army group's center, was to resume the offensive through the Vosges two days later and continue advancing northeast through the Saales and Hantz passes.[22] Devers intended the 6th Corps' advance to constitute the Seventh Army's main effort. Once through the mountains, Brooks' troops would reach the open Alsace Plain and drive to Strasbourg. South of 6th Corps, the French First Army would also mount a series of attacks toward the Rhine.[23] The French 2nd Corps, on the 6th Corps' right wing, was to initiate a three-day attack in the Vosges to protect the 6th Corps' flank and divert enemy attention from the French 1st Corps, which would attempt to breach enemy defenses to the south in the Belfort Gap.

Devers estimated that the 15th Corps would break out onto the Alsace Plain by December 1 and that the French would smash through the Belfort Gap and reach the Rhine near Mulhouse about the same time. He expected the 6th Corps to advance beyond the Vosges as well and capture Strasbourg. And once on the Rhine north of Strasbourg, Devers would cross the river and send his armies up the east and west banks to come in behind the German First Army. He intended to show the big boys in Eisenhower's camp what his underrated army group could accomplish.

If Devers had looked at the situation in Alsace through the eyes of General Wiese and General Balck, he would have been even more optimistic. Wiese's forces had been seriously depleted by the transfer of several Nineteenth Army units to support Army Group B to the north and for use in the coming German Ardennes offensive.[24] He had virtually no reserves, and his defenses were undermanned and could not withstand concerted American attacks. Even the terrain, which should have worked to his advantage, now worked against him. To stem the Americans and French, Wiese needed to shift troops back and forth across his front, and the rugged Vosges Mountains made this extremely difficult.

Despite his optimism, Devers worried about the outcome of the attack in the hours before the November offensive began. The weather was terrible, and the Germans were always formidable. His chief of staff, Maj. Gen. Reuben Jenkins, recalled Devers' concerns the night before the U.S. Seventh and French First armies jumped off. As Devers and Jenkins left the dining room at the palatial hotel/headquarters in Vittel, Devers turned to his aide and said, "Rube, don't forget to say your prayers tonight before you go to bed."[25] The usually smiling Jake Devers had turned somber and emotional. He knew how much was riding on the attack, and he knew that many young men would die the next day. "The Old Man was almost in tears," Jenkins remembered.

# CHAPTER 19

# Moving Out

★ ★ ★ ★

Devers' November offensive began on November 13 in a snowstorm. The troops of Haislip's 15th Corps were under heavy artillery fire as they moved out in the direction of the Saverne Gap. Progress was slow. The enemy fought stubbornly, but by November 18 the German defenses were collapsing. On November 19 Haislip unleashed Leclerc's 2nd Armored Division to exploit the 15th Corps' advances and break through to the Alsace Plain.

Leclerc had every intention of pushing all the way to Strasbourg even as General Patch issued orders that 15th Corps troops were not to take the city. Haislip, however, understood that Strasbourg was nearly as important to the French as Paris, not just for its strategic value but because of what it symbolized. The ancient provincial capital had changed hands between the French and Germans several times in the previous seventy-five years, and it was important to the French that the Tricolour be raised once again as a sign of German defeat and French sovereignty. Haislip also pointed out to Patch that Leclerc was virtually obsessed with the capture of Strasbourg.[1] Haislip persuaded Patch to allow Leclerc at least to send patrols toward the city to test the German defenses. Patch's agreement was all Leclerc needed; he would drive his tanks into Strasbourg under the guise of being a reconnaissance in force.

Leclerc sent out scouts in search of smaller passes through the Vosges to avoid the Saverne Gap, which he knew to be heavily fortified; the Germans would have stopped him cold had he tried to break through there. His map showed numerous small tracks on either side of the gap, and reconnaissance parties found them to be undefended. Leclerc immediately ordered his tanks through these narrow defiles, and within hours they were driving out of the Vosges onto the Alsace Plain, with Strasbourg and the Rhine only twenty miles away.

Leclerc was the perfect commander to take Strasbourg.[2] Of all his days during the previous five years this promised to be one of the sweetest. The capture of Strasbourg would fulfill a promise made in 1941 when, under the heat of the Sahara sun in southern Libya, Leclerc had led his small band of officers in an oath "not to abandon the fight until the flag of France shall fly over Metz and Strasbourg."

Jacques Leclerc's true name was Vicomte Jacques-Philippe de Hautecloque. He had assumed his nom-de-guerre in exile to protect his wife and family, who remained in occupied France. He was a career military officer who had fought the Germans in the month-long Battle of France in 1940 when France collapsed under the Nazi onslaught. He escaped capture twice and fled to Great Britain to join forces with General de Gaulle, who was forming a Free French government in exile in London and building an army to join with Britain and the United States to liberate France. De Gaulle sent Leclerc to Nigeria to consolidate France's African colonies behind the Free French and to overthrow the rule of Marshal Pétain and the German puppet government at Vichy that controlled the French colonies. Leclerc gathered a small force and captured the French colonies of Gabon and Chad, and then led a task force of Free French troops a thousand miles across the Sahara to join with British forces fighting the Germans and Italians in the western Sahara. On the way to Libya, Leclerc seized an Italian garrison at the oasis of Kufra in southern Libya and raised the French flag on behalf of the Free French. It was there that he vowed, in what has been described as "le serment de Kufra," not to lay down arms until the Tricolour once again fluttered over Strasbourg.[3]

Leclerc's forces ranged through the Libyan desert, linking at times with units of the British Long Range Desert Group, harassing the Germans and Italians behind their lines. He later took his command to Tunisia to join the British and Americans fighting Rommel's Afrika Corps. From North Africa, Leclerc transferred his force of Frenchmen to England, where he took command of the French 2nd Armored Division, also known as the "Deuxième DB."

Leclerc was determined to make the 2nd the best armored division in the Allied armies, and he forged Frenchmen from North Africa, Lebanon, and France into a magnificent fighting machine. The power behind the division was Leclerc himself, a man the historian John Keegan describes as "brave with the total indifference to danger of the cavalier, proud without conceit, impassioned without bigotry, selfless, [and] relentless." Leclerc "stamped ruthlessly on all expressions of mutual disregard—'cowards and shirkers' from one side, 'rebels and adventurers' from the other—and drove all to work." Together, Leclerc and his tankers would avenge their humiliating defeat of 1940.

The 2nd landed in France over the Normandy beaches on August 1, 1944, two months after D-day, and immediately went into combat. Attached to Haislip's 15th Corps, Leclerc's men were the first Allied unit into Paris on August 25. Their American M-4 Sherman tanks flew the French Tricolour from their turrets and bore the blue Cross of Lorraine on the sides of their hulls. The 2nd had not initially been picked to move first into Paris, but the determined Leclerc told Bradley that he would go anyway, and Bradley relented. It was only right that a French fighting force be the first to roll down the newly liberated streets of their beloved capital.

Beyond Paris, Leclerc's tankers, by now famous for their élan and courage, raced east into Alsace and Lorraine with Patton's Third Army. On September 29, the 2nd was attached to the 15th Corps and joined to Patch's Seventh Army in Alsace with the objective of reaching the Rhine. The going was slow and the fighting brutal, but by mid-November the Seventh Army was poised on the eastern slopes of the Vosges and struggling to break out onto the Alsace Plain.

Leclerc took aim at Strasbourg. Tanks, armored cars, half-tracks, artillery, mortars, and mechanized infantry charged over the precipitous trails in total darkness, through snow and ice, past the wreckage of German equipment and Wehrmacht soldiers slumped muddied and dead in roadside ditches. By dawn the columns were on the plain and racing to the east through the towns of Phalsbourg and Saverne. The 2nd captured an important German headquarters with its entire staff, who had not anticipated that anyone would send tanks through the Vosges except at the Saverne Gap.

Leclerc's armored columns set out for Strasbourg at 7:15 AM on November 23 and advanced rapidly eastward across the Alsace Plain, with the four separate task forces converging on the city from different directions.[4] They rolled on, brushing aside roadblocks and pockets of German resistance, always keeping an eye out for the spires of the Strasbourg cathedral. Lt. Tony Triumpho, an American liaison officer with the 2nd, recalled the heady charge.[5] "We went roaring across the plain in our jeep along with four or five light tanks and a few half tracks of infantry, about seventy men. We passed working parties and groups of German soldiers . . . they just stood open-mouthed. When they saw it was French troops they were scared to death for they had heard that the French . . . did not take too many prisoners." Triumpho's tiny task force was too intent on getting into Strasbourg to take time to kill Boches. But other French troops, that day and over the next several days, killed German soldiers and French collaborators by the scores.

TF Rouvillois took the enemy by complete surprise when it entered the city at 10:30 that morning. TF Massu, under Col. Jacques Massu, a Leclerc loyalist from the beginning of the war, followed a short time later along with the two other armored columns. Rouvillois' tanks rumbled through the city before the startled Germans knew they were there and before the French population realized they had been liberated. As the first tanks and troops stormed into the city, the day was beginning like any other for the citizens of Strasbourg. Workers were riding their bicycles along the boulevards and German officers were taking their morning coffee in cafés or waiting at bus stops on their way to work. Suddenly tanks appeared out of nowhere and opened fire on anyone in a German uniform. Wehrmacht officers shopping with their wives were cut down on the streets. "It was the most fantastic surprise I ever heard of in the whole war," General Haislip later declared. "The French swept into Strasbourg, going like the wind. The Germans had no idea the French 2nd Armored Division was within fifty miles of them!"[6] Leclerc's aide, Captain Chatel, recalled that when "the townspeople realized we were French many fell to their knees, crying with joy and uttering prayers of thanksgiving."[7]

The tankers captured bridges over the city's canals and raced to take the Rhine highway and railroad bridges connecting Strasbourg with Kehl on the east bank. But some 650 yards short of the objective Leclerc's men ran into stiff German resistance from defensive positions in nearby apartment houses and bunkers and antitank barriers at the bridges' entrances. Over the next forty-eight hours TF Rouvillois made numerous attempts to take the bridges, but all failed.

The Germans quickly reorganized and formed small pockets of resistance in various parts of the city. German artillery across the Rhine in Germany opened up. Dana Adams Schmidt, a war correspondent for the *New York Times*, reported:

> The big guns of the Siegfried Line began firing sporadically across the Rhine into the center of Strasbourg this afternoon while Brig. Gen. Jacque Philippe Leclerc's armored forces completed the town's liberation by mopping up isolated pockets of Germans in the southern and eastern outskirts.
>
> Today's roundup brought the total number of Germans captured in the city to 3,000. I saw French guns as heavy as 105 mm firing from emplacements in the streets and squares of Strasbourg as they answered the Siegfried Line guns with reverberations that sent windowpanes tinkling into the streets. French tanks meanwhile exchanged fire with German anti tank guns across the undamaged road and rail bridges over the Rhine at Kehl. But the Germans still held the bridges and a heavy defended bridgehead of 300 yards on the French side of the river.
>
> If the Germans have any idea of exploiting the bridges they still hold to re-enter Strasbourg or as escape routes for the Germans south of the town they will have to reckon with the American Forty-fourth and Seventy-ninth Infantry Divisions which are mopping up and fanning out behind Leclerc's division. . . . Despite this display of Allied might the Germans have got one important counterattack underway at the northern extremity of the Seventh Army's front that at last reports had advanced in the directions of Eschenwiller, Bearendorf and Gungwiller ten miles northwest of the Saverne Gap.[8]

The Panzer Lehr Division, one of Germany's finest armored units, mounted the counterattack. The division had been withdrawn from the Lorraine front to refit for the upcoming German attack in the Ardennes but was ordered back into action when the Americans began attacking all along the front in Alsace and Lorraine. Its mission was to drive south from the vicinity of Saar-Union into the Seventh Army's left flank in an effort to cut Leclerc's tenuous supply line into Strasbourg and isolate the French armored division from the rest of the Seventh Army. Both Field Marshal von Rundstedt, supreme commander in the west, and General Balck feared that the 15th Corps' eastward drive would split the Nineteenth and First German armies and open the way for Patton's Third Army to carry out an end run around the First Army's left wing and envelop the Saar Basin.

Panzer Lehr scored some early successes as its two columns drove into the Seventh Army's northern flank, but its attacks soon ran out of steam as the 4th Armored Division counterattacked and the weather cleared enough to allow Twelfth Air Force fighter-bombers to pummel the German tanks. Panzer Lehr had the misfortune to run into the best armored division and one of the fiercest commanders in the U.S. Army, Maj. Gen. John S. "Tiger Jack" Wood. A man who was not afraid to upbraid Patton to his face when he believed old "Blood and Guts" was not being aggressive enough, Wood had led the 4th on a rampage across northern France at the head of Patton's Third Army. As the 4th Armored Division lashed back at Panzer Lehr, additional American forces were closing on the Rhine. The 313th Regiment of the 79th Division marched into Strasbourg just behind Leclerc and claimed to be the first Americans to reach the Rhine; other units of the same division were within eight miles of the river north of the city.

As the 15th Corps rolled into Strasbourg, the 6th Corps, reinforced with the 100th and 103rd infantry divisions and the 14th Armored Division, made a final push out of the High Vosges. Once on the Alsace Plain, the 6th fanned north and south. The 36th Division advanced south toward Colmar to support the French drive to the Rhine while the rest of the 6th moved northeast to cover the right flank of the 15th Corps.

Once Strasbourg was taken, Haislip's 15th Corps would reconnoiter northward along the west bank of the Rhine to the Soufflenheim-Rastatt area with orders to force a crossing and establish a bridgehead on the river's east bank. The 6th Corps, coming up from the southwest, would pass through a 15th Corps bridgehead across the Rhine and move northward toward Karlsruhe. The combat-hardened troops of the 6th Corps could be expected to perform like professionals in exploiting any bridgehead across the Rhine.

In southern Alsace, the French First Army had scored a huge victory as well.[9] On November 19, three days before Leclerc's tankers reached the Rhine at Strasbourg, de Lattre's 1st Corps reached the river near Mulhouse. In celebration, French artillery lobbed shells at targets in Germany as patrols crossed the Rhine to reconnoiter the enemy's strength and fortifications.[10] De Lattre had long dreamed of reaching the Rhine and pushing across into Germany. He had far more reason than American and British commanders to target the Rhine and Germany. Large areas of his country were still under German rule, and he and the other French generals would not rest until the Boches—all of them—had been driven out of France. De Lattre advised Devers of his plan to bypass Belfort and drive on Mulhouse. After that, he planned to "force a crossing of the Rhine and drive north through the Black Forest towards Stuttgart."[11] Devers was all for it. "With a team such as I see here now [French and Americans]," he wrote in his diary, "I feel sure we will be able to push across the Rhine."

De Lattre's offensive to the Rhine had begun on September 25. General de Monsabert hoped to surprise the Germans and approach Belfort from the north through the southern Vosges or push directly over the Vosges via Gerardmer and the Schlucht Pass to Colmar and the Rhine. Everything depended on speed, surprise, and the ability to find a weak point in the German lines.[12] The Germans, however, proved too strong. The narrow roads became jammed with tanks and armored vehicles, and the heavily wooded and rugged terrain offered no alternate routes. The French assaults slowed and then ground to a halt. De Lattre lacked reinforcements and supplies. Large portions of his army were still redeploying from the west bank of the Rhone; some units were just arriving from North Africa.

The French tried and failed again in October to dislodge the Germans along the southern front. The troops were exhausted; they trudged through heavy rain and snowfalls and freezing temperatures. Then, on November 16–19, de Lattre's army accomplished what General Truscott had wanted to do two months earlier: it broke through the Belfort Gap and reached the Rhine to become the first Allied troops to reach the river.

De Lattre opened his November offensive on the Sixth Army Group's southern front on November 13 with his 1st Corps attacking across a "Scandinavian landscape."[13] Heavy snow was falling in the attack zone, and visibility was down to zero. De Lattre and his staff went to great lengths to deceive the Germans into thinking that his main attack would be to the north through the Vosges. They developed elaborate deception plans that included misleading documents that were allowed to fall into German hands naming bogus orders for an attack through the High Vosges to Colmar.

De Lattre's troops encountered pockets of resistance, but the French smelled blood and fought with determination. "Our tanks ran amok on touching Alsatian soil," de Lattre remembered.[14] The boundary line of the long-contested province began a few miles west of Belfort. The first Alsatian village the French forces liberated was Seppois. A squadron of Sherman tanks from the French 1st Armored Division under Lt. Col. Louis le Puloch rumbled into the village on the afternoon of November 18, 1944, firing their 75-mm cannons to screen squads of North African colonial troops. The Germans fought hard, first at a roadblock at the Seppois power station and then in the town itself, where they fell back to prepared defensive positions. Le Puloch was determined to take this objective, and the French overwhelmed the enemy in a fight that left some fifty Germans dead.[15] After four years the Tricolour once again flew over Alsace.

De Lattre related the recapture of Alsace and the race to the Rhine in his memoirs: "The Ill [River] was passed. At 1700, almost without further resistance, we were at Jettingen. Then it turned into a charge. At top speed, a detachment under Lieutenant de Loisy, formed from a company of Shermans and a platoon of the First Zouaves, plunged eastwards. Helfranzkirch, Kappelen, Bartenheim. . . . A few bursts of machine-gun fire on isolated enemy troops. . . . Another six kilometers, Rosenau: fifteen astonished prisoners. Another five hundred meters. A screen of trees . . . the Rhine!" Darkness was descending as more tanks and troops approached the river. Guns were wheeled into position and opened fire, "the first salvoes of shells to fall Germany since 1940. In that moment—19 November, 1944, at 1830—what misery was avenged! The first of all Allied Armies, the French First Army had reached the Rhine."[16]

Historian Russell Weigley notes that "General de Lattre's French First Army achieved an astonishing immediate rupture of the autumnal deadlock," then circled northwest to sweep into Mulhouse, where the headquarters of the German Nineteenth Army "had to decamp in disarray."[17] Within a few days the French had outflanked the German position in the High Vosges and controlled both Belfort and Mulhouse and a strip of the Rhine adjacent to Switzerland.

The enemy tried to cut off the French column that reached the Rhine, but de Lattre turned the tables, trapped the Germans, and took several thousand prisoners. "To liberate le beau pays d'Alsace," Weigley writes, "the reorganized French First Army was displaying a boldness of both operational design and tactical execution that Patton could well envy."[18]

The French victories in the south and the American gains in the north around Strasbourg confirmed Devers' belief that his army group could continue to roll up the German army in Alsace. He expected the Nineteenth Army to retreat into Germany, leaving Alsace completely in Allied hands, and was certain that the French First Army with the help of one or two American divisions could mop up the remaining German troops west of the Rhine. More important, Devers believed that his next step was to carry out SHAEF's orders to support the Third Army in its drive to take the Saar. For Devers this meant crossing the Rhine at Rastatt. He had every expectation that his plan to unhinge the southern end of the German front would be successful and might even disrupt the entire German effort along the western front.

# CHAPTER 20

# Finally, the Attack

★ ★ ★ ★

The Seventh Army's immediate objective across the Rhine was Rastatt, a small industrial city on the east bank known for its Baroque architecture. Rastatt began as a market center in the thirteenth century and grew because of its strategic location as a crossing point on the upper Rhine. The city had witnessed war numerous times through the centuries and had been destroyed in 1329, 1424, and 1689. Rebuilt each time, Rastatt flourished and became an important regional administrative center. Bordered by the Rhine to the west and by the upper reaches of the Black Forest to the east, Rastatt was a much less formidable target than the heavily fortified and defended German city of Aachen in the north, which had resisted the American First Army for days in October 1944.

Once the Seventh Army took Strasbourg, its troops continued their advance north along the west bank of the Rhine to Haguenau. There they planned to turn right and cross the Rhine in a zone that Seventh Army planners had chosen from the possible crossing sites along a one-hundred-mile stretch of the Rhine ranging from the Swiss frontier to Speyer, Germany, fifty miles north of Karlsruhe. The Seventh Army diary reports that "Rastatt was selected because it controlled the road network leading to southeastern Germany and its capture would open the way for a Seventh Army advance north along the Rhine valley to Karlsruhe and northeast in the general direction of Nuremberg."[1] Intelligence reports and information from Seventh Army reconnaissance patrols indicated that the German defenses at Rastatt were virtually unmanned.[2] Thus Devers and his commanders believed that nothing lay in the path of the Seventh Army to stop the Americans.

Devers had been getting regular intelligence reports about conditions along the Rhine all the way north from the Mediterranean. The 6th Army Group had made liberal use of Ultra intercepts and information from agents dropped behind German lines who reported on enemy movements and strength.[3] Even before the invasion of southern France, American OSS agents and French underground operatives were feeding valuable information to the Allies on German dispositions from the Italian border to the Atlantic coast.

As the Seventh Army approached Alsace, its intelligence officers were authorized to use carefully screened German POWs to infiltrate behind enemy lines and report back on enemy activity. Most of these agents were soldiers who opposed the war and the Nazi regime and were willing to serve their former enemies to shorten the conflict and reduce the terrible destruction of Germany.

Devers' plan for a cross-Rhine attack was simple and straightforward.[4] A Seventh Army force comprising eight battalions would cross the river, with the advance elements being ferried across in assault boats and the remainder of the attacking force crossing on pontoon bridges.[5] Once across, the Americans troops were to establish a defensive bridgehead in preparation for the advance north along the east bank to Karlsruhe, a junction point of the Siegfried Line defenses. Siegfried Line bunkers and strong points ran straight up the east side of the Rhine in Germany from the Swiss frontier near Basel to Karlsruhe, a distance of about one hundred miles. At Karlsruhe, the line took a sharp left turn to the western side of the river and swung northwest along a line that roughly conformed to the dividing line between the province of Lorraine in France and the German Palatinate.[6] These defenses continued for a distance of about seventy-five miles to the area around Saarbrücken. At the time of the planned attack, the left flank of the German First Army front followed this stretch of the Siegfried Line and formed a shallow salient into the sector held by the U.S. Third Army.

Devers figured that his forces could advance about twenty miles up the undefended east side of the Rhine valley from Rastatt to capture Karlsruhe, then pivot to the west and come in behind the Siegfried Line bunkers and defensive points. The German First Army troops manning the line in this area would then be trapped between the Seventh and Third armies.

An attack up either side of the Rhine might have achieved "significant operational and strategic goals," note historians Clarke and Smith; specifically, the destruction of the German First Army and the capture of Saar industries.[7] It would also relieve pressure on Patton's front and enable the Third Army to break loose and achieve its objective to capture the Saar industrial area, cross the Rhine, and swing north to envelop the Ruhr from the south.

Lt. Col. Willi Kaiser, chief of staff to General Vatterrodt, the German commander in Strasbourg, confirmed that a cross-Rhine assault by the Seventh Army would probably have disrupted defenses in German Army Group G's sector.[8] In a debriefing by Seventh Army intelligence officers after his capture, Kaiser said that the entire river was virtually unguarded, and that opposition to a crossing at any point would have been negligible. The debriefers reported that Kaiser claimed "that there were two logical places to cross, one in the Basle area, a penetration to the East along the Rhine river, subsequently turning north after the Black Forest had been bypassed on the left, and exploiting to the North along the Wutach river axis. The second point of crossing, which he claims to be the better from all points of view, is in the SELTZ–RASTATT–LAUTERBOURG area. This maneuver . . . would entail the capture of KARLSRUHE and the MAXIMILIANSAU bridge-head from the South and permit exploitation to the East towards Stuttgart out-flanking the Black Forest on the North." This was the crossing site chosen by the Seventh Army.

In conjunction with a Rhine crossing and an attack up the Rhine's east bank into the enemy rear from Karlsruhe, Devers' 15th Corps, situated on the Seventh Army's northern flank on the west bank, could have initiated attacks directly north-ward into the flank of the German First Army's Siegfried Line defenses along the German frontier opposite Lorraine. At the same time, Patton's Third Army could have pushed east, resulting in the German defenses being attacked from two sides. Colonel Kaiser identified two sectors along that axis through which Devers' forces could have advanced on the west bank of the Rhine. One was "through the Bien Wald Forest, [an area] similar in terrain to the Haguenau Forest but . . . difficult to outflank because of the OTTERBACH–STEINFELD defenses on the West and lack of maneuver space between the forest and the river on the East." Kaiser be-lieved that three columns of infantry sent, respectively, from Lauterberg to Kandel, from Scheiben-Hardt to Minfeld, and from Bruchwald to Schaidt "would have a good opportunity of breaching the line; and, on debouching from the forest, would be in position to employ armor (subsequently brought up) in exploitation towards the LANDAU–WUERTH–MAXIMILIANSAU bridgehead." The second route Kaiser identified was between Otterbach and Bundenthal. Although the terrain there was difficult, a successful attack would outflank the Germans' main defensive positions. "Simultaneous assault and penetration of both areas," Kaiser believed, would give "the maximum advantage." A breakthrough on either route "and a subsequent exploitation up the valley toward LANDAU and GERMERSHEIM *would jeopardize the entire German position to the West.* The whole SAAR front would likewise be in the greatest of danger because the important [east–west] communication lines over the Rhine near KARLSRUHE, GERMERSHEIM, and SPEYER would be cut."

Clarke and Smith offer another option for the Seventh Army's cross-Rhine op-eration, one they say was "apparently dismissed with little consideration." Patton's Third Army could have supplied the force that drove northward from the 15th Corps' east-bank bridgehead. "Although the redeployments necessitated by crank-ing Third Army forces into the Rastatt bridgehead equation would have created difficult and tactical problems," they note, "such a maneuver was not impossible."[9] Indeed, three weeks later, at the outset of the Battle of the Bulge, Patton performed an even more complex redeployment when he turned around the 4th Armored and the 26th and 80th infantry divisions, and marched them one hundred miles northward within forty-eight hours to help contain the German Ardennes attack on December 16, 1944. The Seventh and 3rd armies together "could easily [have] crack[ed] the German Saar basin defenses, if that was what Eisenhower wanted."[10] Eisenhower and SHAEF also had the option of exploiting the advantageous position of the French army that was poised on the Rhine near Mulhouse, note Smith and Clarke. But Eisenhower "seemed to attach little or no significance to the concomitant First French Army drive through the Belfort Gap to the Rhine and the possible collapse of the [German] Nineteenth Army."[11]

Devers' cross-Rhine assault plan also called for the U.S. 3rd Division to capture the bridges at Strasbourg and cross the river to Kehl, Germany. Devers noted in his diary that the 3rd, "debouching from the Vosges Mountains," would have crossed the Rhine and provided "a blocking force so that any [enemy] troops coming from the south would have had to go back through the Black Forest. This would have automatically relieved the Colmar Pocket and given the French an opportunity to close up on the river."[12] The Colmar Pocket, which contained the remnants of the German Nineteeth Army—some 22,000 men—protruded fifty miles into 6th Army Group territory, forming a wedge between the U.S. Seventh and French First armies and presenting a constant threat to their flanks and rear.

Devers had additional objectives beyond coming in behind the German First Army and unhinging the enemy's entire western front. His secondary line of attack was to unleash his forces into Germany to take Pforzheim and Stuttgart. This advance would open the way for an attack into southern Germany and the capture of Nuremberg and Munich. The advance on Munich, according to a planning report from the Seventh Army chief of staff, "would be nothing more than a flank guard."[13]

The Allies had complete control of the air, and any cross-Rhine attack could have benefited immensely from tactical air support. Winter weather worked against air cover on a daily basis, as it did all across the Allied front, but American fighter-bombers and heavy bombers could probably have supported the Seventh Army's cross-Rhine attack with little or no opposition from the Luftwaffe.

Devers believed that the Seventh Army had the necessary transport to support the offensive. By November the Allied logistical situation all along the western front was improving; supplies had finally caught up to the armies, which had barely advanced in three months. Large depots were being stocked and expanded at Liège and Verdun, and a system of depots was in place in Alsace for the 6th

Army Group. The truck and rail transport necessary to sustain the attack was available as well. During the Battle of the Bulge three weeks later, SHAEF sent thousands of trucks into the battle region, transporting troops and supplies to stem the German advance.

The Rhine crossing at Remagen five months later on March 7, 1945, gives some indication of what might have happened had Devers crossed the river in November or December 1944.[14] The Germans were on their last legs in March 1945 when the 9th Armored Division captured the Ludendorf Bridge at Remagen. But the German Nineteenth Army in Alsace was not much better off in November 1944. Had the Seventh Army crossed at Rastatt, the Germans would have had to react immediately to contain the bridgehead; otherwise they faced the destruction of the already reeling German First and Nineteenth armies. Had these two armies collapsed under Devers' and Patton's blows, the gateway to southern Germany would have been wide open and the war in Europe might have ended within a few weeks.

CHAPTER 21.

# Ike Balks

★ ★ ★ ★

History often plays out in odd twists, and such was the case for Jacob Devers on November 24, 1944. As Seventh Army engineers were preparing to cross the Rhine, Eisenhower was visiting his army and corps commanders on the 6th Army Group front. The supreme commander often used such trips as fact-finding junkets, but they were also morale boosters for the frontline troops. Paul Fussell recalled that the average American GI had a "largely sentimental and quite wonderful" attitude toward the supreme commander. "We knew for example that he had ordered hot Thanksgiving dinners to be served. We never saw him. I had no idea of where his headquarters were. But I thought quite highly of him. We thought he was winning the war. He was a hero to the troops."[1]

Some of the generals, old friends or colleagues of Ike, also looked forward to these meetings either to renew old ties or to discuss the conduct of the war. General Dahlquist, for one, expressed regret that Eisenhower was unable to stop by 36th Division headquarters on his November 24 trip. "General Eisenhower visited Corps Headquarters the other day and sent his special greetings to me and the division," Dahlquist wrote to his wife. "I was sorry he did not come up here to see us. He told Brooks he was specially anxious to see the 3rd [Division] and the 36th."[2]

It was on his tour of the Seventh Army's front on November 24 that Ike learned of the Seventh Army's planned advance across the Rhine—and immediately put a stop to it. The repercussions of that decision echo still. Major Hansen recorded his impressions when Ike and Bradley made their way first to 15th Corps headquarters to confer with General Haislip: "He [Haislip] was small and noisy, he greeted us: 'For God's sake, sir, . . . we don't want you. There is a report of an armored breakthrough on the front held by our cavalry.' Ike laughed, 'Dammit, Ham, you invited me here for lunch and I'm not going to leave until I get it.' Brad laughed and Haislip took Ike and him inside." It was in Haislip's headquarters that Eisenhower got his first inkling of the Seventh Army's plan to attack over the Rhine. Haislip's staff was "busily planning to push their forces farther east, seize bridgeheads over the Rhine, and cross into Germany itself." Ike must have been taken aback, Hansen noted, because he "quickly ended these preparations."[3]

Eisenhower had just come from Third Army headquarters and a visit with Patton, who was mired in the mud and going nowhere. Clarke and Smith believe that Eisenhower had already "made up his mind that something drastic had to be done to assist Patton." In short, he planned to use the Seventh Army to spring Patton loose from the mud and send him on to the Rhine. Eisenhower told Haislip to "halt all preparations for a Rhine crossing, change direction immediately, and advance generally northward astride the Low Vosges Mountains in close support of the 3rd Army. Supporting Patton's advance into the Saar basin was to have first priority."[4]

If there was any discussion about Ike's orders it went unrecorded. The next stop for Eisenhower's entourage was Devers' headquarters in Vittel. Hansen's diary describes the desolate countryside through which they traveled.

> We then mounted again and continued our drive through war torn villages. Everywhere there was evidence of sharp and bitter fighting. The houses were punctuated by bullet holes with gaping boudoirs showing through in holes smashed through the side by cannon fire. Even the road signs announcing the names of the community were punctured by bullets as though French Second Armored had passed through shooting at everything they saw.
>
> Everywhere the rivers were running in swift angry torrents that threatened to wash out our bridges so patiently constructed by engineers who had worked for days in water up to their waists, standing in the chilling river beds with the rains beating in their faces to construct these vital roadways over which we might move our armies to the Rhine.
>
> From the XV Corps we turned down to St. Die, the burned village . . . of utter desolation. In his retreat or withdrawal the Germans had applied the torch to the countryside. The town of St. Die was completely gutted, only the empty walls remained with the people huddled in miserable lumps on the street, shielding themselves and their possessions from the driving rain, looking incomprehensible in their square, impassive Alsatian faces.
>
> Once again we climbed into our cars. . . . We drove through the shot up towns past the trenches the Germans had dug for the winter but never occupied, now standing half filled with water across the rolling hills of that lower section of the front to the resort city of Vittel where Group headquarters is located. Devers lives in the same hotel in which his office is located.
>
> Devers looked happy and boyish as usual and Patch appeared grave, much older and far less jaunty in a doughboy's uniform with steel helmet,

a toga jacket and OD pants. [Patch's son, Mac, had just been killed on the Third Army front.] Last time I saw him [Patch] in England he was a model of uniformity with pink britches and polished boots. There were many photographers about . . . large groups of them with Devers. . . . Brad had a room on the top floor. . . . They had liberal quantities of scotch and we attended a cocktail party where General Frederick, commander of the airborne task force, and others were waiting to meet with General Ike. Brad as usual, clung to the background with his normal great modesty. The party was gay with good conversation and the dinner excellent though without the éclat of our own mess. After dinner, there were wires and whatnot while the Gen. [Bradley] sat up late with Ike and Devers talking late in the wee hours of the morning.[5]

"Talking" is apparently a euphemism for that discussion. The discussions grew intense and heated, and those outside could hear angry, raised voices. Not surprisingly, Devers vividly remembered the meeting and the conversation:

Bradley and Eisenhower came down, had been to my front and looked around, and everybody was pleased with what they saw there. However, they had something on their minds and after dinner we went up on the penthouse of my quarters in the hotel—the Heritage in Vittel—and just General Bradley and General Eisenhower and I were present around that table. In a way, that's unfortunate. I wish I had had another officer there. We talked about the front and pretty soon I discovered Eisenhower wanted me to give up two divisions to Patton's army. He said Patton's army was spread on a thin front and I made some comment, "Well, he's got a tremendous number of troops—and he's in the mud—and he's up against a concrete bastion [Metz]. What I'm trying to do here . . . is loosen this front up so he can move with all those troops he has because I have no reserves of any kind."

Bradley got into this argument, and I got so moved that I let out a secret I had and hadn't told anybody else. I said, "Well, Ike, I'm on the Haguenau River, moving north. I've got everything in the woods there to cross the Rhine. On the other side there are a lot of pillboxes but they're not occupied. I want to cross the Rhine and go up the other side and come back behind their defenses. . . . We've been up there and saw some of them, we got close up. In that way I will force the Germans to lighten up Patton's front and I think I've got enough that I can hold this corridor. Patton can then move and then I can move. If he can get moving and get across [the Rhine] and going, he's got nothing ahead of him.[6]

In his interviews with General Griess years later, Devers made no mention of Eisenhower's earlier order at Haislip's headquarters to cease all planning for a cross-Rhine attack and reorient the Seventh Army's direction of advance from easterly to northerly. Devers spoke as though he thought that this late-night discussion was the first Ike had heard of the plan.

"'Well, I'm thinking of taking two divisions from you, and I wouldn't think of crossing the Rhine,' Eisenhower replied."[7]

Devers was astonished. At that point, Bradley broke in. "You can't cross the Rhine because those pillboxes are like the hedgerows." Bradley was referring to his troops' difficulty in the hedgerow country in Normandy just after D-day.

Devers fired back sarcastically. "Well, Brad, we haven't got any hedgerows. We've got pillboxes and the pillboxes aren't occupied . . . there's nobody in those pillboxes. . . . The point is that I think we can do this with a minimal force—as a raid, really—and this will cause the Germans no end of trouble because they're in trouble all along my front and at the moment I think I have the initiative." Devers was furious because Bradley seemed to be attacking his integrity. "No matter what you think, Brad, I'm not involved with any hedgerows. I'm involved with concrete emplacements and there's nobody in them at this minute."

"How do you know it?" Bradley pointedly asked.

"Because I've been down [to the Rhine] and I saw the patrols," Devers replied angrily. "I talked to some patrols that I found along the river that have just come back from over there [Germany]. Also my intelligence tells me that."[8]

Devers knew that American and French patrols had crossed the Rhine to assess enemy strength, and he believed that Bradley was finding excuses to deny the 6th Army Group the opportunity to cross the Rhine and outdo the other Allied armies along the front. Back in August, at a meeting of war correspondents, Bradley had preached about the importance of invading Germany and had stressed the psychological effect of violating the German border. Now, in Vittel, he was suddenly opposed to doing just that.

Devers turned to Eisenhower, "Furthermore, Ike, I've always been taught that you always reinforce strength. You never reinforce weakness. This is a basic thing of an aggressive commander. Patch is successful. His divisions are all in good strength. Patton's divisions are under strength. They've had casualties. But we're up to strength—that's the one thing we are."

Eisenhower fumed at this rebuke from a subordinate, particularly from the cocksure Devers. Ike was adamant; he would not grant the Seventh Army permission to establish a bridgehead on the east bank. Devers was stunned as well as infuriated. The Seventh Army had a golden opportunity to cross the Rhine and swing in behind German lines and either destroy the enemy's already shattered divisions or force a precipitous withdrawal. That would relieve the pressure on the Third Army and unleash Patton, who might then be able to reach and cross the Rhine farther to the north as the Germans retreated. Devers' attack might also force the Germans to withdraw behind the Rhine all along the western front.

Devers continued to plead his case, telling Ike that he was not planning to use two or three divisions, just a "fast-moving raiding force of tanks, strong infantry, and mortars." And he had no plans of going across and staying. The entire operation would be "a matter of hours." (That was not the whole story. Devers was also planning to allow the Seventh to attack northward toward Karlsruhe to come in behind the German First Army fighting Patton in Lorraine if the conditions were right. He later admitted that if his forces got that far he would have to reinforce them, but he was leaving that decision to Patch and Brooks.) Certainly, he was not going to allow a debacle like Anzio. He was going to cross the Rhine "with a flexible command" that he could call back anytime he wanted. Devers saw his cross-Rhine attack as similar to Patton's amphibious assault behind German lines in Sicily to force a German retreat, and the Allied seaborne attack against Anzio. The Sicilian attack, while perilous, was successful; Anzio was a disaster. "But we did not intend to get caught like we did at Anzio," Devers later stated. "So I was prepared to do this [cross the Rhine] with a flexible command that we could get back across . . . anytime we wanted."

Not only were 6th Army Group's combat troops ready for a Rhine crossing, Devers told Ike; the supply services were prepared to sustain the bridgehead. "We would have had to slow up a little bit before we made a major drive unless the Germans just broke," he later allowed, "which they might have."[9]

But Ike refused to budge.

Devers saw Eisenhower's decision as counter to clear and astute military thinking—and also to SHAEF's own orders to *"advance in zone, secure crossings and deploy in strength across the Rhine."*[10] These orders were supposed to apply to all Eisenhower's generals on the western front. Postwar official histories confirm that "SHAEF directives had provided for the opportunistic seizure of bridgeheads across the Rhine during the November offensive by all participants."[11]

Devers had no doubt that the Seventh was the winning army on the western front at that moment, not Bradley's 12th Army Group or Montgomery's 21st. Ike had just come from visiting Patton's headquarters in Nancy and had found Patton "roadbound and nearly halted." Nor was he likely to get moving anytime soon. The weather was abominable, note Clarke and Smith; "flooding, and military traffic were breaking up what few good roads remained passable in Patton's sector, and elsewhere the ground had turned into a sea of mud. Additional factors delaying Patton's troops just to the north of Seventh Army included a high rate of non-battle casualties (with trench foot predominating), lack of infantry replacements, extensive German minefields, a growing shortage of artillery ammunition, and miscellaneous other supply problems." In contrast, Devers' Seventh Army generals were confidant and ready. Eisenhower had found Haislip "exuberant over the capture of Strasbourg," and even "the usually serious Brooks was more relaxed, elated over his success in finally pushing his command over the Vosges and urging all of his scattered forces to continue the pursuit."[12]

If anything, Devers believed his army should be reinforced. "I felt that my army commanders had demonstrated that they were well out in front in carrying out successful operations. . . . Both Patch and I were set to cross the Rhine and we had a clean breakthrough. By driving hard, I feel that we could have accomplished our mission," Devers wrote in his diary.[13] Clarke and Smith agree. Without Ike's permission to cross the Rhine, on the other hand, "the Seventh Army would lose most of its priceless momentum. Eisenhower's orders required major regroupings within both of the army's corps; as a result, neither corps would be ready to launch another major offensive until 5 December. These delays in turn, would provide the [German] First and Nineteenth Armies with a much needed respite, during which they would be able to rest and reorganize their units and absorb replacements and matériel."[14]

Ike explained that there would be no Rhine crossing until the bulk of German forces on the west bank of the Rhine from the Netherlands to Switzerland had been defeated or pushed back to the river's east bank. Only then would Allied troops cross the Rhine—and any crossings would be against the Ruhr industrial area in the northern sector. Bradley's 12th and Montgomery's 21st army groups would make those attacks. For the time being, Devers' 6th Army Group would remain on the west bank of the Rhine to support the right flank of Patton's Third Army as it advanced across the Rhine to take the Saar. Eisenhower was following his broad front plan to the letter; there was to be no surprise delivered to the Germans in the form of a quick Seventh Army jump across the Rhine, and no possibility of creating a bridgehead that would disrupt enemy defensive strategy all along the western front. The Seventh Army would remain on the west bank of the Rhine instead of conducting an end run around the Siegfried Line by crossing the Rhine, as Montgomery had tried to do at Arnhem. Patch's army would attack northward into the German First Army's prepared left flank defenses in the Siegfried Line. As difficult as this would be, the task would be a lot more difficult if Ike took thirty thousand men away from him.

Devers fought hard to save the two divisions of the 15th Corps that Eisenhower wanted to transfer to Patton. The conversation between the three generals grew even more heated. Devers suggested that rather than transfer the divisions to

Patton, Eisenhower should extend the Seventh Army's front farther north to incorporate some of the Third Army's territory. Devers also noted that he could better supply the 15th Corps because he had an independent supply line to Marseille. If the two divisions were transferred to Patton, they would have to be supplied from the Normandy base area, which was notoriously inefficient. Devers was persuasive on this point; Ike heeded his pleas and left Haislip's corps in the Seventh Army, but it was to take over part of Patton's sector west of the Low Vosges.

Col. Donald S. Bussey, the Seventh Army's Ultra intelligence officer, recalled the aftermath of the meeting between Devers and Eisenhower and "the long faces around the headquarters when we were denied the opportunity to exploit [the] breakthrough to the Rhine." When the meeting ended, relations between Eisenhower and Devers were at their lowest point ever. Ike was "mad as hell" because Devers had criticized his operational strategy along the western front.[15] Devers was equally angry because of Eisenhower's caution and inability to visualize the chaos that a cross-Rhine attack could visit on the Germans. The enemy was not expecting an attack in this area. All the more reason, Devers argued, to breach the Rhine north of Strasbourg.

Devers had every reason to expect support from Eisenhower and SHAEF if he attempted a river crossing. Although Ike's directives to the 6th Army Group about reaching the river and seizing bridgeheads on the east bank were often ambiguous as to the exact time and place of a crossing, they were no less ambiguous than his orders to his other commanders. They were specific about one aspect, however: *"deploy in strength across the Rhine." The Supreme Command,* Forrest C. Pogue's official history of Eisenhower's command in Europe, corroborates Devers' impression that he was both authorized and expected to cross the Rhine if he had the strength and opportunity to do so. "General Hodges was to attempt to establish a bridgehead south of Cologne," Pogue wrote. "Meanwhile General Devers' French and U.S. forces were to attempt to cross the Rhine in their sector."[16]

The September 17 entry in Devers' diary confirms his belief that his mission on the southern flank of the Allied line included a cross-Rhine attack. Devers mentioned a recent meeting between Ike and his commanders. "General Eisenhower had each of the Army Group commanders give us the situation on his front and then proceeded to discuss the strategy in the future. . . . The Sixth Army Group to be reinforced as soon as possible by at least two divisions and possibly three, to drive across the Rhine and through the Vosges Mountains in order to hold as many troops as possible in the south of Germany." An entry two weeks later, on October 5, reported: "The Twelfth Army Group is to capture the Ruhr. The Sixth Army Group is to continue its offensive, cross the Rhine and advance to the northeast. All are to push forward to the Rhine River with a view to crossing it at the earliest possible moment."[17]

The Seventh Army command was also eager to cross the Rhine to forestall possible German counterattacks from German territory across the river. (Such counterattacks would indeed come five weeks later.) U.S. troops heard the revving of engines and the clatter of tanks in Kehl, machine-gun fire rattled back and forth across the river, American mortar crews lobbed their ordnance into targets in Germany, and American patrols found evidence of German infiltration across the Rhine into Seventh Army territory. Enemy aircraft were also active and made sorties against American and French positions in and around Strasbourg.

In the days immediately following the city's capture, the enemy showed no signs of relinquishing the small bridgehead around the railroad and road bridges that linked Strasbourg to Kehl. They had not yet demolished the spans, however, anticipating a counterattack to regain lost ground. But the Americans were clearly entrenched, and while the Germans could harass them with artillery, machine-gun, and sniper fire, and nighttime attacks by reinforced patrols, they had little hope of retaking Strasbourg. Seventh Army troops continued to move up and down the Rhine, taking more territory on the west bank. A British officer who accompanied Leclerc into Strasbourg recalled the arrival of American infantry to ensure control of the city. "We saw the first Americans coming over the hills in single file each side of the road, loping along with that unmistakable long American slouch, how relieved we were! And they continued coming on, all the day long, slouching along, thousands and thousands of them."[18]

Devers had frequently, and often openly, criticized Ike's strategic and tactical thinking, and his staff members worried that the remarks made their way back to Eisenhower. Now, Ike's command decision seemed even more open to question and criticism. Devers was tired of his armies being relegated to a "secondary" and "very minor" role on the western front despite their exemplary record of advances against the Germans all through August, September, and particularly November. Devers confided to his diary that he wondered if he and Eisenhower were members "on the same team."[19]

Devers believed that SHAEF and Eisenhower had become too controlling and that they should decentralize the command structure and give the field commanders more leeway to fight the Germans. In this regard, Devers' thoughts mirrored Montgomery's; he also disagreed with Eisenhower's meddling in the affairs of frontline commanders. As far as Monty was concerned, writes his biographer Nigel Hamilton, "relations between SHAEF and both Bradley and Devers were such that SHAEF was now 'dealing in detail with the moves of individual Divisions inside an Army Group Commander's area, and in telling him in so many words how he should fight his battles,' thus 'interfering with his prerogatives.' . . . The proper method would appear to be that the Army Group Commander should be given a directive and that his conduct of the battle should not be interfered with unless it is seen that his actions are jeopardizing his own or the adjoining armies."[20]

Additionally, Devers believed that Ike's central focus at this point in the war was misguided. Eisenhower wanted to capture the Ruhr and the Saar industrial areas to starve the Germans of munitions and equipment, whereas Devers believed the main objective of all Allied forces was to destroy the German army. The fighting would continue until the Rhine was crossed and the Wehrmacht was finished. A bold strike across the river might collapse the entire German southern front and open the back door to the Ruhr and Saar.

The consequences of Eisenhower's broad front strategy are readily apparent. U.S. troops continued to fight desperate, costly, head-to-head battles of attrition on battlegrounds like the Hürtgen Forest and at Metz against well-entrenched enemy troops where the Americans could not take advantage of surprise and their superiority in manpower, tanks, warplanes, and matériel to mass for breakthroughs. Russell Weigley likens the situation along the western front to the struggles of North and South in Virginia eighty years earlier. "Just as Grant's destruction of the Confederate army in the Wilderness-Spotsylvania–Cold Harbor campaign expended many proud old Union army formations . . . so the autumn attrition of 1944 removed veteran divisions at least temporarily from Eisenhower's line."[21]

SHAEF had already missed the opportunity for a critical strategic breakthrough in the Siegfried Line. The U.S. 5th Corps, under Maj. Gen. Leonard T. Gerow, had breached the line at Wallendorf in the German Eifel in mid-September 1944.[22] The German High Command was in a state of high anxiety, fearing that the entire German western front might collapse if the Americans exploited the breakthrough. But SHAEF was distracted by Monty's disastrous Operation Market Garden to capture the Rhine bridge in Arnhem, and the 5th Corps withdrew. SHAEF also saw no advantage in attacking through the Belfort Gap even as Truscott begged to push through and collapse the German southern front. Now under Ike's guidance, the 6th Army Group was immobilized until the main bulk of the Allied forces reached the Rhine, and until Patton had crossed it first. But that would not be for another five months. In the meantime, U.S. forces would suffer an additional 200,000 casualties in the battles to close on the Rhine.

Devers was not alone in questioning Ike's strategy. Other 6th Army Group generals and officers, as well as Patton, were equally perplexed by Eisenhower's order. Haislip was surprised to learn that the cross-Rhine attack had been aborted. "Our orders were to continue across the Rhine and we had all our plans made, all of our equipment ready, and all our matériel on the ground when suddenly, without warning, we were ordered to turn north," Haislip wrote.[23]

Col. Edward D. Comm of the SOS (Service of Supply), responsible for supplying the Seventh Army in France, believed the Rhine crossing would have been successful. "There wasn't any great opposition on the other side of the Rhine. There couldn't have been. It was the Black Forest area. I think we could have held a bridgehead and then expanded. . . . All I know is that we did not cross the Rhine that night or indeed any other night for a long time to come."[24]

General Davidson also believed a crossing would have been successful. Years later, he recalled what he knew about the events of late November 1944:

> On Thanksgiving Day, General Patch had me go to General Haislip's headquarters [15th Corps] at Sarrebourg to outline the plan to him [for a Rhine crossing] and to get his opinion as to the practicability of such a crossing since his corps is to be given the mission if the idea is approved.
>
> Upon my return to the Seventh Army headquarters that evening [Thanksgiving] I told General Patch that General Haislip considered the idea feasible. The following afternoon Ike, Omar Bradley, . . . and Jakie Devers . . . reviewed the situation . . . and after due deliberation Ike decided against trying to cross the Rhine and instead to have Jakie turn the Seventh Army north to help General Patton envelop the Saar.
>
> I wish I could have been in on the high level meeting for I doubt if anyone there really understood the extent of our engineering preparations and therefore the high probability of a swift crossing in force that could be sustained. . . .
>
> The point of this recitation is that the forethought and planning of the engineer section of the Seventh Army provided the Supreme Allied Commander with an opportunity to depart from his broad front strategy then abundantly apparent to the Germans and make a lightning thrust across the Rhine in the Strasbourg-Rastatt area. Affording him this opportunity seemed to me to be a major contribution to the combat effort.[25]

The quiet, often reticent Patch also obliquely criticized Eisenhower's decision to halt the Rhine crossing. Patch died in the fall of 1945 shortly after the war ended. In August 1945, however, just months before his death, Patch wrote an article about the operations of the Seventh Army in France for the *Army–Navy Journal*. In it he stated, "Instead of crossing the Rhine north of Strasbourg, for which preparations had been made, the Army was ordered to change directions and advance north astride the Low Vosges and generally parallel to the river." Patch added, "This change in direction, which forfeited taking a chance on a short cut to the heart of Southern Germany, gave the Germans much needed time; for the breakthrough to Strasbourg had split the German 1st and Nineteenth Armies and only weak forces were east of the river to contest a crossing."[26]

Even General Patton, the beneficiary of Ike's decision who gained laurels for his crossing of the Rhine five months later, ahead of Devers, expressed surprise at Ike's caution. "I personally believe VI Corps should have crossed the Rhine, but it was stopped by Eisenhower the day he visited Devers."[27] Weigley sums up Patton's attitude: "Ever the opportunist, Patton believed that opportunity in war is too rare to be missed."[28]

Despite Ike's stinging rebuke, Devers remained a consummate team player— unlike many of the commanders in Eisenhower's coterie of generals. He wrote in his diary: "It having been decided to put it where it is, we shall carry on with energy and drive and force the Siegfried Line, carrying out our exploitation to the Rhine near Speyer. In this way, we can shake Patton loose so he can get through the Line also and proceed to the Rhine south of Manheim, crossing it in the vicinity of Worms."[29]

Word of Eisenhower's decision reached the 40th Engineer Combat Regiment on November 26. The equipment and boats were still on the trucks and the men were eagerly awaiting the command to proceed to the Rhine when word came to unload. A regimental historian recorded how the men felt. "The consensus was that the crossing had been called off. This was confirmed on Monday when the boats were hauled to a rear area dump near Luneville. A PFC quipped that this is where SHAEF should be located."[30]

CHAPTER 22.

# Why Not Cross the Rhine?

★ ★ ★ ★

Eisenhower himself said that "against a defeated and demoralized enemy almost any reasonable risk is justified and the success attained by the victor will ordinarily be measured in the boldness, almost foolhardiness, of his movements."[1] But this statement hardly describes the posture of the supreme commander on the western front in the fall of 1944. The words sound more like they were penned by George Patton. Although Eisenhower wrote it four years after the war and was referring to the heady days of August and early September 1944 when the Americans and the British had the German army in full and disorganized retreat across northern France, he could well have been talking about Devers and his plan to cross the Rhine in November of that year.

Did Ike ever comprehend the irony of his own words? He ordered the pursuit of the German army across the Seine but refused to allow Devers to cross the Rhine when the latter was arguably the greater Allied strategic objective. Seine or Rhine, both situations demanded bold action; Ike took it at the Seine but not on the upper Rhine in November 1944. The U.S. Seventh Army faced a "defeated" and "demoralized" foe there as well, and Devers and his subordinate commanders believed that with Patton's help they could wipe out General Wiese's battered German Nineteenth Army and take on and destroy the German First Army. Devers viewed the risks associated with a cross-Rhine attack as "reasonable." If Patch got into trouble, he could retreat back across the Rhine. The Germans crossed the river all the time by barge, ferry, and bridge. Besides, only a portion of the Seventh Army would cross. Haislip's 15th Corps would remain on the west bank protecting the Third Army's right flank.

Why would the supreme commander of Allied forces in Europe prevent his most effective army group commander of the moment from crossing the Rhine? Devers' troops had momentum and were about to accomplish a military goal that would seem universally self-evident to any aggressive commander. There is no question that Patton would have crossed the Rhine once Devers popped him loose; that had been his intention for months. Eisenhower himself had set the Rhine as his armies' objective the summer before. Why not exploit every conceivable strategic and tactical opening, and every enemy weakness when it might mean a strategic breakthrough and perhaps even the end of the war? Ike knew that the area north of Strasbourg was suitable for a Rhine crossing. He said so himself. Of all the natural avenues for crossing the Rhine, Ike stated in *Crusade in Europe*, "southward, in the Strasbourg region, crossings were practicable."[2] Yet he rejected Devers' plan out of hand without even considering how it might have been adapted to benefit the Allied cause. He neither asked to study the 6th Army Group's plans for a Rhine crossing, which were extensive, nor conferred about a crossing with the Seventh Army's commanders, including General Patch and the chief engineer, General Davidson. It is doubtful that Ike gave the proposed crossing much consideration when he first learned of it while visiting his old friend Gen. Wade Haislip prior to his fateful meeting with Devers at Vittel.

Statements by Maj. Gen. F. W. von Mellenthin, Balck's aide in German Army Group G, offer some insight into why Eisenhower rejected Devers' cross-Rhine attack. Mellenthin was analyzing the Americans' capture of the Remagen bridge over the Rhine in March 1945 and Eisenhower's inability to grab the initiative there, but his remarks could pertain as well to the Seventh Army's plan to cross the Rhine at Rastatt in November 1944. "There is no doubt that the Allied strategy was not at a high level at this period of the war," said Mellenthin; "it was rigid, inflexible and tied to preconceived plans. The whole German defense of the Lower Rhine was collapsing, but the Allied leaders would not allow their subordinates to exploit success. Everything had to wait until Montgomery had prepared an elaborate set-piece attack and was ready to cross the river according to plan. Thus Field Marshall Model's [German] Army Group B was given a new lease on life and the long agony in the West was prolonged for a few weeks."[3] Mellenthin was referring to Operation Plunder, Montgomery's plan to cross the Rhine north of Cologne, which was tying up hundreds of thousands of men and vast quantities of matériel.

Gen. Siegfried Westphal revealed the precarious military situation the Germans faced in the fall of 1944. "A 'Remagen' in the autumn of 1944 might have landed the Allied vanguard in a critical position because of the intervention of German divisions which had been transferred from the Eastern Front at that time, but if the Allied nerve held, German resistance could have been extinguished in the same year on both Eastern and Western Fronts."[4]

The *New York Times* certainly realized the significance of French and U.S. forces' arrival on the Rhine. A *Times* correspondent wrote: "The French and Americans will now be able to drive up the Rhine Valley to threaten the flank of the German armies to the north," which would put the entire German army west of the Rhine in danger.[5] Why could journalists see this possibility when SHAEF apparently could not?

In fact, SHAEF's planners were too inflexible to allow for this sort of quick-response maneuver. Even those at the highest levels adhered rigidly to plans. Gen. Walter Bedell Smith, Eisenhower's chief of staff at SHAEF, later wrote with a certain pride that the Allied high command had followed almost to the letter the pre-D-day plan for the invasion of Europe and the destruction of the German army.

> Looking back over the eleven months of fighting which were required to defeat the German armies, I can say very sincerely that I do not believe a great campaign has ever been fought before with so little change in its original strategic plan. The grand strategy for Overlord which was agreed upon at SHAEF before the troops were ever put aboard ship for the invasion was followed almost without alteration. Tactical changes were made as the German reaction called for them, but the strategic plan was not changed. . . .
>
> As a matter of fact, only one really important variation in the tactical plan was made in the entire course of the European campaign. This was General Eisenhower's decision . . . to abandon the operation to clear Brittany of the enemy and use the ports of the peninsula for the supply of American troops. . . . Reviewing the strategic plan . . . I find no point where I really think it might have been improved in the light of subsequent knowledge. I believe it brought victory in the shortest time we could have expected, since every part of it was directed at coming to grips with the German military power and destroying its fighting potential.[6]

At least two Allied generals would have taken issue with Bedell Smith's remarks, particularly with regard to bringing victory in the shortest possible time. Monty wanted to deviate from the Overlord plan and execute his full-blooded thrust because he thought it would end the war before 1945. Devers was just as certain that his cross-Rhine attack would shorten the war.

But even Smith occasionally railed against the supreme command's ponderous decision-making process. When the Germans launched cross-Rhine attacks against the 6th Army Group forces near Strasbourg during Operation Northwind in January 1945, Smith wondered why the Allies could not launch similar waterborne attacks—the very kind that Devers and Patch were prepared to execute at Rastatt. Kay Summersby noted Smith's frustration in a January 15, 1945, diary entry: "Bedell Smith . . . had been struck by the German bridgehead across the Rhine at Strasbourg, a model of pragmatic assault—pushing a motorized battalion across on barges and reinforcing it with a division before the Allies could properly react. Why could the Allies not take a leaf from the German book of warfare and 'if we find a weak spot in the Siegfried Line we might be able to drive a salient into the German Line.'" Mrs. Summersby added that Smith then complained that "we never do anything bold; there are always at least 17 people to be dealt with so we must compromise, and a compromise is never bold."[7]

Even Bradley, who agreed with Eisenhower's broad front strategy, got a taste of SHAEF's rigid devotion to the Overlord plan. When he announced the capture of the Remagen bridge to "Pink" Bull, he was stunned by Bull's reaction. "You're not going anywhere down there at Remagen," Bull scoffed. "You've got a bridge, but it's in the wrong place. It just doesn't fit the plan. Ike's heart is in your sector but right now his mind is up north." Bradley could hardly believe Bull's reaction. "Plan—hell," he fired back. "A bridge is a bridge and mighty damned good anywhere across the Rhine. . . .What in hell do you want us to do, pull back and blow it up?"[8]

Ike, on the other hand, was jubilant when Bradley's troops seized the Remagen bridge. He ordered the 12th Army Group commander to reinforce the bridgehead with five U.S. divisions. Rather than unleash the First Army to smash through the bridgehead and into the heart of Germany or north toward the Ruhr, however, Eisenhower limited Bradley to four divisions in the bridgehead, and Bradley limited their advances to one thousand yards daily. All this was to ensure that the Americans would not detract materially and psychologically from Monty's coming operation to cross the Rhine in the vicinity of Wesel, some thirty miles north of Cologne, for an advance on the Ruhr. Montgomery was preparing a show like none other on the western front. Always known for his "set-piece battles," Monty was putting the finishing touches on Operation Plunder, which was set to go on March 23, 1945, with airborne drops across the Rhine, massive artillery and aerial bombardments, amphibious assault vessels, and fanfare galore. There was so much preparation, in fact, that the enemy could not help but notice.

An official U.S. Army history describes Montgomery's assault planning as excessively cumbersome. Russell Weigley agrees: "The elephantine aspect of Montgomery's generalship was again much in evidence. . . . 21 Army Group proceeded majestically, deliberately even ostentatiously with its elaborate planning and preparation for the crossing of the lower Rhine, Operation Plunder."[9] With the supreme command's acquiescence, Montgomery carried on as though the war had become grand opera. Operation Plunder was to be the last, magnificent act, and Monty was hoping to sing the finale. But the Americans came along and took the bridge at Remagen first. They not only usurped his final lines, they also disrupted SHAEF's and Eisenhower's orthodox thinking and stole Monty's thunder.

If Eisenhower was reluctant to allow his old friend Bradley to break out of the Remagen bridgehead, he certainly was not going to allow Devers to cross the Rhine ahead of everyone else. In his mind, the southern front was a sideshow. Ike saw no material advantage in crossing the Rhine so far from the strategic Ruhr. Likewise, SHAEF still saw the French First Army as a lightweight force good only for a subsidiary role on the western front.

Eisenhower wrote General Marshall on November 27 explaining his refusal to allow the Seventh Army to cross the Rhine: "All current Sixth Army Group operations are, of course, merely for the purpose of cleaning up Devers' area before turning the bulk of 7th Army northward to undertake, in conjunction with Patton's 3rd Army, a converging attack upon the great salient in the Siegfried Line west of the Rhine."[10]

Although Eisenhower may have been correct in thinking that the Seventh Army would bolster Patton's chance of success, he seemed to disregard the fact that an attack northward into the Siegfried Line salient meant a costly offensive against prepared defenses manned by German soldiers with their backs against the wall.[11] It would simply be more of the high-attrition warfare that was consuming American manpower at a prodigious rate while U.S. infantry divisions were desperate for combat soldiers.

Ike's refusal to cross the Rhine at Rastatt may have been deeply rooted in the lesson in logistics he learned painfully when the 12th and 21st army groups pushed beyond the Seine in August and September 1944. After the Allied armies broke out of Normandy and handed the enemy a resounding defeat at Falaise, the German retreat turned into a rout and the end of the war appeared imminent. No commander, not even the cautious Ike, could ignore such an opportunity, and he decided to disregard preinvasion plans that called for Allied forces to pause at the Seine to regroup and resupply before resuming the offensive.[12] He released Bradley and Montgomery immediately to advance over the river to pursue the remnants of the German Seventh Army. Entire enemy divisions had been decimated, and most of those that escaped over the Seine were shells of their former selves without tanks, artillery, vehicles, or unit cohesion. In only two weeks the Allies drove the enemy back from the Seine River to the Reich's frontier; and in early September, U.S. combat patrols crossed into Germany at several points.

But Bradley and Montgomery were soon paying the price for their rapid advances. They had moved well beyond their supply depots, and gasoline and other critical supplies could not keep up with their rapid advances. German resistance stiffened as the German troops reached the Reich's border. One after another, the Allied divisions bogged down. Tanks sputtered to a halt. Ike was forced to restrain some divisions so that others could continue to push forward. Patton, forced to slow his lightning advance into Lorraine, was furious. "No one realizes the terrible value of the 'unforgiving minute' except me," he grumbled to his diary. "If I could only steal some gas, I could win this war."[13]

Field Marshal Montgomery was equally frustrated by the shortages. He urged Eisenhower to give him the troops and gasoline to drive into Germany and take the Ruhr. Once the Ruhr was reduced, Montgomery planned to strike toward Berlin and take the Nazi capital. Of course, this would entail Patton and others ending their offensive operations for an extensive period so that their supplies could be released to Montgomery's forces.[14] Throughout the late summer and fall of 1944, then, logistics trumped bold military planning and maneuver for Bradley and Montgomery. Operation Market Garden was the exception, but that attack was as foolhardy as it was bold.

Eisenhower also understood the importance of national and personal politics in maintaining the alliance, and he knew that he must give Monty and the British a large slice of the glory in winning the war even as their contributions waned. The Americans were now fielding sixty-one combat divisions while the British had about twenty-five. As supreme Allied commander, notes Martin Blumenson, Ike had to prevent the British or the Americans alone from winning the final victory. "Triumph had to be shared."[15]

The struggle to keep the alliance running smoothly exacted a terrific toll on the supreme commander. Clarke and Smith speculate that Eisenhower was so exhausted from his dealings with Monty, the British, Patton, and Bradley that he could not cope with what he perceived as another loose cannon in Devers taking off on a potentially risky cross-Rhine attack. "Eisenhower may have simply concluded that he was having enough trouble dealing with Montgomery and the British without trying to force through such a major change of direction in the main Allied ground thrust. The political demands of waging a coalition war could not be denied. . . . In the upper reaches of the Allied high command, there was room for only a few mavericks, like the irascible Patton."[16]

Xenophobic scheming became rampant as the generals of both nations vied to be first over the Rhine and first to be proclaimed victor over Hitler's Reich. It continued with Eisenhower's apparent acquiescence and was probably the result of his inability to assert his control as field commander. On March 9, 1945, two days after the capture of the Remagen bridge, Bradley met secretly with four of his top generals to lay out a plan to foil Montgomery's demand for more American troops.[17] Ike had promised Monty a reserve of some ten American divisions from the U.S. First Army to assist the 21st Army Group in Operation Plunder. Bradley was incensed that Montgomery should be allowed to tie up so many 12th Army

Group divisions, particularly now that Bradley's troops were already across the Rhine and in a fierce struggle to hang onto the Remagen bridgehead.

Bradley later recalled:

I revealed my desire—and plan—to exploit the Remagen Bridgehead into a full right hook at Kassel. They [the American generals] could not have been more pleased. But I also warned them I did not yet have approval for this plan, that Monty would make the main effort in the north and that not less than ten divisions of the [U.S.] First Army were still earmarked for Monty's reserve. I confided to them my political strategy of gradually increasing the Remagen commitment until it could not be pulled back. Patton summed it up this way in his diary, "It is essential to get First and Third Armies so deeply involved in their present plans that they cannot be moved north to play second-fiddle to the British-instilled idea of attacking with sixty divisions on the Ruhr Plain."[18]

When finally informed of Bradley's scheme, Eisenhower approved the plan and on March 13 issued the following order to Bradley, "The capture of a footing east of the Rhine at Remagen offers an opportunity to exploit this success in order to assist Operations Plunder and Undertone [the Army's March offensive] without detracting from the effort already allocated to them. Twelfth Army Group will firmly secure the bridgehead at Remagen and launch a thrust there from towards Frankfurt."[19]

But Ike still had to mend his fences with the British and Montgomery, who saw his order to move out from Remagen as competing with Operation Plunder. Ike's "order made it clear that Monty's Plunder would still be the main effort, ours secondary," noted Bradley. "To reassure the British, Ike had even labeled our effort an 'assist' to Monty's Plunder and specified that the First Army must still be ready to give Monty 'not less than ten divisions.' But this was all window dressing. . . . Ike knew the operation would develop into a major offensive and that the transfer of ten divisions to Monty was becoming less and less feasible or likely."[20]

If Ike could hold out long enough, the war would be over and all his generals, except Devers and Patch, could claim a share of the victory.

CHAPTER 23.

# Enemies in High Places

★ ★ ★ ★

Would Eisenhower have permitted Lucian Truscott to cross the Rhine at Rastatt had it been Truscott rather than Devers who commanded the 6th Army Group? No one knows the answer, of course, but it is likely that Ike would at least have given the planned attack more consideration. He greatly respected Truscott as a military commander, but he had no such confidence in Devers, despite the latter's reputation for proficiency and the obvious successes of his armies. Eisenhower and the truculent and outspoken Truscott were friends and had previously worked together, and if Ike had refused a request to cross the Rhine, Truscott was the type to let him know the fallacy of his decision. A hard charger like Truscott would not have accepted his fate easily and might even have resigned.

Devers, on the other hand, was the consummate team player who fell into line once the decision was made. Devers' diary entries shortly after his confrontation with Eisenhower and Bradley at Vittel reflect his willingness to carry on without rancor. "I agree we must keep the whole front moving and destroy the Germans west of the Rhine. . . . We shall carry on with energy and drive and force the Siegfried Line."[1]

Devers wrote to Maj. Gen. Wilton Persons, a member of Marshall's staff: "We were poised to dash across the Rhine and then north; and I believe we would have made it for the Germans were completely disorganized; but the weather was so bad that Patton's Third Army had been slowed down to almost a standstill and I think it was wise for us to swing in close to them to break through together."[2] This was Devers the team player speaking, not Devers the military strategist. He was confident that he was right and Eisenhower was wrong. But his years in the military had taught him that when the commander speaks, subordinates follow.

Devers also lacked the cunning of Patton, who would not have hesitated to drive his troops across the Rhine first and ask for permission afterward. In fact, five months after Devers intended to cross the Rhine, Patton did just that—he crossed the river in March 1945 without informing even his immediate boss, Omar

Bradley. "'Brad, don't tell anyone but I'm across,' Patton reported in a telephone call to Bradley on March 23, 1945.

'Well, I'll be damned—you mean across the Rhine?' Bradley asked.

'Sure am,' Patton replied. 'I sneaked a division over last night. But there are so few Krauts around there they don't know it yet. So don't make any announcement—we'll keep it a secret until we see how it goes.'"[3] Patton did not tell Eisenhower that he intended to cross the Rhine because he suspected that Ike would come down on the side of caution and refuse permission. Devers felt that every Allied general's objective should be to cross the Rhine, regardless of the circumstances, and destroy the Germans on the other side. Years later, he said just that in an interview, adding, "I got the idea, however, that Patton's main objective was to drive to the Rhine and get across it without paying too much attention how much he destroyed west of the Rhine."[4]

The journalist Ralph Ingersoll described Devers as a man with "energy, drive, persistence and the courage of his own convictions. He was also naïve, unsubtle and inexperienced in high rank."[5] That was true. Devers should never have let on to Ike that he planned to cross the Rhine. He should have sent a sizable force across and been prepared to withdraw quickly if the Germans mounted a full-scale counterattack or if ordered to backpedal. Fate also played a role in Eisenhower's decision. Had Ike delayed his visit to the 6th Army Group front for several days, the planned cross-Rhine attack might have been in full swing by the time he conferred with Devers in Vittel.

Ultimately, however, Devers may have lost his bid to cross the Rhine and become the hero of the final days of World War II in the ETO simply because Eisenhower did not like him. Exactly why Eisenhower so disliked Devers is not fully known, but they were certainly very different types of men. Nor did Ike make any effort to conceal his feelings—from Devers or his subordinate officers. Devers was something of a "Boy Scout," in the prim and proper sense of the term, and Eisenhower found that annoying too. Ike was quite a brawler in his youth. "You stood up and slugged until one gave way," he wrote of those engagements. The townsfolk of Abilene, Kansas, remembered one fight between Ike and an opponent as the "toughest kid fight" they had ever seen. Ike fought until his eyes were swollen shut, his lips and nose were bloody, and his ears were battered.[6] Although he no longer used his fists, the older Ike was still a very tough man. Told of a German general in 1944 who was refusing to reveal where his men had sewn mines in Cherbourg's harbor, for instance, Eisenhower reportedly barked, "Shoot the bastard."[7] Such behavior was not Jake Devers' way. He had never been a brawler, perhaps because he lacked Ike's solid build. Even as an eighteen-year-old he weighed only 120 pounds.

Ike loved to play poker, enjoyed his drinks, and was not averse to using strong language. In fact, historian Stephen Ambrose writes, he "swore like a sergeant."[8] Devers shared none of these traits. He seldom drank and abhorred bad language. The strongest swear words anyone ever heard Devers utter were, "Gol dang it!" While he was commanding the army's armored forces at Fort Knox in the 1941, Devers refused to allow publication of an article in the *Saturday Evening Post* about his subordinate George Patton because it included Patton's salty language. When Patton asked for an explanation, Devers replied, "Well, George, I'm not interested in what you think about this. I'm just interested in this command, and I'll be doggoned if I'm going to have the mothers of these kids thinking that we have a commanding officer who uses such profane language." Devers' reprimand did not stop Patton from swearing and probably lowered Patton's opinion of him as well. He did nothing to patch up their relationship when he gave Patton a dressing down in front of Patton's wife, Beatrice. "Now, George," he said, "I'm the commanding officer right now, and I'm going to command, and I'm going to make the decisions. . . . Are you going to play ball or aren't you?" Patton, who must have been deeply embarrassed and angered, stood up and said, "Yes, boss."[9]

Devers seems to have engendered dislike in other generals as well, and he was well aware of it. In his diary, for example, Devers acknowledged that Gen. Mark Clark, commander of the U.S. Fifth Army in Italy, "is a bitter enemy of mine."[10] Patton thought Devers was "full of himself . . . but a clever man."[11] Others described Devers as "clever" as well, and it was not meant as a compliment. Many of his detractors saw Devers as scheming, and maybe even deceitful. Devers' constant smile did give him a smug, cat-that-swallowed-the-canary look. Some saw Devers as brash. He brimmed with confidence that others found irritating and considered false bravado. In a letter to Georgie just after Ike rejected his cross-Rhine attack plan he wrote, "We are very proud of our accomplishments. The day before the attack [to reach the Rhine] I told correspondents on this Front what we were going to do and we did it. They didn't believe me that night." Devers added, "Just a little ego for the moment but it gives me pleasure within myself to prove I was right and to make some others wonder if I had been given a little encouragement whether we would not have gone even further to bring the War to a quicker end."[12] This kind of pride and vanity offended Ike and his coterie of northern generals.

Patton in particular bristled at Devers' self-confidence. "Jake, who has at last heard a gun go off in anger, talked in a big way," Patton wrote after one encounter. "He now has become a great strategic expert, but he believes everything he is told until someone tells him different." Patton added, "Ike says that Devers is .22 caliber, and I rather concur."[13] Patton had never taken to Devers even though they had served together; he complained that Devers used "pull" to get what he wanted and to achieve advancement. In a September 23, 1944, letter to Georgie, Devers noted that in a recent meeting with Patton, "he [Patton] was subdued and I got the impression, rather hostile."[14] When the Third Army lost Haislip's 15th Corps to Devers' 6th Army Group, Patton's anger boiled over. "As usual, Devers is a liar and, by his glibness, talked Eisenhower into giving him [15th] Corps," Patton wrote in his diary.[15]

Bradley too had little good to say about Devers, although he admitted that he might have been "initially prejudiced against Devers by Ike." Nevertheless, he insisted that his opinion was his own. "I found him to be overly garrulous (saying little of importance), egotistical, shallow, intolerant, not very smart, and much too inclined to rush off half-cocked." He "was not overjoyed at the prospect of Jake Devers being elevated to high command in Overlord."[16]

Devers' brashness also led him to make what others perceived as snap decisions. While Ike was hesitant, Devers was aggressive, and he admitted that his actions sometimes led to mistakes. During maneuvers before being sent overseas in World War II, he often began his critiques by saying, "I made a lot of mistakes today. So did you." In a short profile of Devers, Hanson Baldwin, the military affairs correspondent for the *New York Times*, called him "a man who makes decisions— some of them wrong, but he makes them."[17]

Devers reacted to Eisenhower's refusal to give his 6th Army Group the role it deserved by becoming more and more independent, which did not help their relationship. Devers had always been known as a man who went his own way, often ignoring Army rules and regulations to accomplish a mission. He used "unorthodox tactics" and "gets things done and worries about the authority for it later," David Wittels observed in his 1943 *Saturday Evening Post* article on Devers' appointment as commander of U.S. forces in Europe.[18]

The historian Charles B. MacDonald suggests that the command structure of the American Army in Europe may have exacerbated the conflict between Devers and Eisenhower. American Army officers simply had no experience with units as large as those operating in Europe in World War II. "There had never been a U.S. army group except in the closing days of World War I," notes MacDonald. "Each army group commander had a measure of autonomy and each led differently. Devers left planning mainly to his army commanders, while he himself, using a liaison plane in all but the worst weather, became a familiar figure at army corps and division headquarters. He authorized his staff to operate accordingly. The staff could seek first-hand information at lower levels and make changes on the spot; the only requirement was to notify Devers immediately." Devers also operated with a very small staff—approximately six hundred officers and men.[19]

Ike's dislike may have begun when Devers was promoted to brigadier general in 1940—over 474 more senior officers—while Eisenhower was still a colonel. Wittels reported that Devers "was long rated in inner circles as perhaps the best organizer and fast action executive in the army." Then President Roosevelt appointed Devers to negotiate a deal with the British: the United States would be allowed to build military bases in the Americas, and the Royal Navy—desperate for ships—would receive fifty World War I destroyers. Devers' subsequent posts included commandant of Fort Bragg and chief of the nation's armored forces. When he was assigned to the European command, he had the blessing of both General Marshall and Roosevelt, who affectionately called him "Jakie."[20]

When Devers took over the European command from General Andrews in May 1943, he believed he had a shot at being named supreme Allied commander for the D-day invasion, or at least command of an army group under Marshall. This undoubtedly did not sit well with Eisenhower. Ike's new command in North Africa was anything but secure. He flubbed Allied dealings with the French Vichy forces that controlled much of North Africa, and his debut as a field commander was close to being a disaster. The U.S. Army was completely unprepared to take on the experienced Rommel and his Afrika Corps. On several occasions, the Germans rolled over the Americans; even the British despaired that the Yanks would ever measure up as soldiers. Roosevelt was prepared to sack Eisenhower, but Ike managed to pull out a victory. On his gloomiest days in North Africa, Ike saw himself being retired to some lackluster staff position back in the States while Devers was one of Marshall's right-hand commanders in the ETO.

After Eisenhower was appointed supreme commander, the War Department asked him to evaluate his generals in the ETO. He placed Devers twenty-fourth on a list of thirty-eight, lower even than many of Ike's corps commanders. And Devers was the only one of the thirty-eight about whom Eisenhower made negative comments. He stated that Devers "was often inaccurate in statements and evaluations." Eisenhower added, "He has not, so far, produced among the seniors of the American organization here [a] feeling of trust and confidence."[21]

Devers was not likely to establish that "trust and confidence" from his base in the 6th Army Group in the fall of 1944. Even after his army group joined up with the other American forces to form a continuous front, Devers was literally kept on the sidelines. A photograph in *The Siegfried Line Campaign*, a history published by the U.S. Army that details the struggles to reach the Rhine in the fall of 1944 and winter of 1945, depicts "The Thirteen Commanders of the Western Front" on October 10, 1944. Devers was one of the top generals on that front, which had been consolidated on September 15, yet he is not in the picture or even mentioned in the caption.[22]

Ike filled many top posts in the ETO with old friends and loyalists—men he knew, trusted, and believed would succeed. Years after the war, Eisenhower wrote: "I have developed almost an obsession as to the certainty with which you can judge a division, or any other large unit, merely by knowing its commander intimately." Indeed, Ike knew most of his ETO commanders very well.[23] He and Bradley had graduated in the same class from West Point, and he and Patton served together during the interwar years. Eisenhower appointed his old friend Maj. Gen. Leonard Gerow to command the 5th Corps, even though Gerow had no combat experience and was not known for his military brilliance. His old friends Gen. Everett Hughes and Capt. Harry Butcher became his trusted aides in Europe.

Monty's biographer Nigel Hamilton reports that "Eisenhower had spoken openly of dismissing Devers and replacing him by General Patch."[24] In the end, Ike did not fire him—no doubt because of Devers' connections to General Marshall and President Roosevelt—but he did relegate Jake Devers and the 6th Army Group to a subsidiary role on the western front. But even so, Devers and his army group of Frenchmen and Americans continued to outshine Eisenhower's cronies. Of all the generals on the western front in the fall of 1944, none had fought as well as Jake Devers, and none but Devers had reached the Allied objective, the Rhine.

# CHAPTER 24

# A Cautious and Inexperienced Commander

★ ★ ★ ★

"**A**ttrition is always a cautious and unimaginative strategy," notes Stephen Ambrose, but Eisenhower believed that the only way to beat the German army was to destroy it; "they must be beaten into the ground."[1] With Ike in command, there would be no grand envelopments, no surprise or bold maneuvers by the 6th Army Group to outwit or outflank the Germans, and certainly there would be no Rhine crossing near Strasbourg in November 1944. Ike's was a strategy of grinding down the enemy in the Hürtgen Forest and on other battlegrounds along the Siegfried Line. The main issues were not whether the Allies would prevail but how long it would take to achieve victory and how many men would have to die.

Ike lacked the boldness of a Patton or a Rommel; and he did not have Montgomery's detailed understanding of tactics and strategy. Ambrose notes that "as early as the fourth day of Torch [the invasion of North Africa], Eisenhower was showing that as a field commander he would not take chances." At the outset of the campaign, he commanded a "floating reserve" of a division of British troops stationed on transport vessels at sea. These men could have been sent to capture Bizerte and then push south to take Tunis to seriously endanger the Germans' position in North Africa.[2] Montgomery's Eighth Army was pursuing Rommel's Afrika Korps through Libya, and American and British Torch forces were attacking through Tunisia from the west. Landings near Bizerte would have amounted to an end run placing Allied troops in the Germans' rear. Eisenhower held back, however, and the enemy quickly began pouring troops into Tunisia through airfields near Bizerte; the fighting in North Africa continued for six more months.

Later, the American and British Combined Chiefs of Staff proposed that Ike capture Sardinia in a lightning strike. The garrison of poorly equipped and trained Italian troops that held the island could not have strongly opposed an Allied invasion. "The potential gain, for such a small investment, was great," notes Ambrose, "—possession of Sardinia would give the Allies airfields from which to attack Tunis,

Sicily, and Italy, and it would threaten the Southern French coast. Best of all, the entire Italian peninsula would be outflanked." But Ike refused to move.[3]

In Tunisia in December 1943, Maj. Gen. Lloyd Fredendall, commanding the 2nd Corps on the right flank of the Allied line, proposed an attack against Sfax or Gabes in Tunisia, but Eisenhower demurred and instructed Fredendall to increase his efforts to secure his existing positions. "Only when . . . the whole region was safe from attack" could Fredendall launch an attack, writes Ambrose, "and even then he was to make certain that no lead elements got cut off and isolated."[4] Less than a year later Eisenhower was following the same "safe" strategy in Europe, demanding that the enemy be driven from all areas west of the Rhine before any Allied troops could cross the river.

Eisenhower also lacked the hard-nosed attributes necessary for effective combat command; Truscott described them best, perhaps, when he said, "No sonofabitch, no commander."[5] After inspecting the 2nd Corps' poorly arranged defenses against an impending German attack in Tunisia and finding Fredendall out of touch and holed up in an underground shelter far from the front lines, for instance, Ike declined to directly criticize the 2nd Corps' commander. Instead, he sent an obliquely censorious letter noting that "one of the things that gives me the most concern is the habit of some of our generals in staying too close to their command posts."[6] Shortly afterward the Germans launched a major attack and broke through American lines at Kasserine Pass, but Eisenhower was still reluctant to fire Fredendall. Ambrose notes, "At the point of attack, [Eisenhower] had shown a lack of that ruthless, driving force that would lead him to take control of the tactical situation and, through the power of his personality, extract that extra measure of energy. . . . He had not forced himself or his subordinates to the supreme effort; there had been an element of drift in the operations he directed."[7]

Ambrose could have been thinking of Patton when he penned these words; Patton was not averse to upbraiding subordinates he believed were failing. In the heady days of the August pursuit of the German Seventh Army across northern France, Patton's corps commander Gen. Manton S. Eddy complained that his tanks would soon run out of gas if he continued his advance. Patton ordered him to do what he, Patton, had done in the First World War, drive on until Eddy ran out of gas and then get out and pursue the Germans on foot.[8]

Certainly, Ike had other things on his mind in North Africa. A substantial portion of his administrative duties was devoted to dealing with the French and smoothing over animosities between the Americans and British. Dealing diplomatically with the French was crucial because the Nazi-backed Vichy government in France controlled French forces in North Africa. Eisenhower had the delicate job of maneuvering touchy French officials into siding with the Allies to avoid having to fight both the French and the Germans. The North African campaign in 1942 and 1943 was the testing ground for Eisenhower as supreme commander, and the traits he developed there characterized his leadership in Europe in 1944 and 1945. His greatest strength lay not in his talents as a superb tactician and strategist, but in his ability to forge a working alliance between British and American forces.

Ralph Ingersoll observes that Ike "had been especially selected for his ability to conciliate, to see both points of view, to be above national interests—and to be neither bold nor decisive, and neither a leader nor a general. . . . A Supreme Allied Commander . . . could have ended the war by Christmas [1944]. . . . But there was no such Supreme Allied Commander. There was no strong hand at the helm, no man in command. There was only a conference, presided over by a chairman— a shrewd, intelligent, tactful, careful chairman."[9]

Ingersoll's description of Ike as CEO is an apt one. Eisenhower was trained as a staff officer, not a field commander, and this more than anything may explain his lack of boldness on the battlefield. In twenty years of service, from 1922 to 1942, Ike had only six months of experience as a battalion commander.[10] Prior to World War II he probably never made a decision that affected more than a few hundred men. Suddenly, after never having commanded a regiment, division, corps, or army, Ike found himself the commander in chief of armies and army groups; his most minor decisions could affect the lives of hundreds of thousands of men.

Eisenhower had never served in combat or in a war zone, and his critics believed that because of this he did not understand the fog of battle. It was not that he actively avoided that experience. In 1916 Lieutenant Eisenhower applied for service with Gen. John Pershing's expedition against Pancho Villa in Mexico but was turned down. He was assigned to a tank outfit in 1918 and expected to be shipped overseas to war, only to be disappointed when his orders were changed. His organizational abilities were so highly regarded that he was sent instead to Camp Colt in Gettysburg, Pennsylvania, to command the largest tank-training center in the United States. He performed so well as an administrator that he was quickly elevated from captain to lieutenant colonel. But World War I ended before he ever got a combat assignment.[11]

The British believed that Eisenhower's lack of experience leading large armies caused his performance to suffer significantly. It was an assessment that had some merit. The U.S. Army had never been a massive force. From the Revolution to the early part of the twentieth century, with the exceptions of the Civil War and a limited appearance in World War I, the U.S. Army was very small. George Washington and the armies of the Revolution defeated the British not with overpowering force but by stealth and maneuver. The Continental Army was a guerrilla force striking only when there was a chance at victory. Throughout most of the nineteenth century, the American army was a collection of infantry and cavalry units scattered about the frontier. They fought roving bands of Indians and adopted their foes' tactics, becoming mobile, light, and swift. Even Pershing's force chasing Mexican bandits in the Southwest in 1916 in no way resembled the vast armies that would fight in Europe in the 1940s. Only with the outbreak of World War II and its aftermath did the U.S. Army and its officers gain any sustained experience in leading large formations.

Eisenhower was not alone in lacking battlefield experience. Many of the leading U.S. commanders had never experienced combat. George Marshall was a staff officer in World War I; he never led men "over the top" and into enemy fire. His only connection to combat was an occasional visit to the front to see and understand the needs of infantrymen and to familiarize himself with the shock and fog of battle. Omar Bradley spent part of World War I guarding copper mines and utilities in Montana.[12] His only combat experience came in 1916 when he was part of Pershing's expedition to Mexico. Patton was among the few senior and well-known U.S. commanders of World War II who saw action in France in 1918. It may be no coincidence that Patton was a superb combat general.

Only at the very end of the war in Europe did the American generals begin to develop a "battlefield sense" that matched that of their German counterparts. The experience they gained in combat combined with the Americans' huge advantage in manpower, equipment, and matériel created an unstoppable force, and the Americans began to outshine their British comrades and overwhelm the Germans.[13]

Nor was Eisenhower encouraged as a junior officer to develop strategy or consider bold tactics; creativity was not considered a command virtue. While he was assigned to the armored forces, Ike and his friend George Patton began developing concepts for the future of armored warfare and published an article in a military journal that detailed their philosophy that the Army should develop bigger, faster, and more heavily armed tanks capable of maneuvering around the battlefield. But the doctrinaire army chiefs considered such proposals heretical and dangerous.[14] Future wars, like past wars, they asserted, would be won by massed infantry attacks.

In 1926 Eisenhower won an appointment to the Command and General Staff School (C&GS) at Fort Leavenworth, Kansas, the Army's most prestigious school. Ambrose writes that the C&GS "did not encourage imagination, independent thought or genius. There was a correct solution and all others were wrong, with no second-guessing or discussion allowed. C&GS was not trying to turn out Napoleons, but rather competent staff officers. . . . The course brought out the best in Eisenhower, his ability to master detail . . . his sense of being a team player."

Ike graduated first in his class, but his classmate, George Patton, cautioned him to "stop thinking about drafting orders and moving supplies and start thinking about some means of making the infantry move under fire."[15]

Henceforth Eisenhower gained a reputation as one of the finest staff officers in the Army. He became an aide to the Army's chief of staff, Gen. Douglas MacArthur, who was so impressed with Ike's administrative abilities that he took him along to the Philippines when MacArthur was given command of the Philippine army. Eisenhower had been hoping for a field command. He returned from the Philippines a colonel, a rank he had always dreamed of attaining and the highest rank he expected ever to hold, and took on more administrative duties.[16] Then World War II broke out and he was quickly advanced. In 1942, General Marshall, who had appointed Ike assistant chief of staff for operations, was so impressed with Ike's organizational skills and easy manner that he sent him to London to be the chief liaison officer when the British and Americans began the planning process for an invasion of Europe. Ike was soon given command of U.S. forces in Europe, and in August 1942 was tapped to lead two field armies in North Africa.

Had he been a civilian, Eisenhower would have been categorized as an "organization man." Indeed, Ingersoll is not the only historian to note that Eisenhower acted more as a CEO in Europe than as the supreme commander. The organization had a plan, and the plan would be followed. So when Jacob Devers proposed to cross the Rhine at Rastatt, Ike's every instinct opposed him. The operation did not conform to the Overlord plan and was thorny with risk. Further, the Seventh Army was too far south of the Ruhr to be of use in destroying Germany's war-making machine. Asked at a press conference just after the Seventh Army captured Strasbourg how he might take advantage of the advance to the Rhine, Ike replied: "That section of the Rhine does not lead as quickly to the definitely decisive areas as some of the other avenues."[17]

One might have thought that Ike was well suited to be a great field commander. He was a superb poker player, and that requires a sense of daring and risk. But he loathed gambling in war. A wilier general might have tried to hoodwink the enemy into thinking that the Seventh Army might cross the river near Strasbourg, just as the Germans had been fooled into thinking that the phantom FUSAG would invade France through Pas de Calais. But Eisenhower made no attempt to disguise his objective or the route his armies would take to achieve it, and the Germans thus knew that they need not reinforce their upper Rhine front to guard against an attack there.

The supreme commander also reasoned that the terrain on the east bank of the Rhine near Rastatt was too rugged and confining, and that the dense Black Forest to the east would block troop movements. Devers' plan to advance up the narrow Rhine Valley to Karlsruhe would "canalize" U.S. troops. A general other than Eisenhower might have seen the Black Forest as an advantage. Devers was not planning to fight through the forest as the Americans had done in the Hürtgen. He planned to advance along the open Rhine River valley using the Black Forest as a shield and then cut west behind the Siegfried Line defenses of the German First Army. The Black Forest would have protected Devers' forces because a German attack against a Seventh Army thrust up the Rhine would have had to come through the forest.[18] Ironically, while Ike considered the Black Forest region unsuitable for an offensive, he approved an attack by Bradley's forces in similar terrain farther to the north. Gen. Lawton Collins' 7th Corps launched persistent—and futile—attacks in the rugged and densely wooded Hürtgen area, particularly from Monschau to Schmidt and Kamersheidt.

Five months after Devers intended to cross the Rhine, Eisenhower authorized Bradley to send four of his divisions across the river into the Remagen bridgehead. This too was densely forested and rugged terrain, filled with rifts and precipitous slopes making it difficult to sustain an advance. Capt. Charles Roland, a battalion operations officer with the 99th Division, which was fighting in the bridgehead, remembered the topography. "Some hills are like mountains and almost straight up," he said.[19]

Field Marshal Brooke complained that Eisenhower's method of command mirrored that of Ulysses S. Grant during the Civil War. Grant attacked relentlessly against Gen. Robert E. Lee's army in the campaigns in Virginia in 1864 and 1865, knowing that eventually his greater numbers would prevail, but he suffered horrendous casualties in the process. His losses were particularly high in the Wilderness campaigns, which took place in terrain that resembled the Hürtgen Forest. Paul Fussell likened the fighting in the Hürtgen to that in the densely wooded Vosges Mountains.[20]

Devers' plan to cross the Rhine was more in line with the imaginative military thinking of Gen. Stonewall Jackson. The Confederates under Lee and Jackson employed ingenuity and stealth to best their enemies, compelled by necessity to maneuver, thrust and parry, and retreat or attack to save their armies. Jackson's attack against Gen. Joseph Hooker's Army of the Potomac at Chancellorsville in 1863 exemplified the bold Confederate tactics. The vastly outnumbered Rebels snuck in behind the enemy through terrain that the Union believed to be impassable and routed the Federals.[21]

Even if he was unwilling to allow Devers the glory of being the first to cross the Rhine in force, Eisenhower could have employed Devers' forces to conduct a diversionary attack to the east bank of the Rhine to draw German forces away from the northern armies and the Ruhr. Had the assault been successful, the Seventh

Army's troops could have advanced up the Rhine to assist Patton's Third Army in Lorraine. Gen. William Slim, commander of the British Fourteenth Army in Burma, employed a similar diversionary attack against the Japanese in the spring of 1945. In a drive to cross the Irawaddy River and capture the city of Mandalay, Slim sent the 33rd Corps in a feigned attack north and west to establish a bridgehead across the river. He also established a dummy corps headquarters to fool the Japanese into thinking the 33rd was to spearhead the main effort. Japanese general Kimura Hoyotaro fell for the deception and rushed reinforcements to contain the bridgehead while Slim's 4th Corps crossed the river farther to the south with Mandalay as its objective. The 4th Corps attack stalled, but the 33rd broke out of the bridgehead and marched into Mandalay.[22]

Eisenhower instinctively discerned that ultimate victory for the Allies was inevitable. In the end, he decided that holding the Anglo-American alliance together was more important than the tactics and strategies the Allies employed on the battlefield. The Allies might suffer setbacks, and the day of Germany's final defeat might be delayed, but the Germans, no matter how valiant and determined, could not withstand for very long the ferocious assaults coming from all sides, particularly on the Russian front where the Soviets were steamrolling through Eastern Europe and threatening the borders of the Reich.

The Allied soldiers also sensed that victory was inevitable. "We knew the Germans had lost the war, and they knew it too," Paul Fussell recalled. "Our inexorable, if snail-like advance, told the story, as did the daily streams of dot-like silver bombers flying toward Germany with none coming the other direction. . . . Since it was clear that we were going to win, why did we have to enact the victory physically and kill them and ourselves in the process?"[23]

Was Ike's decision not to allow Devers to cross the Rhine wise and correct? Some would say yes. Others, including Devers, Patch, Davidson, and Haislip, believed that it was not. Eisenhower might have ended the war sooner and saved countless American and British lives. In his refusal even to consider Devers' cross-Rhine attack, Ike played the part of the quarterback in the championship game who refuses to throw to the open man on the goal line because it's not part of the original game plan. Ike ignored the open man and threw into coverage. And the game on the western front went on for another six months.

# What If Devers Had Crossed in November?

★ ★ ★ ★

What would have happened had Eisenhower permitted the Seventh Army to cross the Rhine in November or December 1944? Would a successful crossing have unhinged the German front and shortened the war, as Devers believed? At least some military historians think that might have been the result. A history put together by members of the West Point history department speculates that German resistance might have broken at various points along the front:

> On the Rhine, opposite the north edge of the Black Forest, Devers was in a position to exploit the most significant gain the Allies had made since crossing the Seine River. . . . Little thought seems to have been given to placing Patton's army under Devers, a logical choice considering how the situation had developed in the south. A speculative question, which requires more scholarly research, particularly in the logistical area, is how a Devers crossing of the Rhine might have affected events. Even reinforced, Seventh Army would have had rough going, but such an advance would have loosened Patton's front and might very well have forced Hitler to unleash the forces he was readying for the Ardennes counteroffensive.[1]

Placing Patton under Devers' command would have been feasible; Devers was an army group commander in charge of two armies while Patton commanded only the Third Army. Most Americans today consider Patton the paramount general on the western front; he wasn't. Devers had a higher rank and—technically, at least—more authority. Whether Patton would have accepted such a transfer is not known. He did not particularly like Jake Devers, but he did not respect Omar Bradley's military thinking, either. "It would perhaps be a mercy if the latter [Bradley] were gathered into heaven—a fine man but not great," Patton wrote of Bradley in his diary. And Patton did see some advantages in going under Devers' command: "I'm not sure that, as the lesser of two evils, it might not be better to be in [Devers'] army group; he interferes less and is not as timid as Bradley."[2]

Given the opportunity to become the principal player in the final drive into Germany, access to the 6th Army Group's separate supply line, and a chance for the glory of being first over the Rhine, Patton might have accepted a transfer. He would no longer have to compete with Montgomery for supplies and glory, and he believed that Devers would give him greater leeway. Eisenhower, however, would probably never have agreed; he was too wedded to his northern strategy. Bradley certainly would have objected strongly to losing his celebrated Third Army to the ".22-caliber" Devers. Nevertheless, a joint attack in the Seventh and Third army sectors had definite merit.

A Seventh Army attack across the Rhine would most likely have forced the enemy to withdraw troops from the northern and central sectors of the western front to contain the bridgehead above Strasbourg. That is what happened five months later in March 1945 when First Army troops established a bridgehead on the east bank of the Rhine at Remagen. Hitler stripped other areas of the German Rhine front of troops—desperately needed where they were—and rushed elements of some twelve divisions (including four panzer divisions) to Erpel on the Rhine's east bank with orders to stop the American breakthrough. The Germans also brought up heavy artillery, aircraft, floating mines, frogmen, and even fired eleven V-2 rockets in attempts to destroy the bridge.[3] The diminishing German forces along the Rhine allowed Patton to break loose and begin advancing through the Palatinate, and he crossed the Rhine at several places south of Koblenz. Hitler summoned Field Marshal Albert Kesselring to command the German troops attempting to contain the breakthrough and to drive the Americans back over the Rhine. Kesselring, known as "Smiling Albert," was one of the Wehrmacht's best generals and an expert in the art of defensive warfare. He had prevented the Allies from advancing out of Italy into Austria and Yugoslavia, but he could not stop the American advance out of the Remagen bridgehead.

SHAEF actually considered shifting the focus of the Allied effort from north to south in November 1944. The Army's official history of the Lorraine campaign notes that with the offensives against the Siegfried Line in the north grinding to costly halts,

> it seemed possible that a stalemate might result at the Roer River [in the First Army sector]; therefore, at the close of November, the SHAEF and Twelfth Army Group staff turned to consider alternative strategy. Progress on the Third Army front and in Alsace, where Sixth Army Group had breached the Belfort Gap position and reached the Rhine, offered some chance of reward. On 27 November Eisenhower ordered

General Devers to attack northward with the object of cracking the West Wall west of the Rhine, thus aiding Third Army in its drive toward the Saar Basin. The SHAEF planning staff on 28 November, considered the possible results of reinforcing a joint offensive by the Third Army and the Sixth Army Group.

While SHAEF's thinking was less bold than Devers', in that SHAEF strategists did not suggest crossing the Rhine, their plan was intended to achieve the same result. In a memo entitled "Immediate Prospects of Western Front," SHAEF planners wrote: "More important than the capture of ground would be the destruction of the Germans in the area between the Moselle and the Rhine. It is probable that this offensive will attract considerable German resources from the northern and central sectors, and it is possible that this movement of reserves may resolve the impasse at the Roer. . . . Although the joint Third-Seventh Army offensive is not the most important sector of the front, it offers the best chance of quick returns and of getting the main offensive underway once more." SHAEF might have implemented this plan had the Battle of the Bulge not occurred less than three weeks later, ending any prospect of focusing the Allies' effort on the Third and Seventh armies.[4]

General Patch believed that a Seventh Army Rhine crossing in late November would have offered a shortcut into southern Germany while unhinging the enemy front.[5] General Davidson, who commanded the U.S. Seventh Army in Europe in the early Cold War years, also speculated about the outcome of a bold attack across the Rhine at Rastatt in November 1944:

It is interesting to conjecture what might have been the effect of the exploitation of an unexpected crossing of the Rhine in the south in late November or early December and an envelopment of the Ardennes to the north along the east bank of the Rhine. The actual preparation for a crossing in the north provided a perfect cover. [Davidson is referring to Allied plans—and the Germans' awareness of them—to cross farther north to capture the Ruhr.] I have often wondered what might have happened had Ike had the audacity to take a calculated risk, as General Patton would have instead of playing it safe. Perhaps success would have eliminated any possibility of the Battle of the Bulge, 40,000 [80,000 actually] casualties there would have been avoided and the war shortened by a number of months at the saving of other thousands of lives.[6]

Clarke and Smith note that "in the end, Eisenhower's Sarrebourg decision [not to cross] also reinforced Hitler's own plans. First, it confirmed the German leader's decision to adhere to a counteroffensive in the Ardennes instead of switching the main effort to Lorraine and northern Alsace. Second, the decision gave the Germans a free hand to continue the Ardennes buildup, which would proceed without facing the crisis that a Rhine crossing by the Seventh Army would have created."[7]

Had Devers crossed the Rhine in November, he would have presented the enemy with a scenario identical with the one the Allies faced when the Germans mounted their Ardennes offensive on December 16, 1944. It took the Allies six weeks of bitter fighting to drive the Germans back to their starting positions, and another month passed before the Allies were prepared to open a winter offensive in late February that led to the crossing of the Rhine in March 1945.

Eisenhower's rush to reinforce the Bulge with American units from other parts of the western front stretched Allied combat capabilities in other sectors to the limit, and all offensive action ceased for nearly three months. Within hours of the German attack, Eisenhower ordered five U.S. divisions to converge on the Ardennes area to stop the German drive. Patton pulled three divisions from Third Army lines, wheeled them around, and hurried them to the north. After a forty-eight-hour forced march, they arrived to attack the southern flank of the German salient. The 101st and 82nd airborne divisions were also ordered from their rest and retraining camps in France—the 82nd to take up positions on the northern flank of the Bulge and the 101st to hold Bastogne, which controlled a strategic road network critical to the Germans' plan to capture Antwerp. The paratroopers arrived within two days of the summons.

Fighting with virtually no air force—the Luftwaffe was no longer a significant factor—and virtually no supplies, the Germans still managed to wreak havoc on American forces in the Bulge. Their gasoline supply was so low that they had to count on capturing American fuel depots to continue their offensive. Most of their supplies were hauled to the front in horse-drawn wagons—as they had been throughout the war. This primitive system of logistics could not sustain the pace of the Germans' attack in the Bulge.

Had Devers launched his own drive north at Rastatt while the Germans were building up in the Ardennes farther north, he could have called on at least one, and probably two, airborne divisions sitting in reserve and looking for a fight, and one or two American tactical air forces as well. The "Mighty Eighth" Air Force could have made it difficult, if not impossible, for the Germans to supply and reinforce any troops moving to contain a Seventh Army advance. The Allies also had thousands of trucks with which to supply a Seventh Army advance. Instead, these vehicles poured into the Bulge in December to ferry troops and supplies around the front.[8] In short, there is good reason to believe that a Seventh Army crossing of the Rhine could have stopped the Ardennes offensive before it ever kicked off. There might have been no Battle of the Bulge in Belgium.[9]

Gen. Hellmuth Thumm, who commanded the German Nineteenth Army's 64th Corps, "expected a critical danger for the entire upper Rhine front" after Strasbourg fell. A lightning attack over the intact Kehl bridges by the Seventh Army in November 1944 would have created a "Remagen" situation. Barring a cross-Rhine attack, Thumm said, the Seventh Army could have moved south along the Rhine and joined up with the French moving north along the river. Such an advance, he believed, would have encircled and destroyed the German Nineteenth Army. Thumm stated that his troops expected to be cut off this way after the Americans reached Strasbourg. Many fearfully complained, "We won't get out of here anymore."[10]

Lt. Col. Willi Kaiser certainly thought a Rhine crossing in November 1944 could have been successful. A Seventh Army intelligence report to General Patch noted: "Colonel Kaiser stated that we made a strategic blunder when we failed to take advantage of the Vosges breakthrough to achieve a quick crossing of the Rhine either in the area N of Strasbourg, or N of Basle." The report added:

> Aside from military considerations, [Kaiser] claims that we missed a golden opportunity because of the political significance of such a maneuver. The people of South Germany, particularly in the Black Forest and Baden areas, have always been very jealous of the Alsatians. Throughout the years both the French and the Germans have wooed this group for obvious reasons. . . . After the fall of France the Germans poured money, industrial equipment, and other economic advantages into the Alsace Plain. The South Germans feel that the Nazis were, therefore, treating foreigners better than their own countrymen. Furthermore, South Germany being predominately Catholic, has been hardheaded about Nazism and has been difficult to bring into line by Hitler and Co. . . . This attitude is reflected in the fact that a great number of SS troops have been employed to effect physical control of SW Germany during the past few months. . . .
>
> Colonel Kaiser . . . felt that the crossing of the Rhine in this area would have found South Germany generally sympathetic or at least, apathetic to the operations; and in all probability would have forced a cleavage between North and South Germany, the consequence of which would have been disastrous to the propaganda pattern of a "United Germany."
>
> Finally, Colonel Kaiser stated that so long as the Rhine River is not crossed, which is a symbol of historical and political importance, the German nation would probably hold out in its present status in the political grip of Nazism. . . . [H]e is convinced, and has been for some time, that

Germany is defeated, but that German troops will continue to fight until the threats against the lives of their relatives have been eliminated.[11]

A successful attack across the Rhine in November or December 1944 could also have galvanized the Russians to increase their attacks on the eastern front.[12] The Soviets were determined to reach Berlin before the Allies, and any American or Allied advance that threatened to capture the capital was a threat to their designs. Berlin had great symbolic value for the Soviets, and its capture would also ensure the occupation of a substantial portion of Germany and much of eastern Europe. Had Devers crossed the Rhine, and had the attack been successful, Stalin might have responded by ordering devastating attacks against already crumbling German defenses on the eastern front. That is exactly what he did in March 1945 when Hodges' First Army crossed the Rhine at Remagen. On March 8, the day after the bridge was taken, Stalin summoned Field Marshal Zhukov, the commander responsible for taking Berlin, to discuss the urgent need to move quickly.

"When we were working on the Berlin operation we took into account the actions of our allies," Zhukov wrote in his memoir. He and Stalin were both concerned that "the British command was still nursing the dream of capturing Berlin before the Red Army reached it." The Russians also feared that once the Germans realized that they were clearly defeated, they would surrender to the Allies or merely retreat and allow the Allies to reach Berlin before the Russians. In March 1945 Stalin's fears were obsessive and he was pitting one general against the other to be first into the enemy capital. "Who is going to take Berlin: are we or are the Allies?" Stalin asked Zhukov and Marshal Konev, both of whom commanded an army preparing to attack Berlin.

"We will," Konev replied, "and before the Anglo-Americans." When cautioned by Stalin that Konev's army was not in position to begin an immediate attack, Konev replied: "You needn't worry, Comrade Stalin. The Front will carry out all the necessary measures."[13]

There is also the question of the Yalta agreement. What impact would a successful Seventh Army advance across the Rhine in November or December 1944 have had on the decisions reached by Roosevelt, Churchill, and Stalin at the fateful Yalta conference in February 1945? One of the main objectives of the conference was to divide Germany into zones of occupation controlled by the Americans, British, and Russians. While the conference was months in planning, the final decisions were not formalized until February 1945. One could argue that if the Allies had broken through the Siegfried Line and crossed the Rhine into Germany in late 1944, the terms of the Yalta agreement might have been different and the USSR might not have received as big a slice of occupied territory as it received at Yalta.

Certainly, Eisenhower's strategy was influenced by the terms of Yalta. Once the Soviet zone of occupation, which included Berlin, was officially established in February 1945, Ike refused to consider advancing on the German capital. Why expend thousands of American and British lives to capture a city that would be handed over to the Soviets? The Russians suffered nearly 75,000 dead and more than 275,000 wounded in taking Berlin, but their reward was great: an occupation zone that included Berlin and reached all the way west to the Elbe River, where Allied forces eventually stopped in late April 1945.[14]

The decision to hold back the Seventh Army ensured that the war of attrition on the western front would continue for months. The Allies' November 1944 offensives had ended with virtually no change in the position of the front line except along the 6th Army Group's front in Alsace and on Patton's right flank in Lorraine. The Allies would not start advancing again until late February and early March 1945.

Devers never understood Eisenhower's decision. In an entry in his diary on December 19, three days after the Battle of the Bulge began, he wrote, "The Seventh Army was poised to strike across the Rhine in the vicinity of Rastatt, turn north and outflank the Siegfried Line. Events at this moment [the Battle of the Bulge] prove that that maneuver, thoroughly planned and taken boldly, would have been successful."[15] A quarter century later Devers was more convinced than ever of Eisenhower's error in judgment. Asked whether a thrust up the east bank of the Rhine would have cut off the German First Army, Devers replied tersely: "That's right."

"And wiped out the German Army there?" asked his interviewer.

"Most of it." Devers asserted also that an attack up the Rhine would have required the Germans "to pull some of those 5th and 6th armored armies that were up there [in the Ardennes] and come down and strike us." He then added confidently, "We wouldn't have had the Bulge!"[16]

# CHAPTER 26

# Breakthrough at Wallendorf

★ ★ ★ ★

The aborted attack at Rastatt was not the only missed opportunity on the western front in 1944. The American attack on the village of Wallendorf in the German Schnee Eifel along the Belgian-German border presented another opportunity to alter the course of the war. Here, in September 1944, American troops actually broke through enemy defenses and advanced beyond the Siegfried Line into Germany. The supreme command ignored—or worse, was totally ignorant of—the penetration as it played out. Properly handled, however, the breach might have been exploited to destroy the German position west of the Rhine.

The breakthrough took place in the early afternoon of September 17, 1944, at the same time that Operation Market Garden began some 120 miles from Wallendorf in the Netherlands. Allied planes by the thousands filled the airspace above the Dutch countryside. Twin-engine C-47 transports and Halifax and Stirling four-engine bombers towed troop- and equipment-filled Horsa, Waco, and Hamilcar gliders. Fighter planes—Spitfires, P-47 Thunderbolts, P-51 Mustangs, and P-38 Lightnings—swarmed in a protective ring around the transports and bombers. There were so many planes in the air that one paratrooper remembered thinking that "we could get out on the wings and walk all the way to Holland." The noise of the armada disrupted church services across southeastern England on this Sunday morning as worshipers rushed outside to watch the aircraft passing overhead.[1] Operation Market Garden—Monty's big show—was under way at last. Along a fifty-mile corridor from Eindhoven to Arnhem, thousands of American and British paratroopers descended on drop zones to begin what the Allied Supreme Command hoped would be the last major act of the war in Europe. The investment of men, machines, and matériel in Market Garden was massive. In all, 4,676 fighters, bombers, transports, and gliders were allocated to the operation.[2] Three Allied airborne divisions and an airborne brigade descended into battle, and on the ground an entire corps of infantry, armor, and artillery—the British 30th—joined the fight, which would last for seven days.

Market Garden was Field Marshal Montgomery's plan to thrust northward along the German frontier with a sizable army, seize the bridge over the lower Rhine at Arnhem, and then turn southeast to outflank the German Siegfried Line defenses. If the operation proved successful, the enemy front would be turned and the Ruhr industrial area could be enveloped and taken. With the Ruhr gone, the Wehrmacht would be without guns and tanks, and Germany's ability to resist would end.

Monty had been badgering Eisenhower to undertake this offensive, or a similar one, since late August and early September as the Allies routed the German armies in France and drove them into Germany and the Low Countries. Montgomery believed the enemy's defenses were in such disarray and the German army so disorganized and demoralized after its defeat in France that little stood in the way of a bold Allied advance along the northwestern German border. Ike, conservative as always, was concerned that the Germans might pinch off any such thrust, leaving thousands of Allied troops stranded behind enemy lines. Montgomery, on the other hand, counseled that only by concentrating their forces and punching through the enemy's defenses could the Allies bring the war to an early end. Ike finally relented and gave his permission for the Market Garden plan, even though a number of his commanders—including his chief of staff, Bedell Smith—tried to convince him that it was destined to fail. General Bradley later wrote that he "objected strenuously" to Monty's plan.[3] While Market Garden did not end in defeat, it was not a victory, either. The offensive gained territory in the Netherlands, but the bridge at Arnhem remained in German hands. The Allies had to look for new ways and avenues to the Rhine and the German heartland.

Ironically, those ways and avenues already existed at various places along the western front, but no one in the high command was paying attention. At the very hour that the paratroopers were floating down in the Netherlands, Field Marshal Gerd von Rundstedt, the German commander in chief in the west, was anxiously looking over situation maps of the Schnee Eifel near Wallendorf. Rundstedt and his staff were alarmed because an American armored force had broken through the Siegfried Line and had advanced six miles inside the Reich. If the Americans took advantage of the breach, there was little the Germans could do to stop them; they had no reserves. The Rhine and the German heartland lay open to Gen. Leonard T. Gerow's 5th Corps, but the supreme command's attention was focused on the Netherlands and Market Garden.

The situation at Wallendorf developed from a reconnaissance in force by the 5th Corps of Hodges' First Army. Its objective was to approach and penetrate the Siegfried Line in preparation for a general attack scheduled to begin on September 14.[4] The German army in the Eifel region was woefully deficient in veteran troops, ammunition stocks, tanks, and guns. The commanders knew that if the Americans probed far enough, they would find many of the Siegfried Line defenses unmanned or manned by overage soldiers, cooks, and clerks with little combat experience. There were also large gaps in the enemy line where division and corps boundaries met and zone responsibilities were vague. The only advantage the Germans had along the 5th Corps front was in the geography and terrain of the Eifel, which was covered with dense forests, deep ravines, and sharp ridges. It was not tank country; nor was it particularly hospitable for advancing infantry.

The 5th Corps' attack began on September 13, 1944, as three separate operations. The 4th Division was to strike on the northern edge of the corps' zone of operation, the 28th Division was to advance in the center, and the 5th Armored Division was to move out along the southern end. Two regiments of the 28th Division—the 109th and the 110th—were to advance through the Siegfried Line defenses toward high ground a few miles inside Germany near the village of Uettfeld. The attacking units lacked the equipment they needed to break through fortified lines—flamethrowers, explosive charges, tanks, and tank destroyers—and they ran into stiff enemy resistance and achieved only partial success. Nevertheless, they punctured the West Wall defenses and for the next two days struggled to break out into Germany. On the fifteenth, the 110th stormed Hill 553, which historian Charles MacDonald calls "a significant objective within the West Wall."[5] But German resistance continued, including a counterattack that wiped out Company F of the 110th Regiment. The loss was a blow to the optimistic spirit of the advance, and despite the fact that the 28th Division had broken through the West Wall and attained high ground a mile and a half beyond the Dragons' Teeth, the attack was called off.

On the 5th Corps' left flank, the 4th Division quickly penetrated the West Wall in the Schnee Eifel on September 14 and continued to widen its gains; by the end of the day, the 4th had punched a two-mile-wide gap in the West Wall defenses. The advance continued into the next day before running into determined German opposition. During four days of combat the 4th tore a hole six miles deep in the West Wall defenses, but the territory they gained offered little advantage.[6]

It was near Wallendorf in the 5th Armored Division's zone where the Americans opened a breach that could have proved fatal to the Germans had the Allies been swift enough to see the advantage. All along the 5th Armored Division's front, patrols and observation posts reported that the Siegfried Line defenses were sparsely held. This area also was the seam between two German corps, and responsibility for its defense was unclear. A reconnaissance by Combat Command R (CCR) on September 13 found many of the pillboxes empty; years' worth of dust coated some while others were flooded. Not a single shot was fired at the recon team.[7]

General Gerow sensed that this was a weak point in the German line and ordered the combat command and the 1st Battalion, 112th Regiment, of the 28th Division to advance through Wallendorf, take the high ground near Mettendorf some five miles inside Germany, and then move on Bitburg, twelve miles inside the Reich. By the afternoon of September 14, CCR had crossed the Sauer River into Germany without opposition and advanced into Wallendorf. A makeshift enemy "Alarmbataillon" put up a fight but was thrown out of the town, which had been set ablaze by artillery and machine-gun fire. CCR's armor rumbled and clanked ahead on September 15, and the best the enemy could do was harass the advancing Americans. U.S. troops seized four villages beyond Wallendorf and took the high ground near Mettendorf. By nightfall on the fifteenth, the command was six miles inside Germany. Although the combat command controlled only the roads in the area, the lack of resistance was a clear indication that the way was clear.[8]

General Gerow devised a plan to seize Bitburg and then swing north to Pronsfeld and Pruem to bring his armor in behind the German forces opposing the 4th and 28th divisions.[9] The Germans were frantic; the Americans were on a rampage behind their lines and they were helpless to stop them. General von Knobelsdorf, commander of the German First Army, sent an urgent plea for help to von Rundstedt, and they cobbled together two grenadier battalions, a flak regiment, and the 19th Volks Grenadier Division to throw against CCR and the U.S. infantry. The Americans kept advancing. On the evening of September 16, the Yanks finally ran into some resistance as the German reinforcements began to infiltrate and attack the undefended flanks of the 5th Armored's advance. Enemy tanks also appeared to oppose a crossing of the Sauer River, and German artillery fire began hitting the CCR. Nevertheless, the U.S. advance continued toward Bitburg, and by afternoon on the sixteenth, troops and tanks from Combat Command B (CCB) were crossing the Sauer into the Wallendorf bridgehead. Division intelligence described the enemy's defenses as "a papier-mâché cordon."[10]

Then the inexplicable happened. The Americans stopped advancing. At the very moment when Gerow had the confused and panicked Germans on the run, he reined in his advancing troops and tanks. "Consolidate your force," he ordered, "and send strong patrols to develop the enemy situation in the vicinity of Bitburg."[11] Gerow ordered the 5th Armored Division to go on the defensive. The order "must have come as a shock to both troops and commanders," MacDonald notes. "That the Germans had not stopped the V Corps Armor was plain." They were barely resisting the Americans. MacDonald attributes Gerow's decision to end his offensive to the overcautiousness of Gen. Courtney Hodges, Bradley's First Army commander, and to Gerow himself. The two had agreed that if the defense proved too stout, the 5th Corps was "not to get too involved."[12]

Hodges did not seem upset by Gerow's decision. He had not been expecting his forces to break through the West Wall, and even the slightest sign of German resistance presaged a major fight for which he did not have the resources. He had deviated from a SHAEF directive by giving the 5th Corps enough gas to even carry out the Wallendorf attack; he was supposed to have given this critical supply to his two other corps, which were covering the flank of the British 21st Army Group. Logistics was the name of the game in the late summer and early fall of 1944. Supplies were so short that SHAEF was allocating limited amounts of matériel, and only to certain units.

The German response to the Wallendorf bridgehead intensified as the Americans dug in, and on the night of September 21 the bridgehead was abandoned. For the next three months the Ardennes-Eifel front remained quiet.[13] One cannot help but wonder what might have happened at Wallendorf had Eisenhower turned down Montgomery's plan to have a go at Arnhem. If only a tiny portion of the vast resources, particularly gasoline, allocated to Market Garden had been available to Hodges to keep the 5th Corps advancing, the Allies might have broken through the Eifel front in force.

After the war, General Westphal portrayed Wallendorf as a missed opportunity for the Allies. Gerow's and Hodges' caution averted a German disaster of immense proportions. "If the enemy had thrown in more forces," Westphal's *History of the German Army in the West* notes, "he would not only have broken through the German line of defenses which were in the process of being built up in the Eifel, but in the absence of any considerable reserves on the German side he must have affected the collapse of the whole West Front within a short time."[14]

The first lift of the Market Garden airborne force carried more than 20,000 men, 511 vehicles, 330 artillery pieces, and 590 tons of supplies; the second lift carried 6,674 troops, 681 vehicles, 60 artillery pieces, and 600 tons of supplies.[15] On the ground, Gen. Brian Horrocks' 30th Corps opened the attack with a 350-gun barrage and fielded a force of some 30,000 men and 20,000 vehicles. SHAEF assured Montgomery that we would have 1,000 tons of supplies per day for the Arnhem operation and stripped three reserve U.S. infantry divisions of their trucks and jeeps to deliver the supplies to the Market Garden front.[16]

What compelled the Allied Supreme Command to squander its airborne reserves in such a questionable operation? Some speculated—then and later— that the airborne forces' commanders were pushing hard to get into the fight, and Market Garden offered a glorious opportunity to show what they could do. British intelligence officer Maj. Brian Urquhart later revealed that "there was a desperate desire on everybody's part to get the airborne into action." He warned his superiors that the operation would not be the "party" some commanders expected, and that the paratroopers could run into far greater opposition than anticipated. But the airborne commanders' "personal longing to get into the campaign before it ended completely blinded them."[17] General Marshall was also urging Eisenhower to make use of his airborne divisions, which were sitting idle.

The paratroopers constituted a strategic reserve available for immediate use. During the Battle of the Bulge, for example, the 101st and 82nd airborne divisions were rushed to the Ardennes. The 101st was later shipped to Devers' 6th Army Group at the tail end of Operation Northwind, the German offensive in Alsace in January 1945. The enemy often used paratroopers as highly trained infantry reserves. In fact, German paratroopers were almost never used in airborne attacks after their debacle in Crete in 1941, when they suffered heavy casualties in taking the island. SHAEF seemed reluctant to use its paratroops except in times of great peril or big public relations opportunities. Market Garden offered the latter.

Like Devers at Strasbourg and Truscott at Belfort, Gerow had an opportunity at Wallendorf to disrupt the German western front. Properly reinforced, the 5th Corps' breach of the Siegfried Line might have broken German resistance in the west; failing that, it might have forced the Germans to quickly fall back to the east bank of the Rhine. The enemy had few reserves with which to stop the American advance, and had they plugged the gap with units from other parts of the front, they would have exposed those areas to Allied breakthrough.

Yet for want of support from Eisenhower and SHAEF, the opportunity at Wallendorf went begging. Ike either did not recognize the opportunity or dismissed it as being too insignificant or too difficult to exploit because his northern troops and matériel reserves were already committed to Market Garden, an audacious but flawed plan. Ironically, the breakthrough SHAEF and Eisenhower desperately sought took place right under their noses in Wallendorf. An extra regiment or two might have held the bridgehead until larger reserve forces arrived. Had SHAEF had those airborne divisions available to commit to Gerow's 5th Corps sector, the course of the war might well have been different.

CHAPTER 27.

# New Orders for the 6th Army Group

★ ★ ★ ★

T he push through southern France in the fall of 1944 had been a long, hard fight. In three and a half months, from August 15 to November 24, 1944, the 6th Army Group had advanced from the Mediterranean coast near Marseille to the banks of the Rhine at Strasbourg, a distance of more than four hundred miles. In terms of speed of advance, distances covered, territory liberated, and casualties and equipment losses inflicted on the enemy, the exploits of the American Seventh and French First armies were equal to or superior to those of the 12th and 21st army groups.

General Devers was pleased with the accomplishments of his comparatively meager forces. His 6th Army Group comprised the equivalent of ten combat divisions, compared with at least three times as many fighting in the 12th Army Group.[1] During the same period, Montgomery's 21st Army Group had only just cleared the banks of the Shelde River to open the port of Antwerp, the First Army had been turned back a second time in the useless struggle to clear the Hürtgen Forest, and Patton's Third Army had advanced no farther than Metz. A week after General Eisenhower refused to allow Patch's Seventh Army to cross the Rhine at Rastatt, Devers reviewed his achievements in a letter to General Persons. Devers was still reeling from what he considered an unwarranted and uninformed decision by the supreme commander to halt his armies. "We of the Sixth Army Group have now taken part in three breakthroughs, and we are a little egotistical at the moment for we did it with the resources given us and without too much help; and we did it in spite of the great strategists who said it couldn't be done. I believe we destroyed the Nineteenth Army for the second time," Devers wrote.[2]

Devers' dream of rolling up the German armies on the southern front and possibly being the catalyst for the final destruction of Hitler's armies in the west was not to be. Instead of pursuing the enemy across the Rhine and coming in behind the German First Army facing Patton, Ike ordered the Seventh Army to pull up under the Third Army's right wing to protect it against a flanking attack and to help ease Patton's troops through the Siegfried Line. Devers' divisions would be used to run interference so that another general and another army could cross the Rhine to glory.

Devers thought that Eisenhower had forfeited two critical elements of any military operation—momentum and surprise—when he aborted the Seventh Army's Rhine crossing. Ike brought Patch's men to a screeching halt in the midst of a rapid advance that had split the German First and Nineteenth armies, leaving both seriously weakened and vulnerable. Between November 15 and November 30, the Seventh had inflicted losses on the Germans amounting to 17,500 troops, 13,000 of whom were taken prisoner. By December, intelligence reports indicated that only 14,000 enemy combat troops were facing the Seventh Army's seven divisions.[3] The supreme commander's order also ensured that the remnants of the German Nineteenth Army would survive and be reinforced in the Colmar Pocket.

On a strategic level, the change in the Seventh Army's direction of advance "forfeited the possibility of a short-cut into the heart of Germany." Tactically, it gave the enemy valuable time to regroup, resupply, and add reinforcements.[4] It took valuable time and energy for the Americans to disengage divisions, regiments, battalions, and companies and shift them to another battle front. Headquarters had to be moved, engineer and intelligence units reoriented, and combat commanders and troops acquainted with a new battlefield and a new enemy. The about face was not complete until December 5, giving the Germans a critical time out.[5] On Eisenhower's orders, Patch turned his army away from the Rhine to face north, along a front perpendicular to the Rhine from a point just north of Strasbourg westward to the town of Sarre-Union. The U.S. line now pressed against the southern flank of the Siegfried Line defenses, which jutted northeast. The crest of the north–south-running Vosges Mountains divided the Seventh Army into two parts, with General Brooks' 6th Corps on the east flank and General Haislip's 15th Corps on the west.

The Seventh Army faced General von Knobelsdorff's First Army in terrain that presented difficult challenges. Brooks' 6th Corps would have to fight its way through the Haguenau Forest, while Haislip's 15th Corps faced some of the strongest positions in the Maginot Line. Many of the fortifications in this complex of pillboxes and underground quarters had been modified to face south and west against the oncoming Americans.

Despite Ike's rebuke, Devers' ego was intact. He believed he still might be able to overshadow Patton in this next round of fighting by beating him to the German border.[6] With the Seventh Army committed to slog along on the Third Army's flank, though, the new drive in early December became a "plodding affair."[7] No fancy stratagems and no bold outflanking moves were allowed. The Americans would bull their way head-on through the German defenses. The fight was gearing up to resemble the bloody struggles of attrition in the Hürtgen.

Along with protecting Patton's flank Devers was to clear the remnants of the German Nineteenth Army from southern Alsace. The bulk of the Nineteenth Army had been squeezed into an 850-square-mile salient that would become known as the Colmar Pocket. The 40-mile-wide, 27-mile-deep pocket protruded from the west bank of the Rhine with its base stretching from the city of Rhinau in the north to Mulhouse and Kembs in the south. SHAEF feared that the 17,000–22,500 German troops in the pocket might break through the encircling French troops and advance northward to threaten Patch's Seventh Army from the rear.[8] Once the Seventh was committed to assisting Patton, Hitler reinforced the zone, and by late January 1945 the number of enemy troops in the pocket had risen to around 50,000.[9]

Devers believed that the pocket was more nuisance than threat. It "seemed to worry the higher headquarters," he later said; "it didn't worry me." And he was prepared for a possible flanking attack out of the salient.[10] Devers had dispatched Leclerc's 2nd Armored Division south from Strasbourg along the west bank of the Rhine to trap the remnants of the Nineteenth Army before they could escape across the river, but Leclerc was delayed by rain and mud and did not arrive in time. Nevertheless, he was present if the Germans tried to leave the pocket to attack the Seventh Army. Devers had calculated that when the Seventh Army crossed the Rhine, the Germans would quickly evacuate the Colmar area and pull their forces back across the river; otherwise, they faced encirclement and certain destruction.[11] But with the Seventh Army now advancing to the north on Patton's flank, the Colmar Pocket would have to be cordoned off for the time being. The French would have to reduce the pocket without much help from the Americans.

On December 5, the 15th Corps began advancing north on Patton's flank. The going was easy for a time, but enemy resistance stiffened. The Germans defended every village and hamlet, and each isolated farmhouse became a stronghold that had to be reduced before the corps could proceed. The retreating enemy blew all the bridges in the wake of its retreat, cratered roads and highways, and left booby traps and mines everywhere.[12] The weather also hindered the Americans' advance. The rain was incessant, fog blanketed the battlefields, and overcast skies limited air support to only four days from December 5 through December 20. The Germans were determined to hold the Maginot Line in the area around Bitche, and Haislip was forced to destroy those positions before continuing his advance. This consumed ten days of intense fighting before the last fort was overwhelmed on December 20.

On the eastern side of the Vosges, the 6th Corps made steady progress in its push north along the Rhine and through the Haguenau Forest, which the Germans had abandoned because they lacked the strength to hold it. By December 12, enemy forces were rapidly falling back and the Americans were within four miles of the German frontier. The 45th Division captured Philippsbourg on the 6th Corps' left flank, while the 79th and 103rd divisions took Surbourg on the northern edge of the Haguenau Forest and advanced through Soufflenheim to Niederrödern and Seltz. Bad weather, rough terrain, mines, and roadblocks combined with stout enemy defenses to hinder the drive. By December 13, the Wehrmacht in front of the 6th Corps was essentially routed and was rapidly falling back before the American onslaught.

By December 15, the 6th Corps was preparing to cross the German border in strength to confront the pillboxes, tank traps, and enfilading fields of fire of the Siegfried Line.[13] By that afternoon, troops had reached or crossed the German border at half a dozen locations, and the German commander, Lt. Gen. Gustav Höhne, ordered his forces to withdraw back into the Siegfried Line fortifications. Nevertheless, his forces had done what was expected of them: they had delayed the Seventh Army until Hitler launched his Ardennes offensive on December 16. And once hunkered down in their concrete bastions and launching local counterattacks, the enemy became very difficult to dislodge.

That the Germans still had the will to continue fighting was remarkable. Morale at all levels was low; and the number of desertions, defections, and surrenders to American forces was "sobering."[14] Army Group G was constantly being robbed of units that were sent north to participate in the Ardennes campaign. Among those redeployed from the German First Army were the Panzer Lehr Division, the 11th Panzer Division, and 401st and 404th Volks Artillery Corps. Commanders struggled to keep their units intact.

When the Ardennes offensive began on December 16, 1944, Devers momentarily believed that it would work in the Allies' favor by weakening German resistance facing the Seventh Army. Patch's forces once again had been advancing at a faster pace than Patton's and threatened to slide past the Third Army's right flank, break through the Siegfried Line, and advance into Germany. They were doing the job they had been asked to do, and even Patton admitted that the Seventh Army's successful drive had loosened the German defenses on his front. Like Devers, he thought the Third Army might be first to break through into Germany.[15]

It soon became apparent, however, that the Ardennes attack threatened the entire Allied line, and that offensive operations all along the front in Lorraine and Alsace had been halted. SHAEF ordered Patton to redeploy forces north to help contain the Bulge, and on December 19 Eisenhower ordered the 6th Army Group to take over the Third Army's vacated positions. Priority in supplies would also go to U.S. forces in the Ardennes. There was little Devers could do in the face of the massive attack in the Ardennes. He was a good soldier; he would follow orders and do what was asked of him and his troops.

CHAPTER 28.

# Northwind—Devers Saves the Day

★ ★ ★ ★

The Germans' Ardennes offensive convinced Jacob Devers that the supreme commander had blundered when he put a stop to the Seventh Army's cross-Rhine attack. A bridgehead on the east bank of the Rhine could have forced Hitler to divert some of his divisions to the south and possibly to limit his Ardennes attack; he might even have aborted the offensive altogether. As Devers read the military situation, the Battle of the Bulge was the result of Ike's and SHAEF's failure. They had left a section of the front from Trier to Monschau weakly defended with four battered or untested divisions stretched to their limits, and the Germans had taken advantage of the situation. Patton also believed the Battle of the Bulge was avoidable. "Had the V and VIII Corps of the First Army been more aggressive, the Germans could not have prepared this attack; one must never sit still," Patton wrote in his diary on December 17, 1944.[1]

Ike had seen the danger too, but he failed to take steps to strengthen the Ardennes front. He seemed far more concerned by the remnants of Wiese's Nineteenth Army in the Colmar Pocket. When the attack came through the Ardennes forest and the enemy poured through the American lines making for Antwerp, Eisenhower immediately ordered Patton to send the 80th and 26th infantry divisions and the 4th Armored Division north to help blunt the German advance. He ordered Devers to expand the Seventh Army's lines to defend the Lorraine front that Patton had evacuated. The Seventh Army and French First Army were now more extended than any other Allied army on the western front. The 6th Army Group's eight-plus divisions each held a stretch of front 15.1 miles long, while the divisions of the French First held 18 miles of front. The Third Army held some 12.4 miles of front; the Ninth Army, 8 miles; and the American First Army, 5.2 miles.[2] The line stretching from Lorraine into Alsace was so porous that it virtually invited a German attack. Nevertheless, SHAEF further reduced the Seventh Army's strength by stripping it of some two thousand replacements and sending them to the Ardennes to serve as infantrymen.[3]

Devers believed his army group was now being asked to save the day on the western front. As the Seventh Army grew weaker, there was growing evidence that Hitler was planning to attack the overextended 6th Army Group to force the Americans to draw reserves away from the Bulge. On Christmas Eve 1944, General Patch's intelligence chief, Col. William W. Quinn, warned of a German buildup in the Black Forest. Quinn usually gleaned his information from infantry patrols, POW interrogations, refugee reports, and aerial reconnaissance. Suddenly all those sources dried up. U.S. patrols ran into superior strength and were unable to capture prisoners; the usual enemy radio signaling ceased, as did Ultra traffic. The flow of refugees stopped, and bad weather curtailed reconnaissance flights.

"I began to suspect we were in for a big surprise," Quinn reported. "It was just too quiet out there." Quinn also noted that Allied intelligence could not account for some twenty-two German infantry and panzer divisions on the western front. Where were they? Quinn wondered. "It occurred to me," he added, "that they might well be on our front." On Christmas Day 1944 there was a break in the weather and the Seventh Army asked for reconnaissance flights. Photos taken near the town of Bitche "revealed newly dug enemy artillery emplacements, forward of the normal reserve unit positions," Quinn reported. The Seventh Army artillery section suggested that these were positions the enemy planned to occupy in an upcoming offensive operation. Quinn was convinced. On December 26 he paid a visit to General Patch. "General," he said, "we're going to be hit. We're going to get clobbered."

"When?" Patch asked.

"New Year's Eve," Quinn replied. His intuition turned out to be dead on.[4]

There was also disconcerting intelligence from the Black Forest area on the east bank of the Rhine, duly recorded in Seventh Army reports. "An urgent message (BAX 25282) from Six Army Group was received at 1718A today: 'Excellent agent source reports enemy units building up in the BLACK FOREST area for offensive.' Other indications for imminent enemy aggressive action exist. Imperative that all defensive precautions be immediately effected."

News of an impending German offensive in Alsace sent shock waves through SHAEF, already reeling from the surprise Ardennes offensive. The last thing Eisenhower needed was another serious disruption or defeat on the western front. In a meeting with Devers in Paris shortly after Christmas, the supreme commander had asked him to be prepared to yield ground in the expected German offensive. Ike wanted Devers to pull the Seventh Army back across the Alsace Plain and take up defensive positions in the eastern slopes of the Vosges Mountains. Eisenhower was particularly concerned about the exposed Lauterbourg salient, where Seventh Army lines turned sharply left from the Rhine.[5]

Devers saw no reason to concede ground already paid for with American blood, but he planned three defensive fallback lines for the Seventh Army just in case, the first being the Maginot Line from Sarreguemines to Sessenheim, and the last being the Vosges foothills. General Patch also saw SHAEF's new retreat order as "a terrifically difficult proposition." He felt it was wrong "to give up a strong defensive position when you feel confident that you can hold it."[6] Devers and Patch ignored the supreme commander's requests, or at least delayed carrying them out, but not for long. On New Year's Day, Devers received an angry call from Bedell Smith "relaying the supreme commander's displeasure over Seventh Army's failure to carry out the withdrawal and ordering Devers to issue the necessary instructions at once."[7]

Devers was still reluctant to withdraw. The French had gotten wind of the plan, and they were outraged. A retreat to the mountains would expose Strasbourg and the entire population of the Alsace Plain to Nazi retribution. The Germans would hunt down and kill any French man or woman thought to have aided the Allied cause. French authorities feared a bloodbath in Strasbourg should the Americans abandon the city. More important, the city of Strasbourg was the symbol of French resurrection. General de Gaulle and his army commanders refused to tolerate an Allied retreat from the city and threatened to pull out of the Allied command and defend Strasbourg and Alsace with the French First Army. De Gaulle sent a communiqué to General de Lattre ordering him "to take in hand and assure the defense of Strasbourg" if the Allied forces withdrew.[8]

Gen. Alphonse Juin, chief of staff of the French Ministry of Defense, met with Bedell Smith to emphasize the French plans to withdraw from SHAEF if the Seventh Army retreated to the Vosges. Juin also reported that de Lattre had orders to begin planning to pull the 3rd Algerian Division from the line in the High Vosges and send it to Strasbourg to defend the city if the Americans began a withdrawal. Smith retorted that if the French were foolish enough to do that, they would receive no more supplies from the Americans. Juin fired back that the French would deny the Americans use of the French national railroads.

The supreme command faced a crisis of potentially catastrophic proportions. Eisenhower realized that this dispute with the French could affect Allied communication lines throughout France and might well affect the conduct of the entire campaign.[9] If the French withdrew from SHAEF, the entire western front could be in jeopardy. The Americans were taking heavy casualties in the Bulge—80,000 by the time the battle ended—and they suffered from a critical shortage of manpower, infantrymen in particular, for the coming battles in Germany. De Gaulle appealed to President Franklin Roosevelt to intercede in favor of the French, but the president deferred to Eisenhower because it was a military matter. De Gaulle refused to concede French territory—which Alsace undoubtedly was—to Germany. "To the allied high command this would be only a defensive maneuver," notes author Lise Pommois. "But for France, it would be a national disaster and a strategic defeat. Alsace was sacred ground."[10]

Would de Gaulle really have carried out his threat to withdraw the French First Army from SHAEF command? Undoubtedly. The general had more than enough French pride and "hauteur" to match his great size. Twenty-five years later, at the height of the Cold War, President Charles de Gaulle yanked France from the integrated military command of NATO and set up an independent command to direct French military policy.[11]

Ultimately, Eisenhower relented. He gave Devers the flexibility to hold the territory he had taken or withdraw to defensive positions in the Vosges if he had to. Devers did not think that would be necessary; he was convinced that his commanders and troops could stop the Germans. Charles Peake, a British political adviser, believed that Eisenhower backed off because he realized he was about to make "one of those blunders which are so easily made when the supreme power is in the hands of the military who lack political experience."[12] In her book *Winter Storm*, Lise Pommois suggests that Ike "yielded to the arguments presented by his staff who had insisted on the 'grave repercussions of the withdrawal.'" Ike's stature had been tarnished by the Battle of the Bulge. Had the southern front virtually collapsed as well due to a retreat by Seventh Army and the withdrawal of the French First Army from Allied command, the consequences for Eisenhower could have been dire.

As the political and personality struggles played out in late December all along the Alsace front, the attack Quinn had anticipated finally materialized. Just after midnight on New Year's Day 1945, elements of the German 13th SS Panzer Corps, spearheaded by the 17th SS Panzer Grenadier and 36th Volks Grenadier divisions, attacked the 44th Division in the center of Haislip's 15th Corps between the towns of Sarreguemines and Rimling. The German 90th and 89th corps launched a simultaneous second blow just to the east and pushed south and southeast of Bitche against the U.S. 100th and 45th divisions. The battle the Germans code-named Operation Northwind had begun.[13]

Northwind was the last gasp of the German army on the western front. Stopped and thrown back in the Bulge, Hitler had one final trick up his sleeve. He would attack Devers' greatly weakened and extended 6th Army Group in Alsace, where Devers' divisions covered a 126-mile front, much of it along poor defensive ground. The Germans hoped to seize the Saverne Gap and separate the 15th from the 6th Corps with an attack south through the Vosges Mountains. The 6th Corps would then be trapped on the west bank of the Rhine. If successful, the Germans would turn west to split the Seventh Army from the Third Army. This was to be the second phase of an operation called "Zahnartz" (Dentist) that would push westward into the area between Luneville and Metz.

To command the enemy forces in Northwind Hitler had once again summoned Gen. Johannes Blaskowitz, the man Gen. Hermann Balck had replaced in September. Now Blaskowitz was replacing Balck at the helm of Army Group G. A newly designated "Army Group Oberrhein," commanded by Reichsführer Heinrich Himmler, was positioned to immobilize the Seventh Army's southern flank.[14]

The battered troops at Blaskowitz's disposal were a far cry from the tough Wehrmacht legions of earlier days or the German units fighting on the Russian front. The 416th Infantry Division, for example, was dubbed the "Whipped Cream Division" because of the special diet required by many men in the unit. Many of the troops in the 17th SS Panzer Grenadier Division, considered the strongest unit of the attacking force, were eastern European Volksdeutsche of questionable dependability.[15] All the attacking forces lacked tanks, self-propelled guns, and adequate stocks of artillery ammunition. Blaskowitz had no reserves and no air support; in short, notes his biographer, Richard Giziowski, "Hitler's attack plans were better suited to a fantasy than to the situation in the Alsace area."[16]

Dick Atkinson was a young machine gunner with the 100th Division when the Germans opened their attacks just after midnight on January 1, 1945. "They were drunk and marched toward us in columns of two with their rifles slung over their shoulders," Atkinson recalled in an interview. The winter was one of the coldest ever recorded, and deep snow blanketed the hills and valleys of northern Alsace. As the enemy troops approached the American positions, they formed skirmish lines and advanced over open fields. The dark figures silhouetted against the white snow made easy targets. The Germans rushed on, screaming epithets even as they fell under the hail of gunfire. "I probably killed 150 to 200 of them," Atkinson claimed.[17] The troops Atkinson faced were attached to Lt. Gen. Hans von Obstfelder's First Army striking down the Sarre River valley.

The situation along the Seventh Army's front was precarious. The history of the 141st Regiment, 44th Infantry Division, records that "those first days in the Bitche area were for many the worst of the war. The fact that the Germans were really on the offensive was fully substantiated. Snow lay deep on the hard frozen ground, and the ominous, non-directional sounds of armor echoed through the splintered woods and hollows. Dawn found the situation critical in many sectors."[18] The Germans made narrow inroads against the 44th Division's line near Rimling during fighting characterized by constant American counterattacks supported by French armor and Allied air attacks during clear weather. Advancing through the Low Vosges, the four divisions of the German 90th and 89th Corps gained surprise by forgoing artillery preparations and by taking advantage of fog and thick forests to infiltrate the American positions held by TF Hudelson, a light mechanized force improvised from the 94th and 117th cavalry squadrons. The defenders held only a thin line of strong points, and they were soon forced to retreat by the 559th, 257th, 361st, and 256th Volks grenadier divisions. The situation along this front seemed desperate. The snow was knee-deep, and the conditions were bitterly cold, so cold that Howard P. Schreiver, a sergeant with the 45th Division, never dug a foxhole—the ground was frozen solid—and his canteen burst. Pat Reilly, a sergeant with the 313th Battalion, 79th Division, recalled buddies urinating into their M-1 rifles to unfreeze the firing mechanisms.[19]

Brooks' 6th Corps, comprising the veteran 45th and 79th divisions, held the Seventh Army front from the Low Vosges southeast to Lauterbourg on the Rhine and then southward toward Strasbourg, with the 14th Armored Division held in reserve. Tying the 15th and 6th Corps together was TF Hudelson, reinforced with infantry.[20] Three additional units—TF Linden (42nd Infantry Division), TF Harris (63rd Infantry Division), and TF Herren (70th Infantry Division)—were hastily formed from newly arrived troops to counter the German attack. The fact that these men were thrown right into battle, notes Roger Cirillo, demonstrates "how far Devers and Patch would go to avoid yielding ground."[21] All three task forces were led by their respective assistant division commanders. For the next three weeks the opposing armies struggled in a battle for Alsace "whose ferocity rivaled the Ardennes fighting in viciousness if not in scope and threatened the survival of the Sixth Corps."[22]

On the 15th Corps' front, Devers and Patch reinforced Haislip's forces with Leclerc's 2nd Armored Division, and by January 3 the enemy attacks against the left flank of the Seventh Army began to wane. But the Germans had more in store for the badly stretched Seventh Army. They unleashed the 6th SS Mountain Division to advance on the Saverne Gap in an effort to continue the 13th Corps' attack near Bitche. Patch sent the 103rd Division east from the 15th Corps' northwestern wing to hold the southeastern shoulder of the Vosges defense. The 6th SS Mountain Division had made it to Wingen-sur-Moder by January 5, but there they were stopped, ten miles short of Sauverne. The Allies still controlled the passes, and Northwind had failed.[23] On January 5, with Northwind's main effort contained, Himmler's 14th SS Corps of Army Group Oberrhein attacked out of the Black Forest and across the Rhine into the southern flank of Brooks' 6th Corps between Strasbourg and Gambsheim. Two days later, the German Nineteenth Army launched Operation Sonnenwende (Winter Solstice) out of the Colmar Pocket, attacking north along the Rhine with the objective of connecting with Himmler's army and recapturing Strasbourg. Cirillo notes that the 6th Army Group "had too few divisions to defend every threatened area. With Brooks' VI Corps now engaged on both flanks, along the Rhine at Gambsheim and to the northeast along the Low Vosges mountain exits, Devers transferred responsibility for Strasbourg to the French First Army, and de Lattre stretched his forces to cover both the city and the Belfort Gap 75 miles to the south."[24]

The greatest danger to the American position was northeast of Strasbourg where the 15th SS Corps had carved out a ten-mile bridgehead around Gambsheim in an area crisscrossed with canals and waterways.[25] On January 7, the German 21st and 25th panzer grenadier divisions launched a fifth attack, striking south toward Hatten and Rittershoffen. Pat Reilly recalled the 313th Regiment falling back before the new onslaught through the Haguenau Forest to the town of Haguenau. The fighting raged in small pockets and in villages as the Americans withdrew to better defensive positions. "It was a weird battle," Reilly recalled. "One time you were surrounded, the next you weren't. Often we took refuge in villages where the Germans were upstairs in the same house. We heard them and could see them and vice versa. If they didn't make a move we left and if we didn't make a move they left."[26]

The 6th Corps' well-organized front turned into a free-for-all, with fierce battles between smaller units raging all along the line. "The battleground now began to resemble a general melee," note historians Clarke and Smith. "Along the entire front of the VI Corps, division and regimental commanders gradually lost control over the battle, and the struggle devolved into a fierce tactical conflict between opposing battalions, companies, platoons and smaller units."[27] The final German attack came on January 16 when units of the 10th SS Panzer and the 7th Parachute divisions attacked south along the Rhine from Lauterbourg. The enemy hoped to consolidate the Gambsheim bridgehead and then drive west behind the 6th Corps. Over the next four days, Brooks found himself outflanked on his right and elected to withdraw to new defensive positions on the Moder River. The withdrawal took the Germans by surprise, and by the time they reengaged the Americans they had lost their momentum. By January 25 Patch's forces began counterattacking along the Seventh Army's front. "Repulsed once more and with the Americans still game," write Clarke and Smith, "the German high command had had enough and on 26 January with their reserves exhausted, finally called a halt to what had clearly become a battle of attrition. As suddenly as it had begun, the German offensive was over."[28]

The victory in the Battle of Alsace was a tribute to Devers and his 6th Army Group. Devers was noted for his hands-off method of command and for the confidence he placed in his field commanders. He counseled, he supervised, and he oversaw, but he seldom interfered. His troika of generals—Patch, Haislip, and

Brooks—performed admirably. Luck certainly played a part in the victory, but skill was the determining factor. Devers and his generals had proved their ability to maneuver their forces as the situation demanded—the mark of a superior commander.[29] Devers singled out General Brooks for his performance in Northwind. "Ted Brooks . . . fought one of the great defensive battles of all times with very little," Devers later wrote.[30]

The American GI also showed his mettle in Alsace. "For many 7th Army soldiers, this had been their first real engagement with attacking German forces whose strength was equal or superior to their own."[31] Devers' disagreement with SHAEF over the conduct of the war in Alsace and his reluctance to withdraw when ordered to do so lowered his stock even more in Eisenhower's camp. But in refusing to withdraw Patch's Seventh Army, Devers may well have saved Eisenhower from a serious political and military mistake. Devers has received very little if any credit for his military insight and ability during the intense and hard-fought Battle for Alsace. In the end, however, his confidence, military planning, political insight, and ability to win when the chips were down, particularly with a denuded and overextended Seventh Army, won the day. The general whom Eisenhower loved to disparage had saved Ike's backside, not only militarily, but politically as well.

CHAPTER 29.

# The Colmar Pocket

★ ★ ★ ★

How critical was the Colmar Pocket to the outcome of the war on the western front? General Eisenhower and SHAEF viewed this 850-square-mile bulge in the Allied lines, named for the medieval city of Colmar in southern Alsace, as the final major obstacle to victory in Europe. And they held Devers accountable for failing to destroy this enemy salient in November 1944 and later in January 1945. On a visit to 6th Army Group headquarters in January, Ike complained that it was the only "sore point" on the entire front and ordered Devers to excise it immediately.

Devers, on the other hand, did not regard the pocket as a dangerous threat, and he believed that Ike was responsible for its presence.[1] Devers was convinced that the pocket would not have existed if the supreme commander had allowed him to pursue his cross-Rhine strategy. Had the Seventh Army crossed the Rhine, the Germans would have been forced to evacuate southern Alsace to salvage what was left of their Nineteenth Army. When Ike instead ordered the Seventh Army to turn north and assist Patton's Third Army, the Seventh Army units engaged in eliminating the pocket withdrew and were relieved by the French, who lacked the necessary punch to finish the job.

Historians Jeffrey Clarke and Robert Smith agree that Eisenhower was at least partly responsible for the pocket's presence in January 1945: "The formation of the pocket was . . . a product of two factors: Eisenhower's eagerness to have Patch's 7th Army turn north, and Hitler's determination to hold onto at least a portion of southern Alsace at all costs." They add, "A 7th Army crossing of the Rhine at Rastatt or its penetration of the German West Wall immediately west of the Rhine would have made the German defensive buildup in the Colmar region extremely unlikely and, at best, a waste of the Wehrmacht's declining manpower resources."[2] General von Mellenthin likewise believed that Eisenhower's order to the 15th Corps to swing north and support Patton "did relieve the situation in southern Alsace and enabled Nineteenth Army to establish itself firmly in the Colmar Pocket."[3]

With the cross-Rhine threat eliminated, Hitler saw great strategic value in preserving and reinforcing the Colmar Pocket. He was about to embark on the Ardennes offensive, and the salient offered a springboard from which to launch diversionary attacks on the Allies' southern front. In mid-November, German troop strength in the Colmar Pocket was estimated to be between 17,000 and 22,000; two months later the pocket held an estimated 50,000 enemy troops.[4]

The French First Army tried and failed to drive the Germans from the Colmar region in December, while the French still held the advantage in numbers and matériel. General de Lattre believed he would have been successful had he been given the opportunity several weeks earlier, when the 6th Army Group had the Germans on the run. The furious French general is reported to have responded to Devers' order to clear the salient, "Non! They wouldn't let me fight when I wanted to fight."[5]

When the Battle of the Bulge began on December 16, 1944, all thoughts of clearing the pocket were placed on hold. The 6th Army Group was stretched to its limits as the Seventh Army took over large sections of the Third Army's former front, and the bulk of the supplies and infantry replacements allocated for Devers' forces were diverted to American units fighting in the Bulge.

Was Ike correct to be so concerned about the Colmar Pocket? A salient ties up many more troops than a linear front, and this case was no exception. And as the most pronounced German enclave on the west bank, the pocket made Ike and SHAEF nervous. Eisenhower's concern about the dangers of the Colmar Pocket was somewhat selective, however. Other areas on the front where the enemy was positioned in greater strength were potentially more vulnerable and more dangerous in the fall of 1944. Ike and General Bradley had been aware for some time of Allied weakness in the Ardennes on the 1st Army's front, for example. Bradley admitted that the sector was held by "fledgling divisions" in the north, and although the southern front was defended by two veteran divisions, they were not at full strength and had not yet recovered from the mauling they received in the Hürtgen Forest.[6] The Ardennes front extended some eighty-eight miles, giving each division more than twenty miles to defend. A major attack in the Ardennes—a traditional route of German attack—would be far more disruptive than one out of the Colmar Pocket. It would be aimed at vital centers such as the port of Antwerp, while an attack from the Colmar Pocket would gain the Germans nothing but the territory the Allies had taken in front of the Vosges Mountains. Even if the Germans broke through the Vosges, they would have had to advance many miles to the north and west to take objectives with strategic value. Nevertheless, Bradley and Eisenhower considered the Colmar salient the more serious threat. They "acknowledged the risks" in the Ardennes, Bradley later said, "but accepted them as part of the price to be paid for resumption of the winter offensive."[7]

Eisenhower was aware of the intelligence reports indicating a buildup of German forces in the Ardennes, but he chose to look to the south and the Colmar pocket.[8] Ike thus "authorized" Devers to concentrate American and French forces on the pocket and eliminate the salient and ignored or failed to see the greater danger brewing in the Ardennes. On the morning of December 15, the day before the Ardennes offensive began, writes historian Forrest Pogue, "the SHAEF G-3 [operations branch] briefing officer, though presumably aware of the current intelligence estimates, said that there was nothing to report from the Ardennes sector."[9] In any case, Bradley was convinced that the Ardennes could be defended with relatively few troops because the Allied armies massed in western Europe were highly mobile and could converge on and destroy an enemy attack with very little notice.

As the Germans' Sonnenwende offensive in early January 1945 proved, even a reinforced Nineteenth Army under Lt. Gen. Siegfried Rasp was not much of a threat. Rasp's attempt to link his army with Himmler's division moving down the Rhine from the north and create a bridgehead that would include Strasbourg appeared for a time to be on the verge of success. Rasp failed to achieve his objective, however, and Strasbourg remained in Allied hands. Rasp and General Thumm, the commander of the 64th Corps, never had much hope of success. They recognized from the beginning that the Nineteenth Army could not go far without reinforcements and that Himmler's forces would have to do most of the fighting.[10] Ultimately, the Nineteenth Army simply lacked the strength to conduct large-scale operations out of the pocket. German reserves were being fed into the Ardennes offensive. And although the French were not able to eliminate the pocket, they did keep the Nineteenth Army busy with their attacks.[11] In the end, Operation Sonnenwende only made the pocket larger and gave the Germans a longer front to defend. After Sonnenwende failed, the mission of the Nineteenth Army was primarily to get as many troops back across the Rhine into the Black Forest before the pocket collapsed and to tie down as many Allied soldiers as possible.

The battle for the final destruction of the Colmar Pocket opened January 20 when Gen. Antoine Béthouart's French 1st Corps launched a series of attacks against the salient's southern shoulder with the objective of taking the two remaining Rhine bridges that supplied the German Nineteenth Army. But bad weather and stiff enemy resistance conspired to limit Béthouart's gains.

To the north, Monsabert's 2nd Corps, which included the U.S. 28th and 3rd divisions, attacked on the northern edge of the pocket on January 22 with the ultimate objective of meeting up with Béthouart's corps and trapping the Nineteenth Army on the Rhine's west bank. The Americans ran into determined German resistance, particularly at the Maison Rouge bridgehead on the Ill River. The fighting seesawed back and forth for several days, but the Germans did not have the resources to blunt the Allied drive, which pushed slowly forward. To assist in the reduction of the Colmar Pocket SHAEF transferred five combat divisions to Devers' front: the 78th, 35th, and 75th infantry Divisions; the 101st Airborne Division; and the 10th Armored Division. The 6th Army Group now had overwhelming power to drive out the Germans.[12]

By early February it was obvious to Field Marshal von Rundstedt, Germany's supreme commander in the west, that the pocket would soon collapse and the soldiers within would become prisoners unless they were evacuated. The Germans began withdrawing, and after February 9 the only Germans left behind in Alsace became POWs.

The reduction of the Colmar Pocket cost both sides dearly. The Allies suffered 18,000 casualties but inflicted at least 22,000 on the enemy and took some 16,438 German prisoners. Clarke and Smith estimate that Rasp managed to save no more than 10,000 of the Nineteenth Army's troops. "Certainly no more than 400 to 500 combat effectives from each of the eight divisions managed to escape across the Rhine. . . . As an effective fighting force the Nineteenth Army had ceased to exist."[13]

Although the Colmar Pocket had been a thorn in the side of the Allies and had distracted Eisenhower from the more serious threat in the north, Russell Weigley believes that in the end it cost the Germans "more than it was worth."[14] A contrarian's view is that ultimately the pocket was something of a boon to Allied fortunes on the western front in December and January 1945. This wooded fortress tied up considerable numbers of German troops who might have been much better used elsewhere on the crumbling German front. If Hitler had used them during the Battle of the Bulge to reinforce the advance on the Meuse River and Antwerp, the outcome of the battle might have been different. When the Germans finally withdrew, von Rundstedt deployed the main body of the Nineteenth Army's remnants along the east bank of the Rhine opposite the former Colmar Pocket. Other elements were absorbed into divisions needing replacements.[15]

After the battle for the Colmar Pocket ended in early February, Devers was criticized for being unable to handle the defensive effort in Alsace without help. Bradley in particular was miffed that SHAEF had sent Devers rested divisions from the 12th Army Group that Bradley had been planning to use in the upcoming offensive into Germany. But Bradley's criticism was hardly fair. While the 6th Army Group did not send any divisions to assist in the Bulge, it took over a sizable portion of Patton's front so that the Third Army could rush troops to the Ardennes to help rectify Bradley's mistakes. "Devers," asserts the Army's official report of events, "noted only that his own forces had repeatedly supported the northern army groups when they were in trouble and that it was unfair to begrudge the 6th a few divisions when they were desperately needed."[16]

By February 1945, the battles for the Ardennes and Alsace were over and the American armies on the western front were poised for one last assault to defeat the German army and bring down the Nazi regime. The U.S. Seventh and French First armies had been largely out of the spotlight over the previous three months, but they deserved as much praise as the American units that had fought and prevailed in the Bulge.

CHAPTER 30.

# "Bayonets Will Be Sharpened"

★ ★ ★ ★

By mid-February 1945, the German offensives in the Ardennes and Alsace had been turned back, but the Allies still had not penetrated the Siegfried Line and advanced to the Rhine. Eisenhower ordered Bradley and Devers to plan a late-winter offensive to clear the Saar-Palatinate, the German district that borders Lorraine in eastern France. That had been Patton's objective as he advanced through Lorraine in the early fall of 1944, but the tenacious German defense at Metz prevented him from capturing the region and using it as a springboard to cross the Rhine on the Palatinate's eastern boundary. The Saar had been the secondary Allied objective in Operation Overlord plans. The factories that made the Saar a valuable Allied military target fed off iron ore from Lorraine and coal from the Saar River basin. The region accounted for some 10 percent of Germany's iron and steel production. It was the site of a synthetic fuel plant in Homburg; and 40–50 percent of Germany's chemicals were produced at the I. G. Farben plant at Ludwigshafen.[1] Despite the proximity of American forces in Lorraine and Alsace and constant air attacks, however, the Saar continued to produce war matériel for the hard-pressed Wehrmacht.

Heavily fortified stretches of the Siegfried Line defended the Saarland, and the landscape—deep valleys, twisting rivers, and streams punctuated by mountains, some rising to heights of two thousand feet—presented a formidable obstacle. The densely clustered towns and factories favored the defenders as well; the Germans could be expected to use every street and every building to frustrate an American advance. "Saarbrücken, the 'Little Pittsburgh,' was apparently to be another Aachen, a building-to-building battleground," wrote a *Time* magazine correspondent prior to the American offensive.[2] It was into this treacherous zone that the U.S. Seventh Army would venture.[3]

Devers and Patch devised a plan, code-named Operation Undertone, that would launch the Seventh Army's three corps northeast from northern Alsace into the Palatinate. The French First Army would guard the rest of Alsace while one of its divisions would clear a narrow strip along the Rhine north of Strasbourg still held by the Germans from their Northwind incursions. The Third Army would make diversionary attacks across the Moselle River and protect the Seventh Army's left flank.[4] The ultimate objective of Undertone was to establish bridgeheads over the Rhine between Mainz and Mannheim. Ike approved this plan on March 8, and it seemed that SHAEF and Eisenhower were finally treating the 6th Army Group as a full-fledged member of the Allied command. Eisenhower had already promised Field Marshal Montgomery that he would be the first to cross the Rhine, but Devers might still be the first American general to cross.

Once again, however, politics trumped strategy. If Undertone were allowed to proceed, Bradley's 12th Army Group would be overshadowed and Patton's Third Army would be relegated to the status of substitute player. Too much glory was at stake in the attack on the Palatinate for Bradley and Patton to remain passive, and they devised a bold and imaginative envelopment that would eclipse anything Devers and his armies did. The Third Army would be the mobile force, swinging in behind the German First and Seventh armies and enveloping the enemy defending against the U.S. Seventh Army attacking from the southwest. The U.S. Seventh would be the anvil on which Patton would crush the Wehrmacht.

The Patton-Bradley plan so impressed Eisenhower that he immediately approved it "without qualification."[5] The plan was unquestionably an excellent one, but both Bradley and Patton had ulterior motives for advancing it. Bradley was concerned that he could lose divisions to Montgomery's upcoming Operation Plunder, which was scheduled to begin March 23. SHAEF had earmarked some ten of Bradley's divisions as a strategic reserve for Monty's operation. If these troops were employed in a critical operation in the Palatinate, they would not be available to Montgomery. The ever impatient Patton also realized that if his Third Army were tied up as a flank guard for a Seventh Army offensive, he would not be in a position to be first to reach and cross the Rhine. Devers and Patch were concerned about the new plan because the Third and Seventh Armies could converge and collide in the Palatinate, which would confuse and slow down the advance. This issue was resolved, however, when Ike authorized Patton and Patch to communicate directly with each other rather than have every tactical move approved by SHAEF. For Patton it was a wonderful coup. The best Rhine crossing sites all lay within what had been the Seventh Army's zone of operations and was now his. He had finagled SHAEF and Eisenhower into giving him a straight shot at the river.[6]

The Third Army's three corps struck first on March 13 in a southeasterly direction across the Palatinate. Gen. Walton H. Walker's 20th Corps held the right flank and generally made rapid progress against the German First Army except where the 80th Division ran into a regiment of the 6th SS Mountain Division. Maj.

Gen. Manton S. Eddy's 12th Corps, in the center, made good progress against the exhausted German Seventh Army, which had been in the fight against the Allies since D-day. "Except for a few reinforcements such as elements of the 6th SS Mountain Division," reports Russell Weigley, "the army that had contended against the Western Allies since D-Day in Normandy had at last been harried and pounded beyond its capacity to put up a good fight."[7]

Despite the good progress, Patton was impatient—particularly when Devers' Seventh Army began its offensive on March 15. Might not Patch and Devers still reach the Rhine before he did? The race to the river was on. Patton was still steaming from a remark by Patch, who had stood on the banks of the Rhine in November and teased, "George, I forgot to congratulate you for being the last man to reach the Rhine." The ever clever Patton fired back, "Let me congratulate you on being the first man to leave it."[8]

Among the U.S. Seventh Army divisions making the attack was Maj. Gen. John W. O'Daniel's battle-hardened 3rd. Before they moved out to meet the enemy, he called on his men to remember their past battles in North Africa, Sicily, and Italy. "Destroy all enemy encountered," O'Daniel's orders began. "The attack will be pressed with the ruthless vigor that has routed every enemy formation opposing the 3rd Div. All men will be brought to the highest possible state of offensive spirit prior to the jump-off. Bayonets will be sharpened. Maximum effort will be exercised at all times."[9]

Patch's Seventh began its assault against the German First Army in a northeasterly direction, hoping to break through the formidable West Wall defenses and force the enemy into a trap as Patton's Third came at their rear. It was essentially the same plan that Devers had proposed in November when his troops reached the Rhine, but in reverse. If Ike had approved it then, it would have been the Seventh coming at the rear of the enemy while the Third came from the west. Patch made good progress. Gen. Frank W. Milburn's 21st Corps had a hard fight to breach the Siegfried Line defenses in the area around Saarbrücken on the Seventh Army's left flank, and finally broke through after a four-day fight. In the east along the Rhine, 6th Army Group troops ran into stiff opposition. The 3rd Algerian Division had to fight its way across a flat floodplain and through easily defended urban areas.

By March 20, however, the German defenses were crumbling and troops were abandoning the Siegfried Line fortifications all along the U.S. Seventh Army line. The Third Army was completing its encirclement of the German Seventh Army and swinging in behind the German First Army. In the late afternoon of the twentieth, the Third Army's 90th Division reached high ground overlooking the Rhine near Mainz. The 4th Armored Division took Worms on the Rhine, and the 10th and 12th armored divisions were also approaching the river. For the Germans the campaign was over; a general withdrawal was authorized. The Germans began crossing the river "that night on ferries, rafts, small boats, almost anything that floated."[10]

General von Mellenthin attributed much of the Allies' success in the Palatinate to the fact that Eisenhower and SHAEF allowed the generals in the field to command. Weigley sees the short-lived Battle of the Saar-Palatinate as a triumph of American arms representing a newfound maturity among U.S. generals. "The campaign was notable for its display of the American army's sharpening instinct for the jugular. . . . The campaign's two envelopments, of the German 7th Army by two columns of Patton's 3rd Army, and then of the German 1st Army by Patton's 3rd and Patch's 7th Armies, were models of how not only to gain ground but to destroy enemy forces."[11] And destroy the enemy they did. The Third Army took 68,000 prisoners; the Seventh took 22,000. The Third Army estimated that total German loses were 113,000 versus its 5,220 casualties. The German First and Seventh armies, for all intents and purposes, had ceased to exist. "The American victory was in large part the product at last of a thoroughly mobile form of warfare genuinely aimed at the destruction of the enemy forces. Even in the glorious late summer of 1944, the American command had too often paid only lip service to the later classical objective."[12]

CHAPTER 31.

# Finally, the Rhine and into the National Redoubt

★ ★ ★ ★

In late March 1945, the Americans in the U.S. Seventh and Third armies were approaching the Rhine with plans to cross and pursue the disintegrating Wehrmacht while the French First Army in Alsace was also preparing to breach the river and take the fight into the German heartland. The Allies were on the threshold of Nazi Germany in awesome power. Eisenhower commanded some 4 million men, almost 3 million of whom were Americans. His forces, reports historian Charles MacDonald, included "three army groups, seven armies, . . . twenty-one corps, and seventy-three divisions, twenty of which were armored. . . . Of the six tactical air commands, four were American, and of the more than 17,500 combat aircraft in the Allied arsenal, 5,000 were U.S. fighter-bombers, and almost 7,000 were U.S. medium and heavy bombers."[1]

The Allies and Germans alike realized that the end of the war was near. One of the few issues remaining was how the glory of victory would be distributed. Patton was determined to take advantage of his position in the Palatinate to jump the Rhine before Patch and Devers did, and even before Field Marshal Montgomery, although Eisenhower had already promised Monty that he would be the first to cross. But Patton would not be the first across the Rhine; nor would Montgomery. The 9th Armored Division in Gen. Courtney Hodges' First Army captured the Ludendorf Railroad Bridge at Remagen on March 7, and the Americans in the First Army zone were sending men across to the east bank by the thousands.

After the Americans captured the Remagen bridge, Bradley and Patton could contemplate a Rhine crossing in conjunction with Monty's upcoming extravaganza near Wesel. But neither American general was certain that Eisenhower would allow crossings in the 12th Army Group's zone.[2] He might yet give all the glory to Monty. In fact, though, Eisenhower seemed eager to get the Americans across the river. On March 19, SHAEF issued a directive ordering both Patton and Patch to advance "vigorously with the object of establishing a firm bridgehead across the

Rhine in the Frankfurt area from which an advance in strength can be made at a later date in the general direction of Kassel."[3]

On March 23, Patton ordered Maj. Gen. LeRoy Irwin, commanding the 5th Infantry Division, to cross that same night with his 11th Infantry Regiment fording at two spots: the 3rd Battalion crossing at Nierstein and the 1st Battalion at Oppenheim. Patton's "jump" was no spur-of-the-moment operation; it had been months in the planning. Like Devers, Patton had long anticipated a Rhine crossing and had trained thousands of troops for the assault. He had even hidden bridging equipment during the Battle of the Bulge so that Devers' troops could not make off with it while Patton's troops were in the Ardennes.[4] When the time came, Patton could dedicate several thousand engineer troops to the task of getting the 5th Division across the river.

The 5th Division met only sporadic German resistance crossing the Rhine. So confident was Patton that he and his men stopped to urinate in the river. When he reached the east bank, the flamboyant Patton stooped down and scooped up German soil in the manner of William the Conqueror when he arrived in England.[5] The Americans' worst enemy that night was a bright, nearly full moon that illuminated the river while the men crossed. By midnight, however, the battalions were on the east bank and moving ahead into Germany. The next morning, Patton telephoned Bradley to gloat: "I sneaked a division over last night. There were so few Krauts around there they don't know it yet. So don't make any announcement—we'll keep it a secret until we see how it goes."[6] But both Patton and Bradley soon decided to go public lest Montgomery steal the limelight with Operation Plunder. Patton's divisions soon found other crossing sites and streamed over the Rhine near Bingen, Boppard, and Saint-Goar.[7] In some places the Germans put up a stiff fight, but as always now, they lacked the strength to stop the American onslaught.

But Devers and Patch would not be denied their opportunity. The Seventh Army had reached the river at various locations, and Haislip ordered a two-division amphibious attack for March 26 at Worms. The 45th Division would cross just north of the city, the 3rd Division just to the south. Both divisions had the support of DD tanks that could cross the river under their own power. The 45th surprised the enemy and met little resistance. The 3rd ran into mortar and air-burst artillery fire. The Americans responded with "a drumbeat of fire," unloading some ten thousand shells into the landing zone. When the shelling lifted, the American assault boats made the east shore almost unopposed.[8] By March 27, enemy resistance in the bridgeheads was collapsing and Haislip's 15th Corps was preparing for a breakout.

As the Americans celebrated their Rhine crossings, the French fretted and waited for their chance. Their concerns were more political than military at that point. General de Gaulle feared that unless de Lattre and his French First Army crossed and joined in the conquest of Germany, the French would be denied a voice in ruling Germany after the war, because they had not been awarded an occupation zone at the Yalta Conference in February 1945. "My dear General," he wrote to de Lattre, "you must cross the Rhine, even if the Americans do not agree and even if you have to cross it in rowboats. It is a matter of the greatest national interest." Devers could easily have turned the Seventh Army right at Worms and advanced up the east bank of the Rhine toward Switzerland, cutting off the French First Army advancing out of the Black Forest and denying the French access to southern Germany. Luckily he was attuned to the needs and desires of the French, and with his acquiescence de Lattre began crossing near Speyer in the early-morning hours of March 31. The invasion was not exactly on the scale of Patton's and Patch's. The 3rd Algerian Division rowed across in a single boat, repeating trips until a company-size force was established. The assault was so insignificant that the Germans missed it altogether. A second French crossing at Germersheim by the 2nd Moroccan Infantry Division ran into a hail of German artillery fire, but by nightfall a bridgehead was firmly established. A third French crossing took place at Leimersheim on April 2, and another at Strasbourg on April 15.

With much of the 6th Army Group across the Rhine, Devers' intent was the complete destruction of Army Group G—the German First, Seventh, and Nineteenth armies. All three were so battered that they hardly existed as coherent formations, but some units could still put up a fight. Devers planned to send Patch's Seventh Army attacking south and southeast behind the enemy armies to cut them off from the rest of Germany.

Eisenhower had other ideas. His major objective along Devers' southern front was to invest the so-called National Redoubt in the Alps of southern Germany, the last bastion of Nazism where Hitler and his henchmen were believed to be planning to hold out. Allied intelligence reports indicated that the Germans could be storing huge caches of arms, ammunition, food, and fuel in mountain strongholds, and that underground factories there would continue to turn out weapons and aircraft. The idea had been planted by Goebbels' propaganda machine.[9] Colonel Quinn, Patch's intelligence chief, did not put much stock into the notion of a redoubt. After all, the enemy could barely equip the troops in the field, much less stockpile supplies in vast quantities. Nevertheless, Quinn and other intelligence officers could not entirely dismiss the reports. In his memoir, Eisenhower notes that in the spring of 1945 he believed that "the strong possibility still existed that fanatical Nazis would attempt to establish themselves in the National Redoubt, and the early overrunning of that area remained important to us."[10]

By this point in the war, Ike and SHAEF no longer considered Berlin their ultimate objective. The German capital lay in the proposed Russian zone of occupation, and the Soviets were intent on taking the city. A rush by the Americans and British to capture Berlin would result in heavy casualties for no strategic advantage. Ike instead focused his attention on the elusive National Redoubt. The logical commander to advance on this bastion was Devers. The 6th Army Group was pushing into southern Germany and could seal off the region and then reduce it if necessary. Matters came to a head in a meeting between Ike and Devers on March 31. Devers presented a proposal to have Patch's Seventh Army attack the German First and Nineteenth armies from the rear, preventing them from withdrawing and retreating into the redoubt. The French First Army would go south along the eastern bank of the Rhine to mop up any enemy troops remaining on that side of the river.[11] Once these pockets of resistance were reduced, Devers planned a drive to the southeast to link with the Russians on the northwest frontier of Austria.

Ike's fear of the redoubt was not sufficient to outweigh political considerations, however. He ordered the Seventh Army to guard the right flank of Bradley's 12th Army Group as it swept into central Germany. "So much did Eisenhower's strategy in early April emphasize the offensive of his favored, Central Group of Armies rather than any help Devers could offer against the threat of the Redoubt," asserts Russell Weigley, "that Devers' army group received territorial responsibilities considerably disproportionate to its numbers."[12] Stretched out to defend the 12th Army Group, the Seventh Army's front extended some 120 miles, a distance almost twice that of Bradley's armies.

SHAEF's new orders directed the U.S. Seventh Army to take Nuremberg, one of the sacred cities of Nazism. Haislip's 15th Corps held the Seventh Army's left flank, Milburn's 21st Corps was in the center, and Brooks' 6th Corps held the right. Haislip's 157th Regiment, 45th Division, encountered fanatical resistance from Hitler Youth and grenade- and rifle-toting civilians, who held off the Americans for six days. The fighting was house to house, with U.S. forces employing heavy doses of artillery and aerial bombardment to roust the enemy. The rest of the 15th Corps had relatively easy going as its troops advanced through a "near-vacuum" in the seam between the German First and Seventh Armies.[13] The 21st Corps ran into a bitter fight at Königshofen but otherwise advanced smoothly. The 6th Corps encountered the stiffest opposition in trying to establish bridgeheads across the Neckar River near Heilbronn.

On April 11, the 15th and 21st corps swung southeast toward Nuremberg to avoid a collision with Patton's Third Army. Würzburg was cleared, and then Schweinfurt after a stout defense by German military students and one more plastering by aerial bombing. By now, the 12th Army Group had reached the Elbe, the farthest extent of the American advance, and SHAEF issued new orders holding the U.S. First and Ninth armies along the Elbe and the Mulde rivers. A reinforced Third Army was to turn southeast toward the National Redoubt.

On April 16, Patton, Devers, and Bradley met to negotiate the boundary changes needed to keep the Third and Seventh armies from stepping on each other's feet. Responsibility for investing the National Redoubt, if it proved real, was handed to Patton's Third, now beefed up to fifteen divisions. As Patton moved south, he wrote his wife, Beatrice, "the country here is the most beautiful I've ever seen. All the trees are in bloom and there are yellow fields of mustard."[14] The Third Army liberated slave labor camps as it advanced. Patch's Seventh also overran labor camps and hospitals. In a letter to General Marshall, Devers described what he had seen: "Recently we overran a hospital at Heppenheim which contained 288 of our American wounded, along with French, Russian, Polish and Italian prisoners. I found that the men had been literally starved for lack of food and that this had been deliberate. . . . The hospital was in frightful shape. The men were so happy at being rescued that I think the recovery of most will be rapid." Devers added, "The roads are crowded with displaced persons working their way towards the Rhine river. Seventy-five percent of them are Russians; fifteen percent French; five percent Poles; and the rest Italians, Czechs, Dutch, Belgians. Our advance is so rapid that this makes a terrific problem for us."[15]

"Push on and push on. This is a pursuit, not an attack," General Brooks exhorted his 6th Corps troops as the Seventh Army moved south in mid and late April. The Americans were closing on the retreating Germans in every vehicle they could find, including "borrowed" and captured enemy vehicles. Augsburg fell on April 27. Munich, another sacred shrine of the Nazis, fell on May 3 as the 3rd and 45th divisions fought isolated pockets of enemy troops within the city, but also passed through streets decked with white flags and lined with cheering crowds.

As Munich fell, elements of the Seventh Army reached the Alps and passed into Austria. By May 4, Berchtesgaden was in American hands. O'Daniel's 3rd Division troops posed on the terrace of Hitler's mountaintop retreat, the Eagle's Nest, sipping from bottles of beer and wine.[16] Berchtesgaden "was a weird jumble of twisted and burned buildings," wrote Sgt. Harry Sions for *Yank* magazine. "It was hard to tell which caused more damage to this palatial hideout in the Bavarian Alps—the 350 Lancasters which bombed it on April 25, or the 2,000 SS men who looted and burned it a few days before the Americans arrived. . . . The roads and woods were littered with empty wine bottles. 'It looks to me,' said a sergeant, 'like they were expecting to defend the place with wine bottles.' One GI swigging from a bottle of Moselle spoke up. 'Heil Hitler, the bastard' was the GI's toast."[17]

The Third and Seventh armies were unstoppable now. Historians Clarke and Smith write that they "spread in an irresistible flood through a picturesque Bavarian countryside ripe with spring. Daffodils bloomed, farmers tilled the land, cows grazed. Only in bomb-blasted cities did war seem to have any place; yet at the next hill, ridge, village, stream, wherever a group of Germans with a will to fight elected to stand, there still might occur a flurry of fighting. Everybody knew the war was over; but somehow, at one isolated spot or another, the war went on, real enough for the moment and sometimes deadly for those caught up in it."[18]

The Allies had literally looked high and low, but no one had found evidence of the National Redoubt. Was it a figment of SHAEF's imagination, an unfulfilled plan, or simply German propaganda? As the U.S. Seventh and Third armies advanced into the German and Austrian Alps in late April, no one was quite certain. Weigley suggests that Bradley and the Americans were taken in by Goebbels' propaganda campaign to disrupt Allied strategy. Weigley notes that Bradley told a visiting congressman that the redoubt might lengthen the war by another year.[19] Hansen wrote in his diary that General Bradley "persists in his contention that the Germans will run to the redoubt with what SS units he can salvage from the front."[20] Was Bradley simply looking for an excuse to persuade Ike and SHAEF to allow Patton to swing southward, so that Patton would capture headlines in the event that the redoubt really did exist?

Devers' troops pushed on into southern Germany and Austria. They reached the Brenner Pass on May 4, 1945, and linked up with U.S. troops from General Truscott's Fifth Army, which had finally swept through the Italian peninsula. For all intents and purposes, the 6th Army Group's war was ended. Devers' function now was to accept surrender delegations from the various isolated German armies—the German Nineteenth and First armies and Army Group G. As the Americans moved south into Bavaria, it became clear that the National Redoubt was a myth. There was no glory for Patton in rounding up broken bands of Germans, most of whom were surrendering in droves to the advancing Americans. On April 27, the Third Army processed 600,000 prisoners of war.

Some German troops actually joined with the Americans to help defeat fanatical SS troops determined to die rather than surrender. In the Itter castle near the Austrian town of Wörgl, which housed such high-profile French prisoners as General de Gaulle's sister and French generals Maurice Gamelin and Maxim Weygand, Seventh Army soldiers joined with German guards to fend off attacks from SS troops who had rejected the camp commandant's surrender to U.S. forces.[21]

Patton now turned his sights to the east toward Czechoslovakia, which offered him the possibility of embarking on "the last offensive of the war."[22] On May 5,

Bradley authorized Patton to advance eastward into Czechoslovakia but set a halt line stretching from Karlovy Vary through Plzn to Ceské and Budejovice. Try as he might, Patton could not get Eisenhower to approve an advance on Prague. The Soviets were advancing from the east, and Ike decreed the Czech capital off limits for political and military reasons.

While Patton captured headlines for some of the final skirmishes of the war, his Czechoslovakian incursion may be best known for saving many of the Lipizzaner horses that had been corralled in the Czech countryside to keep them safe from Allied bombings in Austria. When the onetime cavalry officer heard that the Russians would turn the prized stallions into meat rations if they got there first, he ordered a cavalry squadron to get the horses back into Austria. At considerable risk from the disintegrating but still fighting German Seventh Army, Patton's cavalrymen rode, herded, and transported the horses back into Austria on a nocturnal ride that would be celebrated twenty years later in the Disney film *Miracle of the White Stallions.*

If destroying and capturing the remnants of the German army presented a problem for Devers in the waning months of the war, controlling the French may have been an even greater difficulty. Once across the Rhine, de Lattre moved on Stuttgart, which was clearly in the Seventh Army's zone of operations. It was one of numerous independent actions taken by de Lattre and de Gaulle in an effort to reassert the declining prestige and power of France. When Roosevelt, Churchill, and Stalin had divided Germany into three occupation zones, one for each power, at the Yalta Conference, the French did not get a share, and their pique was considerable. If the other Allies would not give them their own zone, they intended to carve one out from territory allocated to the Americans.

Devers accepted the French incursion into Stuttgart but ordered de Lattre to remove his troops from the city when American forces entered. De Lattre ignored the direct order and thus set off a political-military crisis that grew to involve Eisenhower and President Harry S. Truman. De Gaulle refused to budge until the French were awarded an occupation zone. The Americans and British finally agreed to de Gaulle's demands, but that did not stop French intransigence. De Lattre then proceeded to advance on the German city of Ulm, fifty miles southeast of Stuttgart and forty miles inside the Seventh Army's zone of operation. Ulm was the site of Napoleon's victory over the Austrian army in 1805 and thus symbolized French power. "The Americans will perhaps dislodge us from it," de Lattre declared, "but the French flag will have flown there."[23] As the French First Army approached the Austrian frontier, its troops passed through an American bridgehead on the Danube, risking an inadvertent clash. Once again Devers ordered de Lattre to withdraw, and this time he did, but he took his time getting out.

Difficulties with the French threatened to jeopardize a highly secret Seventh Army operation to gather information in Hechingen, some seventy miles southwest of Stuttgart, where U.S. intelligence believed the Germans had been trying to develop nuclear fission. A special intelligence mission, code-named Alsos, had expected to make its way unimpeded to the city but found the way blocked by the French army operating in the area. Mission members bluffed their way through French checkpoints and got to the research center first.

The French were also intent on reaching Landeck in Austria so that their army could reach the Italian frontier, another symbolic and status-building move. When Devers refused to permit the incursion, de Lattre moved ahead anyway and beat the Americans into Landeck—or so he thought. When a French ski patrol approached the town, the platoon leader placed a call into the town on the civilian telephone network. The voice on the other end was American; U.S. troops of the 44th Division had reached the objective the day before. The Germans surrendered a few days later, and the games between the French and Americans ended.

CHAPTER 32.

# Could the French Have Crossed the Rhine?

★ ★ ★ ★

One more question remains about the 6th Army Group's operations in November 1944. Could General de Lattre and his French First Army have been the first Allied force to cross the Rhine? Certainly he wanted to cross. As his troops reached the river on November 19, 1944, he saw his mission as preparing "for the hour when the French would be able to avenge 1940, invade Germany and, with all their allies, give the coup de grace to the Nazi beast in its lair."[1] But reaching the Rhine was mostly a symbolic victory for French forces. De Lattre might send patrols across the river to reconnoiter, and he could order artillery strikes against enemy targets on the east bank, but the French were not in a position to strike over the river and into the Reich by themselves.[2] Although the courage of his troops was not in question, de Lattre's logistical situation was precarious. The French relied on the Americans for most of their equipment and were usually the last to be supplied. When they reached the Rhine, the French had only enough reserves to sustain an advance for another ten days, two weeks at best.[3] They lacked the bridging equipment, the DUKWs, the assault boats, and the pontoon units to make the crossing. They also lacked the transportation facilities and communications capabilities of their American counterparts, and did not have the training to use them in any case. Many of de Lattre's top units lacked seasoned infantry, officers, and noncommissioned officers.[4]

The French had begun to run out of trained replacements, and many of their colonial troops, although ferocious fighters, were used to a warmer climate and were ineffective in the Alsatian winter. These men were slowly being pulled off the line and sent to less harsh duty guarding the Franco-Italian border. French recruits took their place, often acquiring their complete uniforms, helmets, and overcoats. Many of the new recruits from the resistance forces had to be trained before they could become effective soldiers. But first they had to be integrated into units that might be led by officers and noncommissioned officers who had served in Vichy units—men they had considered enemies just a few months earlier. Many FFI recruits were leftists while their leaders were more conservative North African army cadre.⁵ The new recruits also had to be trained to use unfamiliar American and British weapons and equipment and given American uniforms with American helmets. The one item that was supplied by the French army—the soldiers' boots—caused difficulties when the French and Americans served side by side. French boots had hobnails on the soles, as did those of German soldiers. On night-time patrols, American scouts who heard the distinctive clacking of hobnail boots did not know whether they were being approached by friend or foe.⁶

Myriad other difficulties constrained de Lattre as well. The Germans still held the Colmar Pocket, for one, and the pocket held thousands of enemy troops prepared to attack any French cross-Rhine expedition from the rear. But even if these had not been issues, SHAEF had no plans for the 6th Army Group to undertake such a bold stroke, and there was little maneuver room that far south in the Black Forest on the Rhine's east bank. De Lattre also contemplated a drive up the west bank of the Rhine in Alsace in November after he had reached the Rhine, but his commanders discouraged this action. With the area around Mulhouse still in German hands, any such move would be subject to flank attacks by enemy troops still in and around the city.

De Lattre was threatened with the loss of several of his best units, which were slated for reassignment to other parts of France under Operation Independence. Two divisions were scheduled for redeployment to the Bordeaux area, where the Germans still held the city and the surrounding estuary. The continued occupation of France's second largest port was an affront to French honor, and de Gaulle wanted the port cleared. The Allied command, for its part, feared that the Germans in the sector constituted a threat to the 6th Army Group's left flank. Other French combat units were to be reassigned to maintain order in various cities where unrest was brewing. De Gaulle wanted some of de Lattre's troops to be withdrawn from the front to maintain internal security in southwestern France, where Communist resistance movements threatened to take over local governments. Armed clashes had occurred between various Resistance factions, and the more conservative Frenchmen feared a Communist-led revolution. De Gaulle also wanted the French 1st Infantry Division redeployed to Paris to ensure the security of the capital city.

On the eve of de Lattre's November offensive to breach the Belfort Gap, Devers asked him to take responsibility for protecting the southern third of the 190-mile front along the Franco-Italian border. The sector had been guarded since the Operation Dragoon invasion by the American 1st Airborne Task Force.⁷ When de Lattre objected to this new responsibility, Devers agreed to hold off the redeployment until after the November offensive. Operation Independence would have left de Lattre with little offensive punch to pursue the Germans on the 6th Army Group's southern end. Furthermore, it disrupted his command's planning process because staff officers never knew which divisions would be in the line to fight. The threat of losing troops was a constant distraction at French First Army headquarters.

If the logistical and political problems were not enough, SHAEF was also concerned about the loyalty of the French high command. Further, the French took offense easily, and Devers found himself treading lightly with de Lattre and making concessions to him as the two armies advanced into Alsace. Often, Devers found himself prodding the French to push harder. "I'm not happy about the French troops fighting in the south. They don't have the punch and willingness to go all out as have the American troops," he confided to his diary.[8] Devers also held the French accountable for their own supply difficulties. He noted that they failed to build up a surplus and that their officers did not properly supervise their distribution system. They also expended prodigious amounts of ammunition, particularly artillery ammunition.[9] Generally, however, Devers was pleased with the competence of the French commanders and their soldiers and was somewhat amused by de Lattre's behavior, which was often stereotypically French.

De Lattre did not speak English. "At least we didn't think he did," Devers later mused. Devers employed the services of American aristocrat Henry Cabot Lodge, a former U.S. senator and future vice presidential candidate, as his interpreter and liaison. Devers also recalled that de Lattre "was a brilliant orator. He would pace the floor very much like General MacArthur used to pace—and he would pour out great torrents of French. Cabot Lodge would stand behind me and interpret." Devers and his staff were often spellbound as de Lattre paced back and forth waving his arms and gesturing as the French do, and when it came time for the Americans to respond to de Lattre's speech-making, they found themselves using the same gestures.

De Lattre could be something of a martinet. "Sometime at the end of a conference he would be furious when he'd leave the room," Devers remembered. "He would go to the door. I'd stand up. He'd turn around, salute me, walk out, and slam the door. And he might not speak for another five or six days, but he always came around, and we got to know and understand each other."[10] In the end, despite all the difficulties they posed for the Americans and British, the French proved to be worthy allies.

# Epilogue

★ ★ ★ ★

From the day that Allied troops landed in Normandy on June 6, 1944, the outcome of World War II in Europe was seldom in doubt. Once the Allies got the hang of fighting the Germans, victory was only a matter of time. There were dark and frustrating periods before the enemy surrendered in May 1945, as when Rommel's Seventh Army contained the Americans and British in the Normandy bridgehead for nearly two months. But studies of the German situation after the war revealed that the German Seventh in Normandy was stretched to its limit, and Rommel knew that it was only a matter of time before his troops gave way. He was taking severe casualties and receiving virtually no reinforcements. When Hitler attacked in the Ardennes in December 1944 hoping to take Antwerp and split the Allied armies, Patton reacted almost with glee as he saw the opportunity to attack at the base of the German salient and trap thousands of enemy troops.[1]

Ironically, American POWs captured in the Bulge may have had a better sense of the inevitable German defeat than the Allied generals did. As they were marched deep into Germany to POW compounds, they saw firsthand the plight of the German Army. Raymond Christman, an infantryman with the 28th Division captured near Wiltz, Luxembourg, on December 19, 1944, was amazed to see German army trucks a few miles behind the lines being pulled by teams of horses and supplies heading to the front in horse-drawn wagons. The enemy had no gasoline. "I knew the war was over for them," Christman said. His opinion solidified as he and hundreds of other GIs were marched for days through the devastation of German cities.[2]

General Eisenhower also knew that victory was inevitable. "From the start of OVERLORD, we knew that we would win—but we knew it not factually but with faith," Eisenhower wrote in *At Ease*.[3] By summer's end the Allies were preparing for victory before Christmas. No modern army, not even the best—as the Wehrmacht was—could win against such numerical and material odds. The wonder is that the Germans held off their enemies for so long.

In all probability, the war in Europe would have been fought very much the same way had an American general other than Eisenhower been the supreme commander. The Americans did not have a tradition of maneuvering huge armies, spearheading in tandem as the Germans did in Russia, and they seemed to shy away from the concept of concentration at the point of attack. Raw power was the name of the game for the U.S. Army. Attack in force along a broad front and grind down the enemy.

Was Eisenhower correct in his broad front strategy in Europe? Based on the traditions of the American army in modern massed warfare, he probably was. With the knowledge that he would eventually win regardless of the strategy he employed, his forces bulled their way to victory while he concentrated on holding together the fragile coalition of the British and American armies.

If victory was assured, what difference does it make whether or not Eisenhower allowed Devers to cross the Rhine in late November 1944? The answer is simple: the historical record needs to be set straight. General Devers and his 6th Army Group are almost forgotten participants in the European war. They should be remembered. Additionally, it must be noted that even successful campaigns such as Operation Overlord have their shortcomings. Military personnel should be acquainted with all facets of a military campaign. Seeing the war from a different perspective can be enlightening.

Armies and generals must adapt and learn from their past mistakes. Eisenhower did not readily adapt to changes. He was cautious and often indecisive, and these traits may have cost the army thousands of unnecessary casualties and prolonged the war. Devers' planned attack might have shortened the war. But would it have cracked the German front? Who can say? The facts have been presented. It is up to a future generation of soldiers and historians to decide.

★ ★ ★ ★

# NOTES

CHAPTER 1. Victory Assured

1. Bradley, *A Soldier's Story*, 521.
2. Ibid., 502–11.
3. Weigley, *Eisenhower's Lieutenants*, 640, 641.
4. Ibid., 299.
5. Ambrose, *Eisenhower*, 14.
6. Colley, *Blood for Dignity*, 120.
7. Bradley, *A Soldier's Story*, 510.
8. Ibid., 21.
9. Ambrose, *Eisenhower*, 49.
10. Bradley, *A General's Life*, 35.
11. Atkinson, *Army at Dawn*, 486.
12. Chester B. Hansen diaries, U.S. Army Military History Institute (USAMHI), Carlisle, Pa. [hereafter Hansen diaries].
13. Atkinson, *Army at Dawn*, 486.
14. Bradley, *A Soldier's Story*, 14.
15. Ibid., 173.
16. Ibid., 510, 511.
17. Hechler, *The Bridge at Remagen*, 54–69, 137–46.
18. Colley, *Blood for Dignity*, 91.
19. Rooney, *My War*, 252.
20. Weigley, *Eisenhower's Lieutenants*, 727.
21. Bradley, *A Soldier's Story*, 511.
22. Hill, "Germans Bomb Bridgehead," 1.
23. Bradley, *A General's Life*, 407.

CHAPTER 2. First to the Rhine

1. Griess interview with Devers, tape 21, side 1, p. 53 of typed transcript, box 87, York Heritage Trust Library/Archives [hereafter Griess interview]; Jacob L. Devers Papers 1943–1987, USAMHI; Markey, *Jake: The General from West York Avenue*.
2. Griess interview with Miss Devers, box 92, tape 61.
3. Griess interview with Devers, tape 21, side 1, p. 53 of typed transcript, box 87.
4. Griess interview with Miss Devers, box 92, tape 61.
5. Markey, *Jake: The General from West York Avenue*, 11–25.

6. Griess interview with Miss Devers, box 92, tape 61.
7. West Point Year Book, 1909.
8. Griese interview with Devers, box 92.
9. Ibid.
10. Griess interview with Miss Devers, box 92, tape 61.
11. Ibid.
12. Drummond, "A Soldier's General."
13. Ibid.
14. Baldwin, "Our Generals in the Battle of Germany."
15. Devers diary, November 29, 1944, York Heritage Trust Library/Archives [hereafter Devers diary].
16. Griese interview with Devers, box 92, tape 4, March 28, 1964.
17. Ibid.
18. Weigley, *Eisenhower's Lieutenants*, 402.
19. Clarke and Smith, *Riviera to the Rhine*, 193, 229.
20. De Lattre, *The History of the French First Army*, 29.

## CHAPTER 3. What History Doesn't Tell Us

1. Chandler, ed., *Papers of Dwight Eisenhower*, 4:2258–59; Devers diary, September 23, 1944; *The Seventh United States Army in France and Germany 1944–1945*, 2:413, 414; *History of 6th Army Group*, chaps. 1 and 2.
2. Griess interview with Devers, box 83, p. 56 of typed transcript.
3. Maule, *Out of the Sand*, 247–56.
4. *The Seventh United States Army in France and Germany 1944–1945*, 2:414.
5. Maule, *Out of the Sand*, 239–63.
6. Combat History 324th Infantry Regiment.
7. Taggart, *History of the Third Infantry Division in World War II*, 276–77; The Cross of Lorraine, 83.
8. Daily diary of the 117th Cavalry Reconnaissance Squadron (Mecz), November 1– November 30, 1944.
9. Griess interview with Devers, tape 29, side 2, p. 40 of typed transcript.
10. Bradley, *A Soldier's Story*, 420.
11. Griess interview with Devers, box 92.
12. Griess interview with Devers, tape 42, side 1, p. 126 of typed transcript.

## CHAPTER 4. Devers Gets in the Act

1. *Christian Science Monitor*, June 19, 1943.
2. Ziegler, *London at War*, 222–26.
3. Author interview with Ruth Martin, 1987.
4. *New York Times*, November 11, 1943.
5. Griese interview with Devers, box 82, p. 99 of typed transcript.
6. *New York Times*, July 7, 1943.
7. Griess interview with Col. and Mrs. Alexander Graham Frances, March 7, 1975, box 57, York Heritage Trust Library/Archives.
8. Devers diary, August 25, 1944.
9. Markey, *Jake: The General from West York Avenue*, 36.

10. Clarke and Smith, *Riviera to the Rhine*, 29.
11. Pogue, *George C. Marshall, Organizer of Victory*, 374.
12. Clarke and Smith, *Riviera to the Rhine*, 4–22.
13. David Eisenhower, *Eisenhower at War, 1943–1945*, 321–25.
14. Bradley, *A Soldier's Story*, 316.
15. De Lattre, *History of the French First Army*, 50.
16. Clarke and Smith, *Riviera to the Rhine*, 77–80.
17. Devers diary, August 20, 1944.
18. Eisenhower cable to Marshall, Cable W 9737, Secret, January 18, 1944, National Archives and Records Administration [hereafter NARA].
19. *Time*, August 28, 1944; *New York Times*, August 18, 1944.
20. Griess interview with Devers, box 92.
21. Second Lt. A. M. Patch war diary, Patch Papers, U.S. Military Academy Archives/Library, West Point, N.Y. [hereafter USMA].
22. *Time*, August 28, 1944, 24; Spillar, General Patch, in *Dictionary of American Military Biography*.
23. Col. Russell Reeder to Gen. Jacob Devers, February 27, 1946, Patch Papers, USMA.
24. De Lattre, *History of the French First Army*, 53.
25. A. M. Patch to Gertrude Stein, September 17, 1944, Patch Papers, USMA.
26. A. M. Patch telegram to his wife, October 26, 1944, Patch Papers, USMA.
27. Patch Papers, USMA.
28. Oral history interview with Devers in Eisenhower Library, tape 5, May 1969, box 82, York Heritage Trust Library/Archives.

## CHAPTER 5. From Marseille to Alsace

1. Truscott, *Command Missions*, 412.
2. Clarke and Smith, *Riviera to the Rhine*, 92; de Lattre, *History of the French First Army*, 51.
3. Truscott, *Command Missions*, 412.
4. Murphy, *To Hell and Back*, 170.
5. John E. Dahlquist Papers, USAMHI.
6. Clarke and Smith, *Riviera to the Rhine*, 108–25.
7. Ibid., 122.
8. Ibid., 80.
9. Ibid., 79.
10. Weigley, *Eisenhower's Lieutenants*, 229.
11. Ibid.
12. Botsch, "The Story of the 7th American Army in War," 28.
13. Atkinson, *Army at Dawn*, 141.
14. Ibid., 141.
15. Weigley, *Eisenhower's Lieutenants*, 223.
16. DePastino, "The Day the General Apologized to the Dead."
17. Weigley, *Eisenhower's Lieutenants*, 229.
18. Ibid., 232.
19. Murphy, *To Hell and Back*, 187.

20. Parton, *Air Force Spoken Here*, 364.
21. Devers to Georgie, Devers Papers, York Heritage Trust Library/Archives.
22. De Lattre, *The History of the French First Army*, 135.
23. Clarke and Smith, *Riviera to the Rhine*, 252.
24. Devers diary, September 8, 1944.
25. Clarke and Smith, *Riviera to the Rhine*, 40.
26. Devers diary, August 29, 1944.
27. Clarke and Smith, *Riviera to the Rhine*, 358, 359; *History of the Headquarters 6th Army Group*, USAMHI.
28. Clarke and Smith, *Riviera to the Rhine*, 171–73.
29. U.S. Seventh Army press release, September 19, 1944.
30. Weigley, *Eisenhower's Lieutenants*, 236.
31. Botsch, "198th Reserve Infantry Division, July–Oct. '44."
32. Botsch, "The Story of the 7th American Army in War."
33. Dwight D. Eisenhower, *Crusade in Europe*, 294.
34. Griese, ed., *The Second World War*, 350.

## CHAPTER 6. To the Siegfried Line

1. *Yank—The GI Story of the War*, 114.
2. Keegan, *The Second World War*, 389, 394.
3. Bradley, *A Soldier's Story*, 330–37.
4. Pyle, *Brave Men*, 434.
5. Keegan, *The Second World War*, 394.
6. Ibid., 396–97.
7. Dwight D. Eisenhower, *Crusade in Europe*, 279.
8. Weigley, *Eisenhower's Lieutenants*, 241–48.
9. Blumenson, *Breakout and Pursuit*, 688–89.
10. Ibid.
11. Pogue, *The Supreme Command*, 244, 245.
12. Hamilton, *Monty: Final Years of the Field Marshall*, 3.
13. Colley, "Deadly Accuracy," 44.
14. Hamilton, *Monty: Final Years of the Field Marshall*, 3.

## CHAPTER 7. Broad Front or Single Thrust?

1. Esposito, *West Point Atlas of American Wars*, map 59.
2. Weigley, *Eisenhower's Lieutenants*, 298.
3. Ibid., 278–80.
4. Clarke and Smith, *Riviera to the Rhine*, 225–30.
5. Dwight D. Eisenhower, *Crusade in Europe*, 226.
6. Crosswell, *Chief of Staff*, 253.
7. Hamilton, *Master of the Battlefield*, 707–8.
8. Ambrose, *Eisenhower*, 340.
9. Ibid., 344; Ingersoll, *Top Secret*, 219; D'Este, *Crisis in Command*, 668.
10. Ambrose, *Eisenhower*, 151.
11. Ibid., 151, 359.

12. Ibid., 151.
13. Weigley, *Eisenhower's Lieutenants*, 266.
14. Pogue, *The Supreme Command*, 543.
15. Hamilton, *Monty: The Making of a General*, 560.
16. Ambrose, *Eisenhower*, 233–34.
17. Ibid.
18. Weigley, *Eisenhower's Lieutenants*, 81.
19. Irving, *The Trail of the Fox*, 80–99.
20. Bradley, *A General's Life*, 196.
21. Hansen diaries, June 9, 1944.
22. Bradley, *A Soldier's Story*, 209.
23. Hamilton, *Monty: The Final Years*, 7.
24. Ibid., 44.
25. Bryant, *Triumph in the West*, 195.
26. Information about Montgomery in these paragraphs is from Hamilton, *Monty: The Making of a General*, 36–45.
27. Ambrose, *Eisenhower*, 348.
28. Ibid.
29. Crosswell, *Chief of Staff*, 267.
30. D'Este, *Eisenhower*, 603.
31. Bradley, *A Soldier's Story*, 398.
32. Blumenson, *Patton Papers*, 523.

## CHAPTER 8. The Enemy Waits for the 6th Army Group

1. Giziowski, *The Enigma of General Blaskowitz*, 15–188.
2. Mellenthin, *Panzer Battles*, 371.
3. Ibid., 373.
4. Kemp, *The Unknown Battle, Metz, 1944*, 224; Blumenson, *Patton Papers*, 576.
5. Truscott, *Command Missions*, 441.
6. Clarke and Smith, *Riviera to the Rhine*, 193.
7. Postwar interview with General Wiese, manuscript B-787, p. 30, USAMHI.
8. Ibid.
9. Clarke and Smith, *Riviera to the Rhine*, 232.
10. Truscott, *Command Missions*, 441–43.
11. Ibid., 442–44.
12. Bonn, *When the Odds Were Even*, 4–5.
13. MacDonald, *The Siegfried Line Campaign*, 9–65.
14. Clarke and Smith, *Riviera to the Rhine*, 297–300.
15. Ibid., 372.
16. Ibid., 373; Cole, *The Lorraine Campaign*, 230.
17. First Army (German) Estimate of the Situation, September 10, 1944, Historical Division, Headquarters U.S. Army Europe.
18. Mellenthin, *Panzer Battles*, 371–85.
19. Headquarters 6th Army Group, Letter of Instructions, September 26, 1944, to Seventh Army and First French Army.

## CHAPTER 9. Into the Vosges

1. Clarke and Smith, *Riviera to the Rhine*, 314.
2. Devers to Georgie, September 29, 1944, York Heritage Trust Library/Archives.
3. Author interview with Fussell, 2005.
4. Ibid.
5. *Foreign Military Studies*, D739.F6713 no. B-518, USAMHI.
6. Ibid.
7. Weigley, *Eisenhower's Lieutenants*, 252.
8. Clarke and Smith, *Riviera to the Rhine*, 36, 37.
9. Operations Report, Headquarters 30th Infantry Regiment, box 6386, NARA.
10. Clarke and Smith, *Riviera to the Rhine*, 238–51.
11. Murphy, *To Hell and Back*, 196.
12. Clarke and Smith, *Riviera to the Rhine*, 238–51.
13. 36th Infantry Division Assoc./Texas Military Forces Museum, 141st Infantry Regiment, 6th Infantry Division, http://www.texasmilitaryforcesmuseum.org/gallery/36div.htm.
14. Postwar interview with General Wiese, manuscript B-787, USAMHI.
15. Clarke and Smith, *Riviera to the Rhine*, 254.
16. Blumenson, *Patton Papers*, 557.
17. Chandler and Ambrose, *Papers of Dwight Eisenhower*, 4:2599.
18. Blumenson, *Breakout and Pursuit*, 690.
19. Author interview, 1994.
20. Clarke and Smith, *Riviera to the Rhine*, 254, 255.
21. Biography/history, Wade H. Haislip Papers, USAMHI.

## CHAPTER 10. Logistics

1. *Seventh Army, Report of Operations*, 3:897, 898.
2. Ibid., 1:316.
3. Ibid., 1:316, 317.
4. Clarke and Smith, *Riviera to the Rhine*, 196.
5. Ibid., 220.
6. Ibid., 195.
7. Ibid.
8. Ruppenthal, *Logistical Support of the Armies*, 2:124.
9. Clarke and Smith, *Riviera to the Rhine*, 575.
10. James Huston, *Sinews of War*, 533.
11. Bykofsky and Larson, *Transportation Corps, Operations Overseas*, 312.
12. Devers diary, September 13, 1944.
13. Pogue, *The Supreme Command*, app. B, 535.
14. Ruppenthal, *Logistical Support of the Armies*, 2:123.
15. Marshall, Arnold, and King, *War Reports*, 192.
16. Ruppenthal, *Logistical Support of the Armies*, 2:123.
17. *Seventh Army, Report of Operations*, 315–33.
18. Esposito, *West Point Atlas of American Wars*, 2:59.
19. Dwight D. Eisenhower, *Crusade in Europe*, 292.
20. Griess, *The Second World War*, 350.

21. Griess interview with Devers, box 92.
22. Ibid.
23. Ibid.
24. Ibid.
25. Ibid.
26. Ibid.
27. Huston, *Sinews of War*, 531.
28. Griess interview with Devers, box 87, tape 21, pp. 57, 58.
29. *Time*, December 1, 1947; Griess interview with Palmer re Devers, box 83, tape 21, p. 58.
30. Griess interview with Palmer.
31. Beck et al., *The Corps of Engineers*, 452.
32. Bykofsky and Larson, *Transportation Corps, Operations Overseas*, 319.
33. Griess interview with Devers, box 83.
34. Beck et al., *The Corps of Engineers*, 453.
35. Palmer interview with Devers, box 83.
36. Clarke and Smith, *Riviera to the Rhine*, 351.
37. *The Seventh United States Army in France and Germany 1944–1945*, 3:898.
38. Blumenson, *Patton Papers*, 586–87.
39. Van Creveld, *Supplying War*, 228.
40. Ibid., 225.
41. Ruppenthal, *Logistical Support of the Armies*, 2:178.

CHAPTER 11. On to Strasbourg
1. Clarke and Smith, *Riviera to the Rhine*, 263.
2. Murphy, *To Hell and Back*, 198.
3. Thirty-sixth Infantry Division Assoc./Texas Military Forces Museum, 141st Infantry Regiment.
4. Ibid.
5. Clarke and Smith, *Riviera to the Rhine*, 322.
6. Griess interview with Devers, box 92, tape 7.
7. Ibid.
8. Ibid.
9. Shirey, *Americans: The Story of the 442nd Combat Team*, 51–73.
10. Clarke and Smith, *Riviera to the Rhine*, 329–33.
11. Author interview with Elsner, 2005.
12. John E. Dahlquist Papers, USAMHI.
13. Clarke and Smith, *Riviera to the Rhine*, 333.
14. Ibid., 269.
15. Ibid., 361.

CHAPTER 12. Whither the 6th Army Group?
1. Clarke and Smith, *Riviera to the Rhine*, 349–54.
2. Weigley, *Eisenhower's Lieutenants*, 580.
3. D'Este, *Crisis in Command*, 670.

4. David Eisenhower, *Eisenhower at War*, 8–9.
5. Griess interview with Devers, February 4, 1975, box 87.
6. Ambrose, *Eisenhower*, 296.
7. Hamilton, *Monty: Final Years of the Field Marshall*, 329.
8. Devers diary, August 20, 1944.
9. Clarke and Smith, *Riviera to the Rhine*, 229.
10. Ibid., 229, 230.
11. Butcher, *My Three Years with Eisenhower*, 704.
12. Clarke and Smith, *Riviera to the Rhine*, 226.
13. Bradley, *A Soldier's Story*, 171.
14. Clarke and Smith, *Riviera to the Rhine*, 229–30.
15. Devers diary, September 19, 1944.
16. Letter of Instruction, Headquarters 6th Army Group to Commanding Generals, Seventh and French First armies, and 1st Airborne Task Force, September 22, 1944, to seize bridgeheads across the Rhine.

## CHAPTER 13. The Prickly French

1. Griess interview with Devers, July 2, 1975, box 87.
2. Author interview with Paul Fussell, 2005.
3. Col. Villarat, "Friction between French and Americans," 7th Army report, box 59, York Heritage Trust Library/Archives.
4. Hansen diaries.
5. Leckie, *Delivered from Evil*, 177–82.
6. Devers diary, November 7, 1944.
7. Esposito, *West Point Atlas of American Wars*, map 17.
8. De Lattre, *History of the French First Army*, 29.
9. Ibid., 30.
10. Headquarters 7th Army, Public Relations Office, press release, September 15, 1944.
11. Ibid.
12. Clarke and Smith, *Riviera to the Rhine*, 355.
13. De Lattre, *History of the French First Army*, 30.
14. Ibid., 170.
15. Maule, *Out of the Sand*, 260.
16. Griess interview with Palmer, box 83, side 4, p. 56.
17. Maule, *Out of the Sand*, 230.
18. Weigley, *Eisenhower's Lieutenants*, 250–51.
19. Ibid., 554.

## CHAPTER 14. The Greatest Obstacle

1. Caesar, *The Gallic War and Other Writings*, 81.
2. Ibid., 82.
3. Bryant, *Triumph in the West*, 328.
4. *The Seventh United States Army in France and Germany 1944–1945*, 3:744.
5. Cole, *The Ardennes*, 13.

6. Ibid., 12.

7. Hechler, *The Bridge at Remagen*, xiii–xvi.

8. Ibid.

9. Westphal, *The German Army in the West*, 195.

10. Memorandum from Col. William W. Quinn, headquarters Seventh Army, Office of the A.C. of S., G-2, 22 December 1944.

## CHAPTER 15. Cross the Rhine!

1. Headquarters 6th Army Group, Letter of Instructions, September 26, 1944, to Seventh Army and French First Army; see Devers' diary regarding the meeting at SHAEF on October 5, 1944, Re: "cross the Rhine."

2. Clarke and Smith, *Riviera to the Rhine*, 352–53.

3. Ibid.

4. Blumenson, *Patton Papers*, 547.

5. Ibid.

6. Hansen diaries.

7. Devers diary.

8. Letter from Supreme Headquarters to General Devers, October 19, 1944, box 87, York Heritage Trust Library/Archives; Clarke and Smith, *Riviera to the Rhine*, 352–53.

9. A History of the Headquarters Sixth Army Group, entry 155, USAMHI.

10. Ibid., entries 156–57, p. 53.

11. Devers diary, October 5, 1944.

12. Ibid.

13. Weigley, *Eisenhower's Lieutenants*, 404.

## CHAPTER 16. Planning the Crossing

1. Sixth Army Group diary, 247–53, USMA.

2. Ibid., September 25, 1944, 264.

3. "Special Study: The Assault Crossing of the Rhine from Basle to Manheim," 5–23.

4. Sixth Army Group diary, 310.

5. Seventh Army Diary, 389, November 21, 1944.

6. "Special Study: The Assault Crossing of the Rhine from Basle to Manheim," 5–23.

7. Ibid.

## CHAPTER 17. The River-Crossing Schools

1. "History of River Crossing School," Headquarters 2nd Battalion, 40th Engineer Combat Regiment, December 2, 1944.

2. Alexander French, *History of the 40th Engineer Combat Regiment in WWII*, 84.

3. Ibid., 85.

4. Weigley, *Eisenhower's Lieutenants*, 642.

5. "History of River Crossing School"; Report on the Operations of Seventh Army River Crossing Schools at Dole and Camp de la Valbonne, September 26–October 18,

1944.

6. French, *History of the 40th Engineer Combat Regiment in WWII*, 85.
7. Author interview with James Seitzer, 2005.
8. Ibid.
9. Seventh Army diary, October 4, 1944, 286.
10. Davidson, *Grandpa Gar*, 94.
11. Seventh Army diary, November 18, 1944.
12. Chandler and Ambrose, Papers of Dwight D. Eisenhower, 4:2162; Seventh Army Engineering Division, Weekly Reports, June 1–November 15, box 220, NARA.
13. Seventh Army diary, November 22, 1944, 393.
14. Ibid., 319.
15. Ibid., 396, 389.
16. Ibid., 389.
17. Headquarters Seventh Army, Office of the Engineer, Re: River Crossing Equipment, November 18, 1944.

## CHAPTER 18. Moving Up

1. French, *History of the 40th Engineer Combat Regiment in WWII*, 96–97.
2. Ibid.
3. Griess interview with Edward D. Comm, tape 67, side 2, p. 35 of typed transcript, York Heritage Trust Library/Archives.
4. Clarke and Smith, *Riviera to the Rhine*, 438, 439.
5. Weigley, *Eisenhower's Lieutenants*, 383; Bradley, *A Soldier's Story*, 434.
6. Clarke and Smith, *Riviera to the Rhine*, 352; Weigley, *Eisenhower's Lieutenants*, 383.
7. Clarke and Smith, *Riviera to the Rhine*, 353.
8. Weigley, *Eisenhower's Lieutenants*, 383.
9. Butcher, *My Three Years with Eisenhower*, 679.
10. Bradley, *A Soldier's Story*, 435.
11. Hansen diaries, October 23, 1944.
12. Weigley, *Eisenhower's Lieutenants*, 383–84.
13. Clarke and Smith, *Riviera to the Rhine*, 351–54.
14. Devers to Georgie, November 19, 1944, York Heritage Trust Library/Archives.
15. Devers to Vice Adm. A. G. Kirk, November 13, 1944, York Heritage Trust Library/Archives.
16. Devers to Georgie, November 8, 1944, York Heritage Trust Library/Archives.
17. Brown, *The Diary of Hallet K. Brown*.
18. Devers to Georgie, November 19, 1944, York Heritage Trust Library/Archives.
19. General Dahlquist to Ruth, John E. Dahlquist Papers, USAMHI.
20. J. Glenn Gray, *The Warriors*, 5.
21. Devers diary, November 11, 1944.
22. Clarke and Smith, *Riviera to the Rhine*, 365, 366–88.
23. Ibid., 406–28.
24. Ibid., 377–79, 409–16.
25. Griess interview with Lt. Gen. Reuben Jenkins, York Heritage Trust Library/Archives.

## CHAPTER 19. Moving Out

1. Maule, *Out of the Sand*, 245.
2. Ibid.
3. Keegan, *The Second World War*, 325
4. Clarke and Smith, *Riviera to the Rhine*, 374–76.
5. Whiting, *America's Forgotten Army*, 89.
6. Maule, *Out of the Sand*, 254.
7. Ibid., 252–55.
8. Schmidt, "Strasbourg Rocks under Shellfire."
9. De Lattre, *History of the French First Army*, 249.
10. Clarke and Smith, *Riviera to the Rhine*, 297.
11. Devers diary, September 18, 1944.
12. Clarke and Smith, *Riviera to the Rhine*, 298.
13. Ibid., 413.
14. De Lattre, *History of the French First Army*, 249.
15. Ibid.
16. Ibid.
17. Weigley, *Eisenhower's Lieutenants*, 403, 404.
18. Ibid.

## CHAPTER 20. Finally, the Attack

1. Official diary for the Commanding General, Seventh Army, 287–88, USMA Archives/Library.
2. Griess interview with Devers on 6th Army Group Offensive, tape 29, side 2, p. 40 of typed transcript.
3. Ibid., tape 21, side 1, box 87, p. 57 of typed transcript.
4. Ibid., tape 29, side 2, p. 39.
5. *The Seventh United States Army in France and Germany 1944–1945*, 3:744; Seventh Army, Office of the Engineer, Historical Report, General Narrative for November 1944, 8 pp.
6. Esposito, *West Point Atlas of American Wars*, map 59.
7. Clarke and Smith, *Riviera to the Rhine*, 563.
8. Memorandum, Headquarters Seventh Army, Office of the A.C. of S., G-2, December 22, 1944, folder 107–0.3.0, RG 407, entry 427, box 2571, NARA.
9. Clarke and Smith, *Riviera to the Rhine*, 444.
10. Weigley, *Eisenhower's Lieutenants*, 500–501.
11. Clarke and Smith, *Riviera to the Rhine*, 442.
12. Devers diary, December 19, 1944.
13. Official diary for the Commanding General, Seventh Army, September 30, 1944, USMA Archives/Library.
14. Colley, *Blood for Dignity*, 87–126.

## CHAPTER 21. Ike Balks

1. Author interview with Paul Fussell, 2005.
2. John E. Dahlquist Papers, USAMHI.
3. Chester B. Hansen Papers, USAMHI.

4. Clarke and Smith, *Riviera to the Rhine*, 438, 439.
5. Hansen diaries, 1944, 1945.
6. Griess interview with Devers, tape 29, p. 35, box 88.
7. Ibid., tape 42, side 1, box 89.
8. Ibid.
9. Ibid.
10. Official diary for the Commanding General, Seventh Army, USMA Archives/
    Library; 268; A History of Headquarters 6th Army Group. (Italics added for emphasis.)
11. Clarke and Smith, *Riviera to the Rhine*, 439.
12. Ibid., 438, 439.
13. Devers diary, October 5, 1944.
14. Clarke and Smith, *Riviera to the Rhine*, 438.
15. Ibid., 440.
16. Pogue, *The Supreme Command*, 310.
17. Devers diary, September 17 and October 5, 1944.
18. Maule, *Out of the Sand*, 258.
19. Devers diary, November 25, 1944.
20. Hamilton, *Monty: The Final Years of the Field Marshall*, 329.
21. Weigley, *Eisenhower's Lieutenants*, 438.
22. MacDonald, *The Siegfried Line Campaign*, 56–64.
23. Corps in Combat, Wade Haislip Papers, USAMHI.
24. Griess interview with Comm, tape 67, side 2, box 91.
25. Davidson, *Grandpa Gar*, 95.
26. Alexander Carrel Patch file, cu 5187, box 6, USMA Archives/Library.
27. Blumenson, *Patton Papers*, 583.
28. Weigley, *Eisenhower's Lieutenants*, 407.
29. Devers diary, November 24, 1944.
30. *History of the 40th Engineer Combat Regiment in WWII*, 97.

## CHAPTER 22. Why Not Cross the Rhine?

1. Dwight Eisenhower, *Crusade in Europe*, 289–90.
2. Ibid., 225.
3. Mellenthin, *Panzer Battles*, 415.
4. Westphal, *The German Army in the West*, 176.
5. "The French and the Rhine."
6. Smith, *Eisenhower's Six Great Decisions*, 21, 211, 213.
7. Hamilton, *Monty: Final Years of the Field Marshall*, 329.
8. Bradley, *A Soldier's Story*, 511.
9. Weigley, *Eisenhower's Lieutenants*, 639.
10. Clarke and Smith, *Riviera to the Rhine*, 445.
11. Ibid.
12. Weigley, *Eisenhower's Lieutenants*, 241.
13. Blumenson, *Patton Papers*, 531.
14. Weigley, *Eisenhower's Lieutenants*, 262.
15. Blumenson, *Patton Papers*, 527.
16. Clarke and Smith, *Riviera to the Rhine*, 443.

17. Bradley, *A General's Life*, 408, 409.
18. Ibid.
19. Ibid.
20. Ibid.

## CHAPTER 23. Enemies in High Places

1. Devers diary, November 24, 1944.
2. Devers to Maj. Gen. Wilton Persons, Office of the Chief of Staff, November 30, 1944, York Heritage Trust Library/Archives.
3. Bradley, *A Soldier's Story*, 521.
4. Griess interview with Devers, tape 29, side 2, p. 38.
5. Ingersoll, *Top Secret*, 33.
6. Ambrose, *Eisenhower*, 29.
7. Hanson diary, July 1944.
8. Ambrose, *Eisenhower*, 267.
9. Hirshson, *General Patton: A Soldier's Life*, 245.
10. Devers diary, November 1, 1944.
11. Blumenson, *Patton Papers*, 565.
12. Devers to Georgie, November 26, 1944.
13. Blumenson, *Patton Papers*, 414.
14. Devers to Georgie, Sept. 23, 1944.
15. Ibid., 558.
16. Bradley, *A General's Life*, 210.
17. Baldwin, "Our Generals in the Battle of Germany."
18. Wittels, "These Are the Generals—Devers."
19. MacDonald, *The Mighty Endeavor*, 408.
20. *Saturday Evening Post*, June 19, 1944.
21. Irving, *The War between the Generals*, 323.
22. MacDonald, *The Siegfried Line Campaign*, 22.
23. Dwight D. Eisenhower, *At Ease*, 246.
24. Hamilton, *Monty: Final Years of the Field Marshall*, 329.

## CHAPTER 24. A Cautious and Inexperienced Commander

1. Ambrose, *Eisenhower*, 357.
2. Ibid., 210–11.
3. Ibid., 211.
4. Ibid., 213.
5. Atkinson, *Army at Dawn*, 141.
6. Ambrose, *Eisenhower*, 227.
7. Ibid., 214–15.
8. Blumenson, *Patton Papers*, 531.
9. Ingersoll, *Top Secret*, 219.
10. Ibid.
11. Ambrose, *Eisenhower*, 126.
12. Bradley, *A General's Life*, 45.

13. Weigley, *Eisenhower's Lieutenants*, 639.

14. Ambrose, *Eisenhower*, 72.

15. Ibid., 80, 82.

16. Ibid., 101.

17. Butcher, *My Three Years with Eisenhower*, 704.

18. Griess interview with Devers regarding the way to invade Germany, tape 21, side 1, p. 54 of typed transcript.

19. Colley, *Blood for Dignity*, 95.

20. Author interview with Paul Fussell, 2005.

21. Catton, *The Army of the Potomac*, 171–218.

22. Spector, *Eagle against the Sun*, 372–73.

23. Fussell, *Doing Battle*, 125.

## CHAPTER 25. What If Devers Had Crossed in November?

1. Griess, *The Second World War*, 364.

2. Blumenson, *Patton Papers*, 588.

3. Hechler, *The Bridge at Remagen*, 178–84.

4. Cole, *The Lorraine Campaign*, 520.

5. Typescript of "The Seventh Army from the Vosges to the Alps," *Army-Navy Journal*, August 2, 1945, Patch file USMA.

6. Davidson, *Grandpa Gar*, 94.

7. Clarke and Smith, *Riviera to the Rhine*, 445.

8. Colley, *The Road to Victory*, 229–31.

9. Davidson, *Grandpa Gar*, 93.

10. Interview with General der Infantry Hellmuth Thumm, USAMHI.

11. Memorandum from Col. William W. Quinn, Headquarters Seventh Army, Office of the A.C. of S., G-2, December 22, 1944.

12. Toland, *The Last 100 Days*, 243–62.

13. Ibid.

14. Beevor, *The Fall of Berlin 1945*, 424.

15. Devers diary, December 19, 1944.

16. Griess interview with Devers on the way to invade Germany, December 29–30, tape 21, side 1, p. 54 of typed transcript.

## CHAPTER 26. Breakthrough at Wallendorf

1. Ryan, *A Bridge Too Far*, 189.

2. Ibid., 139.

3. Bradley, *A Soldier's Story*, 418.

4. MacDonald, *The Siegfried Line Campaign*, 39, 56.

5. Ibid., 47.

6. Ibid., 55.

7. Ibid., 56.

8. Ibid., 59.

9. Ibid., 60.

10. Ibid., 61.

11. Ibid., 62.
12. Ibid.
13. Ibid.
14. Westphal, *The German Army in the West*, 174.
15. Ryan, *A Bridge Too Far*, 190.
16. Pogue, *The Supreme Command*, 283, 284.
17. Ryan, *A Bridge Too Far*, 132, 133.

## CHAPTER 27. New Orders for the 6th Army Group

1. Clarke and Smith, *Riviera to the Rhine*, 561; Bradley, *A Soldier's Story*, 557.
2. Devers to General Persons, November 26, 1944, box 21, York Heritage Trust Library/Archives.
3. *Report of Operations, 7th U.S. Army*, 2:459.
4. Ibid.
5. Ibid., 457.
6. Clarke and Smith, *Riviera to the Rhine*, 454.
7. Weigley, *Eisenhower's Lieutenants*, 410.
8. Whiting, *America's Forgotten Army*, 96.
9. Weigley, *Eisenhower's Lieutenants*, 597.
10. Griess interview with Devers, box 88.
11. Clarke and Smith, *Riviera to the Rhine*, 484, 485.
12. Ibid., 483.
13. Ibid., 466.
14. Ibid., 489, 490.
15. Ibid., 491.

## CHAPTER 28. Northwind—Devers Saves the Day

1. Blumenson, *Patton Papers*, 595.
2. Weigley, *Eisenhower's Lieutenants*, 551.
3. Ibid.
4. Quinn, *Buffalo Bill Remembers*, 144–45.
5. Weigley, *Eisenhower's Lieutenants*, 552.
6. Clarke and Smith, *Riviera to the Rhine*, 497.
7. Ibid.
8. Ibid.
9. Pommois, *Winter Storm*, 110–12.
10. Ibid., 112.
11. *Newsweek*, March 7, 1966, 50.
12. Pommois, *Winter Storm*, 112.
13. Clarke and Smith, *Riviera to the Rhine*, 505.
14. Cirillo, *Ardennes–Alsace 1944–45*, 37.
15. Giziowski, *The Enigma of General Blaskowitz*, 307.
16. Ibid., 371.
17. Author interview, 1994.
18. Pommois, *Winter Storm*, 101, 102.

19. Author interview with Pat Reilly, 1994.
20. Cirillo, *Ardennes–Alsace*, 39.
21. Ibid., 39.
22. Ibid., 47.
23. Ibid., 42.
24. Ibid., 47
25. Ibid., 48.
26. Author interview with Pat Reilly, 1994.
27. Clarke and Smith, *Riviera to the Rhine*, 519–20.
28. Ibid., 526–27.
29. Ibid., 528.
30. Devers diary, January 17, 1945.
31. Clarke and Smith, *Riviera to the Rhine*, 576, 577.

## CHAPTER 29. The Colmar Pocket

1. Griess interview with Devers, tape 36, p. 56, box 88.
2. Weigley, *Eisenhower's Lieutenants*, 551.
3. Mellenthin, *Panzer Battles*, 401.
4. Clarke and Smith, *Riviera to the Rhine*, 538.
5. Griess interview with Comm, interview tape 67, p. 36.
6. Bradley, *A Soldier's Story*, 451.
7. Ibid., 454.
8. Pogue, *The Supreme Command*, 369.
9. Ibid.
10. Clarke and Smith, *Riviera to the Rhine*, 517.
11. Ibid., 533.
12. Ibid., 556.
13. Ibid., 557.
14. Weigley, *Eisenhower's Lieutenants*, 557.
15. *The Seventh United States Army in France and Germany 1944–1945*, 2:652.
16. Clarke and Smith, *Riviera to the Rhine*, 556.

## CHAPTER 30. "Bayonets Will Be Sharpened"

1. MacDonald, *The Last Offensive*, 236–37.
2. *Time*, December 18, 1944, 44.
3. MacDonald, *The Last Offensive*, 237.
4. Ibid., 239.
5. Ibid.
6. Weigley, *Eisenhower's Lieutenants*, 634–35.
7. Ibid., 636.
8. Ibid.
9. Ibid., 633.
10. MacDonald, *The Last Offensive*, 260.
11. Weigley, *Eisenhower's Lieutenants*, 639.
12. Ibid.

## CHAPTER 31. Finally, the Rhine and into the National Redoubt

1. MacDonald, *The Mighty Endeavor*, 406.
2. Weigley, *Eisenhower's Lieutenants*, 642.
3. Ibid.
4. Ibid.
5. MacDonald, *The Mighty Endeavor*, 451.
6. Weigley, *Eisenhower's Lieutenants*, 451.
7. Ibid., 642.
8. MacDonald, *The Mighty Endeavor*, 451.
9. Quinn, *Buffalo Bill Remembers*, 155.
10. Dwight D. Eisenhower, *Crusade in Europe*, 415.
11. Weigley, *Eisenhower's Lieutenants*, 703–4.
12. Ibid.
13. Ibid.
14. Ibid., 710.
15. Devers to General Marshall, April 3, 1945, York Heritage Trust Library/Archives.
16. *Yank—The GI Story of the War*, 236–37.
17. Ibid., 237.
18. MacDonald, *The Mighty Endeavor*, 493.
19. Weigley, *Eisenhower's Lieutenants*, 716.
20. Ibid., 715.
21. *The Seventh United States Army in France and Germany 1944–1945*, 3:860, 861.
22. Blumenson, *Patton Papers*, 696.
23. MacDonald, *The Mighty Endeavor*, 492.

## CHAPTER 32. Could the French Have Crossed the Rhine?

1. De Lattre, *The History of the French First Army*, 406.
2. Griess interview with Devers, box 89.
3. Clarke and Smith, *Riviera to the Rhine*, 355.
4. Ibid., 431, 432.
5. Ibid., 355.
6. Author interviews, 2006.
7. Clarke and Smith, *Riviera to the Rhine*, 357.
8. Devers diary, January 27, 1944.
9. Ibid., October 1, 1944.
10. Griess interview with Devers regarding relations with the French, tape 3, p. 20.

## Epilogue

1. Blumenson, *Patton Papers*, 598.
2. Author interview with Raymond Christman, September 2007.
3. Dwight D. Eisenhower, *At Ease*, 280.

★ ★ ★ ★

# BIBLIOGRAPHY

## BOOKS AND ARTICLES

"Alsace." *New York Times*, November 23, 1944.

Ambrose, Stephen. *Eisenhower*. New York: Simon and Schuster, 1983.

———. "A Fateful Friendship." *American Heritage*, April 1969, 40–41, 97–103.

Atkinson, Rick. *Army at Dawn: The War in North Africa, 1942–1943*. New York. Henry Holt, 2003.

Baldwin, Hanson W. "Army Comes of Age." *New York Times*, October 9, 1944.

———. "Harder Blows to Fall on Germans in the West." *New York Times*, November 26, 1944.

———. "'Jakie' Devers Bows Out." *New York Times*, August 1, 1949.

———. "Our Generals in the Battle of Germany." *New York Times*, October 22, 1944.

———. *Tiger Jack*. Johnstown, Colo.: Old Army Press, 1979.

Beck, Alfred, Charles W. Lynch, and Abe Bortz. *The Corps of Engineers: The War against Germany*. Washington, D.C.: Center for Military History, 1988.

Beevor, Anthony. *The Fall of Berlin 1945*. New York: Penguin, 2003.

Bland, Larry I., ed. *The Papers of George Catlett Marshall*. Vol. 4: *Aggressive and Determined Leadership, June 1, 1943–December 31, 1944*. Baltimore: Johns Hopkins University Press, 1996.

———, ed. *The Papers of George Catlett Marshall*. Vol. 5: *The Finest Soldier, January 1, 1945–January 7, 1947*. Baltimore: Johns Hopkins University Press, 2003.

"Blaskowitz Out, London Informed." *New York Times*, November 5, 1944.

Blumenson, Martin. *Breakout and Pursuit*. Washington, D.C.: Office of the Chief of Military History, 1961.

———. *The Patton Papers, 1940–1945*. Boston: Houghton Mifflin, 1974.

"Bombs Miss 3 Generals." *New York Times*, August 21, 1944.

Bonn, Keith. *When the Odds Were Even*. Novato, Calif.: Presidio Press, 1994.

Botsch, Walter. "198th Reserve Infantry Division, July–Oct. '44." *Foreign Military Studies*, U.S. Army Military History Institute.

———. "The Story of the 7th American Army in War." *Foreign Military Studies* (1946): 28, U.S. Army Military History Institute.

Bracker, Milton. "Foe Flees in Fog from Strasbourg." *New York Times*, December 3, 1944.

———. "Guns Still Firing Near Strasbourg." *New York Times*, November 29, 1944.

———. "Yankees in Britain to Mark Gala 4th." *New York Times*, July 4, 1943.

Bradley, Omar N. *A General's Life*. Reprint. New York: Simon and Schuster, 1983.
———. *A Soldier's Life*. New York: Henry Holt, 1951.
"British Evacuees Thanked by Devers." *New York Times*, November 16, 1942.
Brown, Anthony Cave. *Bodyguard of Lies*. New York: Harper and Row, 1975.
Bryant, Arthur. *Triumph in the West: History of the War Years*. Garden City, N.Y.: Doubleday, 1959.
———. *The Turn of the Tide*. Garden City, N.Y.: Doubleday, 1957.
Butcher, Harry C. *My Three Years with Eisenhower*. New York: Simon and Schuster, 1946.
Bykofsky, Joseph, and Harold Larson. *The Transportation Corps, Operations Overseas*. Vol. 1. Washington, D.C.: Department of the Army, 1968.
Caesar, Julius. *The Gallic War and Other Writings*. New York: Modern Library, 1957.
Carr, Caleb. "VE Day—November, 1944." In *What If: Eminent Historians Imagine What Might Have Been*, ed. Robert E. Cowley. New York: Berkley Books, 2001.
Catledge, Turner. "Fort Knox Making 'Battle' Veterans." *New York Times*, May 12, 1943.
Catton, Bruce. *The Army of the Potomac*. New York: Doubleday, 1962.
Chandler, Alfred D., and Stephen E. Ambrose, eds. *The Papers of Dwight David Eisenhower*. Vol. 4: *The War Years*. Baltimore: Johns Hopkins University Press, 1970.
Churchill, Winston. *Triumph and Tragedy*. New York: Houghton Mifflin, 1953.
Cirillo, Roger. *Ardennes–Alsace 1944–45*. Washington, D.C.: Center for Military History, 1995.
Clarke, Jeffrey J., and Robert R. Smith. *Riviera to the Rhine*. Washington, D.C.: Center for Military History, 1991.
Cole, Hugh M. *The Ardennes: Battle of the Bulge*. Washington, D.C.: Office of the Chief of Military History, 1993.
———. *The Lorraine Campaign*. Washington, D.C.: Office of the Chief of Military History, 1993.
Colley, David P. *Blood for Dignity: The Story of the First Integrated Combat Unit in the U.S. Army*. New York: St. Martin's Press, 2003.
———. "Deadly Accuracy." *American Heritage of Invention and Technology* 16, no. 4 (2001): 44–50.
———. *The Road to Victory: The Untold Story of the Red Ball Express*. Washington, D.C.: Brassey's, 2000.
"Command: Patch for Patton." *Time*, August 28, 1944.
"Commander of the Seventh." *New York Times*, August 18, 1944.
Crosswell, D. K. R. *Chief of Staff: The Military Career of General Walter Bedell Smith*. New York: Greenwood Press, 1991.
Cullum, George W. *Biographical Register of the Officers and Graduates of the US Military Academy*. Boston: Houghton, 1891–1950. U.S. Army Military History Institute.
Daley, Arthur. "Sports of the Times." *New York Times*, May 11, 1943.
Daniel, Clifton. "With General Eisenhower at SHAEF." *New York Times*, March 4, 1945.
Daniel, Raymond. "Devers Takes Over Andrews Command." *New York Times*, May 11, 1943.
Davidson, Garrison H. *Grandpa Gar: The Saga of One Soldier as Told to His Grandchildren*. Self-published, 1974. U.S. Military Academy/U.S. Army Military History Institute.
DePastino, Todd. "The Day the General Apologized to the Dead." *Chicago Sun-Times*, May 27, 2007.

D'Este, Carlo. *Eisenhower: A Soldier's Life*. New York: Henry Holt, 2002.

————. *Patton: A Genius for War*. New York: HarperCollins, 1995.

"De Gaulle Honors Devers and Patch." *New York Times*, February 12, 1945.

"Devers Appointed to Andrews' Post." *New York Times*, May 7, 1943.

"Devers Clarifies 'Elastic' Strategy." *New York Times*, May 24, 1943.

"Devers Full of Confidence on Anzio Beachhead Visit." *New York Times*, February 22, 1943.

"Devers Meets George VI." *New York Times*, July 8, 1943.

"Devers Pledges Victory in Message to Troops." *New York Times*, December 24, 1943.

"Devers Predicts Hard Land Fights." *New York Times*, November 3, 1943.

"Devers Says Our Men Are Eager to Attack." *New York Times*, November 11, 1943.

"Devers' Yanks Join Leclerc's Troops in Ancient Strasbourg." *New York Times*, November 25, 1944.

Drummond, Roscoe. "A Soldier's General." *Christian Science Monitor*, June 19, 1943.

"DSM Is Awarded to General Devers." *New York Times*, October 20, 1943.

Eisenhower, David. *Eisenhower at War, 1943–1945*. New York: Random House, 1986.

Eisenhower, Dwight D. *At Ease: Stories I Tell to Friends*. Garden City, N.Y.: Doubleday, 1967.

————. *Crusade in Europe*. Garden City, N.Y.: Doubleday, 1948.

"Eisenhower Takes 7th into Command." *New York Times*, September 16, 1944.

"Eisenhower Visits Front during a German Attack." *New York Times*, November 24, 1944.

Esposito, Vincent J. *The West Point Atlas of American Wars*. Vol. 2. New York: Praeger, 1964.

Farago, Ladislas. *Patton: Ordeal and Triumph*. New York: Dell, 1963.

"Foe Tries to Cut Saverne Corridor." *New York Times*, November 26, 1944.

"44th Division, from New York and New Jersey, Wins Praise as Part of the Seventh Army." *New York Times*, November 22, 1944.

French, Alexander. *History of the 40th Engineer Combat Regiment in WWII*. 40th Engineer Combat Regiment National Association, 1995.

"French Drive Cuts Belfort Defenses." *New York Times*, November 20, 1944.

"The French at the Rhine." *New York Times*, November 21, 1944.

Fuller, J. F. C. *The Second World War*. New York: Duell, Sloan, and Pearce, 1948.

Funk, Arthur Layton. *Hidden Ally: The French Resistance, Special Operations, and the Landings in Southern France, 1944*. New York: Greenwood Press, 1992.

Fussell, Paul. *Doing Battle: The Making of a Skeptic*. Boston: Little, Brown, 1996.

————. *Wartime: Understanding and Behavior in the Second World War*. New York: Oxford University Press 1989.

Gelb, Norman. *Ike and Monty*. New York: William Morrow, 1994.

"Gen. Devers Sees Post War Unity." *New York Times*, July 4, 1943.

"Gen. Patch Dies of Pneumonia at 55: Led 7th Army in Victorious Drive." *New York Times*, November 22, 1945.

"General Patch Sees Game." *New York Times*, July 11, 1945.

Giziowski, Richard J. *The Enigma of General Blaskowitz*. New York: Hippocrene Books, 1997.

Glantz, David. *Hitler and His Generals: Military Conferences 1942–1945*. New York: Enigma Books, 2002.

Gray, J. Glenn. *The Warriors: Reflections on Men in Battle*. New York: Harper and Row, 1970.

Griess, Thomas E., ed. *The Second World War: Europe and the Mediterranean*. Wayne, N.J.: Avery Publishing Group, 1989.

Hamilton, Nigel. *Master of the Battlefield: Monty's War Years 1942–1944*. New York: McGraw-Hill, 1984.

————. *Monty: The Final Years of the Field Marshall, 1944–1976*. New York: McGraw-Hill, 1986.

————. *Monty: The Making of a General 1887–1942*. New York: McGraw-Hill, 1981.

Hart, B. H. Liddell. *History of the Second World War*. New York: Putnam, 1970.

Headquarters Seventh Army. Public Relations Office. "Biography of General de Lattre de Tassigny." September 15, 1944.

Hechler, Ken. *The Bridge at Remagen*. New York: Ballantine Books, 1957.

Hill, Gladwin. "Germans Bomb Bridgehead, but Line over Rhine Is Strong." *New York Times*, March 9, 1945.

Hirshson, Stanley P. *General Patton: A Soldier's Life*. New York: Collins, 2002.

Hobbs, Joseph Patrick. *Dear General: Eisenhower's Wartime Letters to Marshall*. Baltimore: Johns Hopkins University Press, 1971.

Huston, James. *The Sinews of War: Army Logistics 1775–1953*. Washington, D.C.: Center for Military History, 1988.

Ingersoll, Ralph. *Top Secret*. New York: Harcourt, Brace, 1946.

Irving, David. *The Trail of the Fox*. New York: Avon, 1977.

————. *The War between the Generals*. New York: Congdon and Lattes, 1980.

Keegan, John. *A History of Warfare*. New York: Alfred A. Knopf, 1993.

————. *The Second World War*. New York: Penguin Books, 1989.

————. *Six Armies in Normandy*. New York: Viking Press, 1982.

Kemp, Anthony. *The Unknown Battle, Metz, 1944*. New York: Stein and Day, 1980.

Larrabee, Constance Stuart. *WWII Photo Journal*. Washington, D.C.: National Museum of Women in the Arts, 1989.

Lattre de Tassigny, Jean de. *The History of the French First Army*. London: George Allen and Unwin, 1952.

Lawler, Nancy Ellen. *Soldiers of Misfortune: Ivoirien Tirailleurs of World War II*. Athens: Ohio University Press, 1992.

Lawrence, W. H. "8th Air Force Gets 'Home Folks' Visit." *New York Times*, August 3, 1943.

Leckie, Robert. *Delivered from Evil: The Saga of World War II*. New York: Harper and Row, 1987.

————. *The Last Offensive*. Washington, D.C.: Office of the Chief of Military History, 1973.

————. *The Mighty Endeavor: American Armed Forces in the European Theater in World War II*. New York: Oxford University Press, 1969.

————. *The Siegfried Line Campaign*. Washington, D.C.: Office of the Chief of Military History, 1963.

MacDonald, Charles B. *A Time for Trumpets*. New York: William Morrow, 1985.

Markey, Michael A. *Jake: The General from West York Avenue*. York, Pa.: Historical Society of York County, 1998.

Marshall, George C., H. H. Arnold, and Ernest J. King. *The War Reports*. Philadelphia: J. B. Lippincott, 1947.

Maule, Henry. *Out of the Sand: The Epic Story of General Leclerc and the Fighting Free French*. London: Odhams Books, 1966.

Mellenthin, F. W. von. *German Generals of World War II: As I Saw Them*. Norman: University of Oklahoma Press, 1977.

————. *Panzer Battles*. New York: Ballantine Books, 1980.

Middleton, Drew. "Allies Slowed Up." *New York Times*, November 28, 1944.

———. "Americans Win Southern Gate to the Saar." *New York Times*, November 22, 1944.

———. "Patch's Men Gain." *New York Times*, December 15, 1944.

———. "Patton Hits Hard." *New York Times*, November 25, 1944.

———. "Rhine City Falling." *New York Times*, November 24, 1944.

———. "10 Forts Captured." *New York Times*, November 27, 1944.

Miller, Donald L. *The Story of World War II*. New York: Simon and Schuster, 2003.

"Mulhouse Near Fall; Allies Gain along Line." *New York Times*, November 22, 1944.

Murphy, Audie. *To Hell and Back*. New York: Holt, Rinehart and Winston, 1949.

"The Nine New Generals." *New York Times*, March 14, 1945.

O'Connor, Richard. *Black Jack Pershing*. Garden City, N.Y.: Doubleday, 1961.

O'Donnell, Patrick K. *Operatives, Spies and Saboteurs: The Unknown Story of the Men and Women of WWII's OSS*. New York: Free Press, 2004.

Parton, James. *Air Force Spoken Here: General Ira Eaker and the Command of the Air*. Bethesda, Md.: Adler and Adler, 1986.

Patch, A. M. "The Seventh Army from the Vosges to the Alps." *Army-Navy Journal*, December 7, 1945.

Pergrin, David E. *First across the Rhine: The Story of the 291st Engineer Combat Battalion*. New York: Atheneum, 1989.

Pogue, Forrest C. *George C. Marshall, Organizer of Victory, 1943–1945*. New York: Viking Press, 1973.

———. *The Supreme Command*. Washington, D.C.: Office of the Chief of Military History, 1954.

Pommois, Lilse M. *Winter Storm: War in Northern Alsace November 1944–March 1945*. Paducah, Ky.: Turner Publishing, 1991.

Pyle, Ernie. *Brave Men*. New York: Henry Holt, 1944.

Quinn, William W. *Buffalo Bill Remembers*. Fowlerville, Mich.: Wilderness Adventure Books, 1991.

Reston, James. "Invasion Leader Pleases British." *New York Times*, December 25, 1943.

Rooney, Andy. *My War*. New York: Public Affairs. 2000.

Ruppenthal, Roland G. *Logistical Support of the Armies*. Washington, D.C.: Office of the Chief of Military History, 1995.

Ryan, Cornelius. *A Bridge Too Far*. New York: Simon and Schuster, 1974.

———. *The Last Battle*. New York: Simon and Schuster, 1966.

Schmidt, Dana Adams. "Strasbourg Rocks under Shellfire." *New York Times*, November 25, 1944.

*The Seventh United States Army in France and Germany 1944–1945*. 3 vols. Heidelberg: Aloys Graf, 1946.

Shirey, Orville C. *Americans: The Story of the 442nd Combat Team*. Washington, D.C.: Infantry Journal Press, 1946.

Smith, Walter Bedell. *The Chief of Staff: The Military Career of General Walter Bedell Smith*. New York: Greenwood Press, 1991.

———. *Eisenhower's Six Great Decisions: Europe 1944–1945*. New York: Longmans, Green, 1956.

Spector, Ronald H. *Eagle against the Sun: The American War with Japan*. New York: Free Press, 1985.

Spillar, Roger J., ed. *Dictionary of American Military Biography*. Westport, Conn.: Greenwood Press, 1984.

Strobridge, Truman R., and Bernard C. Nulty. "General Alexander M. Patch." *Military Review* 61 (June 1981): 823–26.

"Stronger Maginot Faces Americans." *New York Times*, November 15, 1944.

Taggart, Donald G. *History of the Third Infantry Division in World War II*. Washington, D.C.: Infantry Journal Press, 1946.

Thompson, R. W. *Montgomery: The Field Marshal*. New York: Charles Scribner's Sons, 1969.

Toland, John. *The Last 100 Days*. New York: Random House, 1966.

Truscott, Lucian K., Jr. *Command Missions, a Personal Story*. New York: E. P. Dutton, 1954.

Turner, John F., and Robert Jackson. *Destination Berchtesgaden: The Story of the United States Seventh Army in World War II*. New York: Charles Scribner's Sons, 1975.

Van Creveld, Martin. *Supplying War*. London: Cambridge University Press, 1977.

Weigley, Russell. *The American Way of War*. New York: Macmillan; London: Collier Macmillan, 1973.

———. *Eisenhower's Lieutenants*. Bloomington: Indiana University Press, 1981.

———. *History of the United States Army*. New York: Macmillan, 1967.

Westphal, Siegfried. *The German Army in the West*. London: Cassell, 1951.

Whiting, Charles. *America's Forgotten Army: The Story of the U.S. Seventh*. New York: St. Martin's Press, 1999.

Williamson, S. T. "Fighters in Review: These Are the Generals." *New York Times*, October 24, 1944.

Wilmot, Chester. *The Struggle for Europe*. New York: Harper and Brothers, 1952.

Wittels, David. "These Are the Generals—Devers." *Saturday Evening Post*, July 10, 1943.

Wyant, William K. *Sandy Patch: A Biography of Lt. Gen. Alexander M. Patch*. New York: Praeger, 1991.

*Yank—The GI Story of the War*, by the Staff of *Yank, the Army Weekly*. New York: Duell, Sloan, and Pearce, 1947.

Ziegler, Philip. *London at War*. New York: Alfred A. Knopf, 1995.

## COLLECTED PAPERS

John E. Dahlquist Papers. Ca. 1917–1966. U.S. Army Military History Institute, Carlisle, Pa.

Garrison H. Davidson Papers. 1976. U.S. Army Military History Institute, Carlisle, Pa.

Jacob L[oucks] Devers Papers. 1887–1979. York Heritage Trust Library/Archives

Jacob L. Devers Papers. 1943–1987. U.S. Army Military History Institute, Carlisle, Pa.

Wade H. Haislip Papers. Archives Collection 01, U.S. Army Military History Institute, Carlisle, Pa.

Chester B. Hansen Papers. 1898–1952 (includes diaries). U.S. Army Military History Institute, Carlisle, Pa.

Reuben E. Jenkins Papers. 1944–1958. Archives Collection, U.S. Army Military History Institute, Carlisle, Pa.

Alexander M. Patch Papers. U.S. Military Academy Library, West Point, N.Y.

Lucian K. Truscott Jr. Papers. 1947–1965. U.S. Army Military History Institute, Carlisle, Pa.

## MEMORANDA AND REPORTS

Blaskowitz, Johannes von. Answers to questions directed to General Blaskowitz. Foreign
Military Studies, D739.F6713, no. A-916, U.S. Army Military History Institute,
Carlisle, Pa.

Davidson, Garrison H. "Lessons Learned during Operations in France and Germany." Office
of the Engineer, Headquarters 7th Army, 1945 S-3 Report, 7th Regiment, 3rd
Infantry Division. Situation Report for November 27, 1944. National Archives and
Records Administration.

Knobelsdorff, Otto Von. First Army estimate of situation, September 10, 1944. Foreign
Military Studies, D739.F6713, no. B-222, U.S. Army Military History Institute,
Carlisle, Pa.

Memorandum, Col. William W. Quinn, Headquarters 7th Army, to General Patch G-2,
December 22, 1944. Folder 107-0.3.0, RG 407, box 2571, National Archives and
Records Administration.

Operations reports, 117th Cavalry Reconnaissance Squadron (Mecz), November 1–
November 30, 1944. RG 427, boxes 18282–18308, National Archives and Records
Administration.

Operations report, 30th U.S. Infantry, to Commanding General, 3rd Infantry, Division 5,
December 1944. Box 6386, National Archives and Records Administration.

Report by Col. Villarat regarding Friction between French and Americans, September 1944.
Box 59, York Heritage Trust Library/Archives.

Seeger, Willy. Report on Operations of the 405th Division, Strasbourg, summer 1944–spring
1945. Foreign Military Studies, D739.F6713, no. C-027, U.S. Army Military History
Institute, Carlisle, Pa.

Situation Reports, 6th Army Group to Eisenhower, November 23, 1944. RG 338, box 28,
National Archives and Records Administration.

Vaterodt, Franz. Preparations for the defense of the town of Strasbourg in the year 1944, and
the battle for Strasbourg, November 23–25, 1944. Foreign Military Studies, D739.
F6713, no. B-545, U.S. Army Military History Institute, Carlisle, Pa.

## COMBAT HISTORIES

*Combat History, 44th Infantry Division, 1944–1945.* Atlanta: Albert Love Enterprises, 1946.
*Combat History of the 324th Infantry Regiment, 44th Infantry Division.* Baton Rouge:
Army & Navy Publishing, 1946.
*The Cross of Lorraine: A Combat History of the 79th Infantry Division,* June 1942–
December 1945. Baton Rouge: Army and Navy Publishing, c. 1946.
Daily diary of the 117th Cavalry Reconnaissance Squadron (Mecz), November 1– November
30, 1944. Department of the Army, Adjutant General's Office, Departmental
Records Branch, Historical Records Section.
Fisher, George. *The Story of the 180th Infantry Regiment (45th Infantry Division).*
San Angelo, Tex.: Newsfoto Publishing, 1947.
*History 540th Engineer Combat Group, 1945.* Unit History 503-540 1945/46, U.S. Army
Military History Institute, Carlisle, Pa.

*A History of the Headquarters Sixth Army Group, 1945.* Unit History 02-6 1945. U.S. Army Military History Institute, Carlisle, Pa.

"Unit Journal, 7th Infantry Regiment, 3rd Infantry Division, November–December 1944." RG 407, box 6360, National Archives and Records Administration.

Wood, Steling, Edwin M. Van Bibber, Thomas L. Lyons, and Robert G. Deihl. *History of the 313th Infantry in World War II.* Washington, D.C.: Infantry Journal Press, 1947.

## INTERVIEWS

Author Interviews

Raymond Christman. September 2007.

Robert Elsner. 2005.

Paul Fussell. October 2005.

Ruth "Tony" Martin, staff nurse in American embassy, London, 1941–43; personal friend of Ambassador John Winant. 1995.

Pat Reilly, 313th Infantry Regiment, 79th Division. 1992.

James Seitzer. 2005.

Col. Thomas E. Griess Interviews, York Heritage Trust Library/Archives

Gen. Bruce Clark. Box 89.

Col. Edward D. Comm. 1972. Box 91.

Miss Catherine Devers. 1974. Box 92, tape 61.

Gen. Jacob Devers. 1969–74. Boxes 80–98.

Col. and Mrs. Alexander Graham C. Frances. 1972. Box 88.

Lt. Gen. Reuben Jenkins. Box 89.

Henry Cabot Lodge, 1968. Box 82. July 2, 1975. Box 88.

Lt. Col. Palmer. 1973. Box 83, tape 21, p. 58.

## DIARIES

Brown, Hallet K. *The Diary of Hallet K. Brown.* http://www.103rdcactus.com/bio.

Jacob Devers diary. York Heritage Trust Library/Archives.

U.S. 7th Army Official Diary. 3 vols. Single-space typescript, January 10, 1944, to June 2, 1945. U.S. Military Academy Archives/Library, West Point, N.Y.

A. M. Patch Jr. war diary, 18th U.S. Infantry, Douglas, Ariz., November 1, 1915 (regarding Pershing expedition against Villa).

Gen. Alexander M. Patch file, Archives/Library USMA, West Point, N.Y.

## ENGINEERING STUDIES FOR AN ASSAULT CROSSING OF THE RHINE

Headquarters, 2nd Battalion, 40th Engineer Combat Regiment. "History of the River Crossing School," December 2, 1944. Box 19539, National Archives and Records Administration.

Headquarters, 7th Army, Office of the Engineer. Historical report regarding assault crossing of the Rhine, June 13, 1945. National Archives and Records Administration.

Headquarters, 7th Army, Office of the Engineer to Engineer, VI Corps, U.S. Army, subject: River-Crossing Equipment, November 18, 1944. National Archives and Records Administration.

Instruction of Staff Officers in 1927: Memorandum Regarding Exercise in Crossing the Rhine. National Archives and Records Administration.

Operations Instruction 19, regarding assault crossing of the Rhine, November 24, 1944. National Archives and Records Administration.

Report of Operations in Eastern France [September 5, 1944, to December 1, 1944], Headquarters, 40th Engineering Combat Regiment, December 5, 1944. Box 19537, National Archives and Records Administration.

Rhine River Crossing Sites. Engineering Section, 6th Army Group, Intelligence Branch. Box 221, National Archives and Records Administration.

Special Study: The Assault Crossings of the Rhine River Line between Basle and Mannheim. Engineering Section, 6th Army Group, September 1944. Box 221, National Archives and Records Administration.

Supreme Headquarters, Allied Expeditionary Force, Engineer Division. Meteorological considerations affecting the crossing of the Rhine, November 2, 1944. National Archives and Records Administration.

★ ★ ★ ★

# INDEX

**A**

Aduatici people, 1

Afrika Korps, 49, 52, 158

air forces, American: Fifteenth, 35; "Mighty Eighth", 168

Aix en Provence, 73

Albert Kesselring, 166

Algiers, 22, 24, 27, 38, 58, 86

Alsace: American attacks in, 125; as battle-ground, 13, 37, 87–88, 182, 195–98; in Colmar Pocket, 93, 100, 191–94; de Gaulle's demands in, 93, 184–85; French capture of, 127; geology of, 61; German line in, 55–57, 59; German retreat from, 119; logistical advantages, 68, 132; Nineteenth Army in, 17, 39, 57, 60; in Northwind, 177, 183, 186–189; 6th Army Group in, 15; scorched earth in, 118; strate-gic importance, 33–35, 123, 168

Alsace plain: German retreat to, 45, 60, 63; German situation in, 85; German treatment from, 169; as military objective, 56, 64, 68, 81, 119, 121, 123, 125, 169; in Northwind, 183

American Civil War, 46, 50, 60–62, 160, 163

American Field Forces, 7

Andrews, Frank M., 21, 156

Antwerp, 54, 69, 70, 116, 168, 178

Anvil. *See* Operation Dragoon.

Anzio, 34, 63, 138

Armee B. *See* French First Army.

armies, American: First: in battle, 42, 44, 129, 148, 173, 178, 184, 199; under Bradley, 4; in broad front debate, 53; in the Heurtgen, 178; role in operations, 2, 75, 87, 99, 117, 129, 150, 151, 166, 170, 173; at Wallendorf, 175, 182; Ninth: allocated to British, 2; in the Bulge, 182; as flank guard, 117 Seventh: in Alsace, 18, 60, 63, 65, 98, 99, 100; in Colmar Pocket, 190–91; in cross–Rhine attack, 8, 17, 20, 103–109, 111–14, 116–43, 162–63, 165–71; in Dragoon, 68, 73–74, 88; first to the Rhine, 8, 96–103, 106, 110, 123–25, 129, 130–35, 137–41, 143, 145, 146, 159, 164, 178–91, 211; in Germany, 195–97, 200–206; logistical concerns, 69, 74; in Northwind, 182–89; under Patch, 14, 26, 28, 29, 87; under Patton, 14, 26; relations with French, 89, 92–93; 6th Army Group, 17; Third: in the Bulge, 168, 181; in cross–Rhine attack, 87–88, 109, 111, 131, 138; 15th Corps transferred from, 65, 67, 155; flanked by Seventh army, 85, 87, 127, 139, 145; in Germany, 196–98, 202–204; logisti-cal support of, 74; 178–79; in northern France, 37, 42, 44, 54, 56–57, 59, 66, 82, 125; in Northwind, 184, 186, 191, 193; to the Saar, 99, 116, 130, 167

armies, British: Eighth, 49, 52, 86, 158, 168; Fourteenth, 164; Second, 74, 75

armies, Canadian: First, 44

armies, French: First, in Alsace, 95, 100, 110, 125, 127, 132, 182, 195; American attitude toward, 89, 90, 132; as Armee B, 26, 37–38; at Belfort Gap, 58–60, 62, 66; in Colmar Pocket, 191; composition of, 26, 37; under de Lattre, 14; first to the Rhine, 125–27; influence of de Gaulle, 90, 93, 184–85; internal divisions, 92; in Northwind, 184, 188; in November offensive, 100; on the

Rhine, 100; relations with SHAEF, 116,
149; in 6th Army Group, 56; in southern
France, 15 58, 60, 66; in Strasbourg, 93; in
the Vosges, 45, 65, 119–20
armies, German: Fifteenth, 4, 48; Fifth
Panzer, 42, 55, 59, 60, 82, 85; First, destruction of, 138–39, 186, 196–97; Devers as
adversary, 120, 130–32, 171; divisions
removed from, 82; in the Siegfried Line,
131, 163; at Wallendorf, 175; Nineteenth, in
battle, 65, 117; in Colmar Pocket, 182, 190,
192–93; commander of, 25, 33, 36, 38, 45,57,
60; destruction of, 39, 100, 132, 133, 145,
169, 178–80; headquarters, 127; Northwind,
187; retreat of, 17, 32, 35–37, 55–57, 82–83, 93,
119–20; Seventh, 98; Seventh Panzer, 42
army groups, American: Sixth, Bradley reaction to, 2; Devers takes command, 14–17,
18, 20, 25, 36, 37, 38; with French First
army, 14, 89; first on the Rhine, 8, 17, 19,
98, 100, 103, 113, 137–39, 146, 153, 155; logistical concerns of, 68, 69, 70, 72, 74, 116,
140, 142, 156–57, 181; invasion of southern
France, 40; rapid advance of, 15, 36–38,
44, 82; under SHAEF command, 45, 57,
86, 88, 99; Twelfth, Bradley's command,
1–2, 4, 18; in broad front strategy, 45, 53,
54; Devers considered for command, 24;
headquartered at Namur, 44; relationship
with 7th Army, 100, 166; in Rhine crossing, 117, 148, 193, 196, 199; supplies to, 74
army groups, British: 21st, in attack on
Ruhr, 2, 8, 45, 53, 116–17, 150; broad front
strategy, 75; in cross Rhine attack, 139; in
France, 44, 50, 149; logistical concerns of,
66, 71, 74, 176
army groups, German: 5th Armored Army,
171; 6th Armored Army, 171; Army
Group G, 82, 130, 146, 181; Army Group
Oberrhein, 186–87
Army's Infantry School, 4
*Army–Navy Journal*, 143
Arnhem, 75, 139, 142, 172–73
Atkinson, Dick, 186
Austerlitz, battle of, 94

**B**
B–17, 30, 41
B–24, 30, 41
Bailey Bridge, 108
Balck, Hermann, 55, 56, 59, 77, 82, 117, 120,
125
Baldwin, Hanson W., 13, 155
Balkans, 22, 24, 27
Bartenheim, 127
battalions, American, armored: 813th Tank
Destroyer Battalion, 66
battalions, American, infantry: 3rd, 200
battalions, American, ponton: 85th Heavy
Ponton Battalion, 110
Battle of the Bulge 76, 82, 132, 133, 167–69, 171
Bayerlein, Fritz, 41
Beau Geste, 91
Belfort Gap: description of, 36; 24, 33; as mil-
itary objective, 34, 36–38, 56–58, 60, 66,
68, 83, 119, 126, 132, 142, 166, 208; strategic
significance, 33–34, 57, 58, 62
Berchtesgaden, 203
Bethouart, Antoine, 37, 192
Big Bertha guns, 1
Bitburg, Germany, 175
Bizerte, 158
Black Forest, 2, 19, 45, 53, 59, 61, 87, 103–5,
126,
Blodelsheim, 105
"Blood and Guts", 125
Blumenson, Martin, 42, 74, 150
Boche, 126
Botch, Walter, 38, 62
Bradley, Omar N.: commander 12th Army
group, 1–9, 45; in North Africa, 4; rela-
tionship with Eisenhower, 3, 6, 157; rela-
tionship with Devers, 15, 85, 136–37, 155,
166, 193; Rhine crossing, 9, 53, 148, 151–52,
165; in Sicily, 4, 49; at West Point, 3
brigades, American: 3rd Field Artillery, 79
brigades, British: 2nd Independent
Parachute, 32
*Bridge at Remagen*, 8
British Imperial General Staff, 25, 47, 94
broad front approach, 45, 139
Brooke, Alan, 47, 50, 94, 163

Brooks, Edward, 79, 80, 113, 119, 134, 138, 139
Brown, Hallet K., 118
Brussels, 1, 44, 117
Buddhaheads, 81
Bull, Harold R., 2, 3, 5, 6, 148
Bussey , Donald S., 140
Butcher, Harry, 157

**C**

C-47, 74
Cabot Lodge, Henry, 209
Caesar, Julius, 18, 94, 112
Camp Colt, 160
Cannes, 25
Carbine, 92
*Catoctin*, 30
Cavalaire-sur-Mer, 31
cavalry, 11, 29. 32, 34, 91, 134, 161, 187, 205
cavalry squadrons/groups, American: 117th
    Cavalry Reconnaissance Squadron, 19,
    187; 106th Cavalry Group, 67
Central Group of Armies, 70
Chad, 122
Chateau de Namur, 1
Chatel, Jean, 63–64, 92, 124
Cherbourg, 25, 69–70, 153
Chochias, 92
Christman, Raymond, 211
Churchill, Winston S., 22–23, 25, 43, 50, 170,
    205
Cirillo, Roger, 187
Clark, Mark, 154
Clarke, Jeffrey, 82, 88, 97, 130–32, 135, 138, 139
Class of 1909, USMA, 9
Class of 1915, USMA, 3
Cobra, 41
Cold Harbor, 142
Collins, Lawton, 41, 163
Colmar, France, 2, 93, in Alsace, 100, 102,
    125, 190, approach to, 126, 132
Combined Chiefs of Staff, 88
Comm, Edward D., 115
Command and General Staff School, 12, 161
corps, American: 2nd, 4, 26, 159; 5th, at
    Belfort Gap, 56, 57, 58; in Dragoon, 32–34,
    37; under Gerow's command, 157, 173–77;

at Wallendorf 142–43; in WWI, 66; 6th,
    with 1st Armored Division, 26; Truscott
    as commander, 30; with veteran troops,
    62–63, 65; 7th, 41, 163; 12th, 197; 15th, in
    Normandy, 66; in Northwind, 185, 87, 190,
    155; in Rhine crossing, 20, 67, 77, 83; in
    Strasbourg attack, 17, 119, 121–23, 125, 131,
    143; transferred from Third Army, 65–66,
    113; 20th, 97, 196; 21st, 197, 202
corps, British: 2nd, 52; 4th, 164; 30th, 176;
    33rd, 164
corps, French: 1st, 37, 119, 126; 2nd, 37, 83,
    119, 192
corps, German: 13th, 187; 64th, 169, 192; 48th
    Panzer, 59; 13th SS Panzer, 185
Corsica, 30, 62
Cowan, Howard, 6
Cross-Rhine attack 9, 17, 19, 22, 24, 99, 115,
    150, 132

**D**

Dahlquist, John, 31, 82, 118, 134
Dahlquist, Ruth, 31, 82, 118
Davidson, Garrison, 73, 112, 114, 145–46, 164,
    167
D-day, 15, 24, 40, 45, 69, 86, 122, 137, 147, 156
de Gaulle, Charles, 90–93, 112, 184, 185, 201,
    204
de Hautecloque, Jacques-Philippe, 122
De Lattre de Tassigny, Jean: in battle, 126–27,
    191, 201, 205; at Belfort Gap, 58, 60, 62; as
    commander, 14, 25, 27, 36, 37, 90; French
    First Army, 26, 32, 91–92; in Strasbourg,
    184, 188
De Monsabert, Joseph de Goislard, 37, 126,
    192
Dempsey, Miles, 44, 74
deuce-and-a-half trucks, 68, 74
Deuxieme DB. *See* French 2nd Armored
    Division.
Devers, Catherine "Kit" 7, 9–12, 14
Devers, Ella Kate, 9, 10
Devers, Frank, 9
Devers, Georgie, 11, 56, 61, 118, 154, 155
Devers, Jacob L: boyhood, 8–10; in Colmar
    Pocket, 180–81, 190–94; in Dragoon,

24–26; as European commander, 21–23; at Fort Knox, 12–13; in France, 33, 35–39, 44–45, 55; in Germany, 200–6; as junior officer, 10–12; letters to Georgie, 11, 118, 154–55; logistical concerns, 68–76; in Northwind, 182–89; relationship with Bradley, 15, 137, 155; relationship with Eisenhower, 15, 24, 86–87, 134–44, 152–57, 162; relationship with the French, 24, 87, 89–95, 209, 212; relationship with Marshall, 12–13, 22, 23–24, 79, 85–87, 156–157; relationship with Patton, 65, 152, 154–55; Rhine Crossing, 8, 15, 17, 19–20, 58, 64, 87–88, 97–120, 126–33, 145–51, 162–71; as 6th Army Group commander, 15, 61, 82, 85; West Point days, 10–12

Devers, Philip (brother), 9

Devers, Philip (father), 9

Dieppe, 34

Dijon, 15, 37, 102

divisions, American, infantry: 3rd, in Dragoon 32, 34; exhaustion of men, 82; in Germany, 200, 203; relieved in the Vosges, 81; in Sicily 49; in southern France, 63; at Strasbourg, 132; in the Vosges, 64, 192; with Audie Murphy 31; 5th, 200; 9th, 26; 35th, 193; 36th, in Dragoon, 16, 31, 32; Eisenhower visits, 134; in support of the French, 125; in southern France, 64; in the Vosges, 78, 80, 81; 44th, 19, 186; at war's end, 206; in Northwind, 185, 186; 45th, in Dragoon, 19; in southern France 3; in the Vosges, 63–65, 80, 83, 118; 63rd, 187; 75th, 195; 78th, 195; 79th, in Northwind, 187; in Strasbourg, 125; in the Vosges, 66; 85th, 67; 100th, 186; 103rd, in December offensive, 187; in Northwind, 187; relieves 3rd Division, 118; in the Vosges, 81

divisions, American, armored: 2nd, 79; 4th, 174; 5th, 44, 174–175; 9th , 4, 5, 133 199; 10th, 195; 11th, 79; 12th, 197; 14th, 101, 125, 187

divisions, American, airborne: 82nd, 168, 177; 101st, 168, 177, 193

divisions, German, panzer: Panzer Lehr, 41, 125, 141, 163, 181; 11th, 181; 10th SS, 188,

divisions, panzer grenadier: 15th, 82; 21st, 188; 25th, 188

divisions, SS panzer grenadier: 17th, 185, 186, 187

divisions, German, volks grenadier: 19th, 175; 36th, 185; 256th, 187; 257th, 187; 361st, 187; 559th, 187

divisions, German, SS mountain: 6th, 187, 196–97

divisions, German, parachute: 77th, 188; 418th, 186

divisions, French, infantry: 2nd Moroccan, 91, 201; 3rd Algerian, 184, 197, 201; French 14th, 38; French 16th, 38

divisions, French, Armored: 2nd, advance along Rhine, 93, 180; in Northwind, 187; in Strasbourg attack; 17, 18, 66, 79, 121–124, in Vosges; 83

Dortmund, 20

Drabik, Alex, 5

Drummond, Roscoe, 13, 21

Duisburg, 20

DUKWS, 71, 108, 110–11, 115, 207

Dusseldorf, 20

E

Eaker, Ira, 35, 86

Ecole Superieur de Guerre, 66

Eddy, Manton S., 159, 197

Egypt, 4, 25, 52

Eisenhower, Dwight D.: in broad front controversy, 45–46, 117, 148, 150; in Colmar Pocket concerns, 190–94; in cross–Rhine attack, 88, 100, 113, 134, 149, 158–64, 166–71; as European commander, 47; as a leader, 8, 21–23, 45, 48, 50, 53, 58, 71, 74, 146, 179, 198; Northwind, 182–89; as supreme commander, 15, 39, 45, 87, 89; relationship with Devers, 17, 22, 24, 85–86, 155, 157; relationship with French, 89, 95, 132, 134–44; at West Point, 3, 12; as youth, 2

Eisenhower, Mamie Dowd, 66

El Alamein, 50, 52

Elba, 32

Elbe River, 171, 202–3

Elizabeth (wife of George VI), 22

Elsner, Robert, 81
English Channel, 22, 44, 54, 74, 75
Epinal, 57, 64
Erpel, 5, 166
Essen, Germany, 20
ETO, 14, 31, 53, 56–57, 62, 71, 81, 87–88, 97, 153
Evinrude outboard, 111

F

Faucogney, 63
FFI, 36, 92, 207
Foret de la Harth, 105
Fort Benning, 2
Fort Bragg, 12, 13, 156
Fort D. A. Russell, 11
Fort Knox, 13
Fort Leavenworth, 12, 161
Fort Lewis, 34
Fort Myers, 12
Fort Sam Houston, 66
Fredendall, Lloyd, 159
Frederick, Robert T., 136
French army, 89–90
French Free Forces, 92
French general staff, 66
FUSAG, 162
Fussell, Paul 61, 62, 89, 134, 163–64

G

Gabes, 159
Gabon, 122
Garand, 92
Geisswesser, 105
George VI, 21
Gerardmer Pass, 126
German General Staff, 95
Gerow, Leonard T., 142, 157, 173, 175–77
Gerstheim, 106
Gilland, Morris W., 115
Giziowski, Richard, 186
Goebbels, Joseph, 201, 204
Gould, Foster, 66
Grant, Ulysses S., 163
Gray, Carl R., Jr., 72, 73
Grenoble, 32–34, 37, 38
Griess, Thomas E., 137

Guadalcanal, 26
Guderian, Heinz, 59

H

Haguenau Forest, 131, 179–81, 188
Haguenau River, 136
Haguenau, 18, 115, 129, 173, 146, 188
Haislip, Wade: in Germany, 200–2; as 15th
    Corps commander, 65–67, 77, 119, 121, 122,
    185, 200, 202; halts Rhine assault, 135, 137,
    139, 144–45, 164; in Northwind, 179–185;
    relationship with Eisenhower, 146; Rhine
    crossing, 164; transferred to 6th Army
    Group, 155
Hamburg, 105
Hamilton, Nigel, 141
Hansen, Chester B., 3, 50, 89, 90, 99, 134,
    135, 204
Hardt Mountains, 104
Hawaii, 12
Helfranzkirch, 127
Herpelmont. 64
Higgins boats, 30
Hill, Gladwin, 6
Himmler, Heinrich, 55, 186–87, 192
Hitler, Adolf: in Ardennes attack, 165–67,
    181; in battle for France, 41–42, 77, 91;
    Colmar Pocket strategy, 180, 190; defense
    of Germany, 201–203; defense of ports, 32;
    defense of the Rhine, 95; destruction of
    armies, 178; Northwind strategy, 181–86;
    191–93; orders command change, 55, 59,
    81; policy of no retreat, 33, 59
Hodges, Courtney: captures Remagen
    Bridge, 199; crosses the Rhine, 170; as
    First Army commander, 4, 5, under
    Bradley's command, 24, 44, 53, 117, 140; at
    Wallendorf, 173, 175–76, 178
Hooker, Joseph, 163
Horrocks, Brian, 176
Hoth, Herman, 59
Hughes, Everett, 157
Huningue, 105
Hurtgen Forest, 66, 77, 97, 142, 158, 163,
    178–79, 191
Huston, James, 72

**I**

Ill River, 195
Ingersoll, Ralph, 153
Irawaddy River, 164
Irwin, Leroy, 200
Italy: as airbase, 30; as battleground, 24–25, 31, 62,
64, 78, 115, 159, 166, 197; divisions in Italy, 16, 34; Devers in 35; Fifth Army in, 154; the French in, 91; as possible landing site, 22; Sixth Corps in, 57, 74; as training ground, 36, 73

**J**

Jackson, Stonewall, 163
Jenkins, Reuben, 120
Jettingen, 127
Juin, Alphonse, 184
Jura Mountains, 36

**K**

Kaiser, Willi, 130–31, 169
Kamersheidt, 163
Kappelen, 127
Karlsruhe: in cross–Rhine attack, 82, 97, 99, 100, 104, 125, 130–31, 138; on Rhine, 20, 60, 129, 163
Kassel, 151
Kasserine Pass, 159
Keegan, John, 122
Kehl, 18, 104, 124, 132, 141, 169
Kehl bridges, 169
Kembs Dam, 105
Kensington Palace Gardens, 21
Kipling, John, 28
Kipling, Rudyard, 28
Kirk, Alan G., 118
Koblenz, 166
Konev, Marshall, 59, 170
Kufra, 122

**L**

L–5 Cub , 73
Larkin, Thomas B., 72
Lautenbourg, 106
Lavaline du Houx, 64

Le Havre, 69–70
Le Muy, 32
Le Puloch, Louis, 127
Leclerc, Jacques Philippe: 92–93, capture of Strasbourg, 17–19, 121–25, 141; in Colmar Pocket, 180; in Northwind, 187–88, 202; in Rhine crossing, 99, 113; in Vosges, 83
Lee, Robert E., 163
Lehigh University, 8
Leimersheim, 106, 201
Lepanges, 64
Libya, 4, 122, 158
Lipizzaner horses, 205
*Logistical Support of the Armies,* 70
logistics, 68, 71–75, 115, 149, 150, 167, 176
London, 21, 22, 90, 122, 162
Lost Battalion, 81
Loucks family, 9
Ludendorf Railroad Bridge, 5, 6, 133, 199
Lyon, 15, 37, 70, 110

**M**

M–4 Sherman tank, 13, 18, 113, 122, 127
MacArthur, Douglas, 23, 24, 50, 162, 209
MacDonald, Charles, 174
Mackenheim, 105
Maginot Line, 91, 179, 180, 184
Mainz, 97, 196, 197,
Mandalay, 164
Mannheim, 97, 99, 100, 104, 196,
Marseille 15, 17, 30–34, 37, 60, 66, 69–71, 74, 83, 101, 114, 140, 178
Marshall, George C.: in battle of France, 43; Brooke's opinion of, 47; logistical concerns of, 70, 74; Overlord strategy, 22–24; relationship with Bradley; 4, relationship with Devers, 12–13, 22, 23–24, 79, 85–87, 156–157; relationship with Eisenhower, 12–13, 85–87, 149, 152, 156–57, 162, 177, 205; relationship with the French, 90; as Ted Brook's boss, 79–80
Marshall, S. L. A., 95
Martin Blumenson, 74
Massu, Jacques, 123
Mauldin, Bill, 34
Mellenthin, F. W., 55–56, 59, 60, 146, 190, 198

Merovingians, 1

Messerschmitt 262, 5

Metz, 8, 56, 97, 122, 136, 142, 178, 186, 195

Meuse–Argonne Offensive, 66

Meuse River, 1, 59, 66, 193

Milburn, Frank W., 197, 202

Model, Field Marshall, 146

Monschau, 163

Monte Cassino, 31, 35, 63

Montelimar, 33–36, 39

Montgomery, Bernard L.: in Arnhem operation, 75, 139, 142; in battle of France, 40, 50, 51–52, 74; childhood and youth 51–53; Churchill's description of, 50; as commander, 48–50, 141, 149; as commander, 21st Army Group, 8, 45; in cross–Rhine attack, 2, 146, 148–50, 196; in France, 40, 74, 116; intention to cross the Rhine, 17; logistical concerns, 68, 75; in Market Garden, 173, 176; in Normandy, 40, 44–54; opinion of Eisenhower as general, 50, 151; in Operation Plunder, 196, 199, 200; personality problems of, 47, 51; relationship with Eisenhower, 2; relationship with U.S. generals, 49, 50–53, 166; in Sicily, 49; single thrust strategy, 45–46, 117; as tactician, 58, 14

Moselle River, 38, 63–65, 167, 196, 203

mules v. horses, 11

Mulhouse: on Alsace front, 82, 102–103, 127; in Colmar Pocket, 180, 208; near the Rhine, 20, 57, 100, 119, 125, 126, 132

Munchhouse, 106

Murphy, Audie, 31, 35, 63, 77

### N

Namur, 1, 4, 44

Nancy, city of, 73

Napoleon, 32, 88, 94, 161, 205

National Redoubt, 201–4

NATOUSA, 24, 71

Neuwied, 94

*New York Times,* 6, 13, 124, 146, 155

Newhausen , 106

Niffer, 105

Noir Gueux, 64

Normandy: allies bogged down in, 22, 24, 40; armies supplied by, 70, 140; arrival of new divisions, 66, 83; breakout from, 149; hedgerows in, 137; Ike visits, 71; Leclerc lands at, 93, 125; Operation Cobra, 41; Overlord planning for, 74; planning for attack, 46; second invasion force, 48; size of bridgehead, 44; transfer of troops to, 25

North Africa: Bradley in, 3, 4; bomber transfer to, 86; de Lattre forces in 62; Devers' command in, 21; Eisenhower commands troops in, 4, 156, 158–62; engineers in, 115; Japanese–Americans in, 79; French army in, 91–93, 126, 208; General Gray in, 72; Germans in Tunisia, 52; Leclerc arrives in, 122, 158, 159, 162; NATOUSA, 71; Seventh Army in, 25; U.S. divisions in, 16; Von Manteuffel in, 59; Westphal in, 96

### O

O'Daniel, John W., 197, 203

OP pipeline, 76

Operation Dragoon: controversy over, 25; formerly Anvil, 24; on French coast, 27, 30–32, 38, 39; French involvement in, 25; as left hook, 24; logistical concerns, 69–71; SHAEF ignores, 88; ultimate objective of, 99

Operation Husky, 26

Operation Independence, 208

Operation Northwind, 93, 147, 177, 185–87, 189, 196

Operation Overlord: 86, as codename, 24; in change of plans, 42, 45–46, 96, 147–48; Devers' role in, 155, 162; secondary objective of, 195

Operation Plunder, 146, 148–51, 196, 200

Operation Sonnenwende, 187, 192

Operation Torch, 158

Operation Undertone, 151, 195–96

Operation Zahnartz, 186

### P

Palestine, 25

Pas de Calais, 162

Patch, Alexander M.; in advance on

Strasbourg, 121; in cross–Rhine attack, 18, 19, 96, 100, 102, 114, 123, 138–39, 145–46, 147, 164, 167, 169, 178; description of, 135; early career, 26, 27–29; in Germany, 199–206; in Northwind 183–89; as replacement for Devers, 157; as 7th Army commander, 14 25–29, 33, 36, 57, 60, 62, 87, 123; in the Vosges, 63, 68,–69

Patch, Alexander M., Jr., 28

Patch, "Little Mac", 29

Patch, Julia, 28

Patton, Beatrice, 15, 154, 203

Patton, George S. Jr.: advancing to the Saar; 87, 181; in Ardennes attack 193, 211; in battle for France, 44–45, 47, 54, 57, 59; command philosophy, 48, 85, 150, 152, 158–59, 162; as commander of 3rd Army, 55–56, 82, 142; in cross Rhine attack, 17, 99–100, 111, 116–17, 125, 130–31, 135–140, 142, 144, 146, 153, 165–68, 171; as Devers' classmate 10; feared by Germans, 82; idiosyncrasies of, 5, 50; linkup with Seventh, 102; new orders for, 178–82, 190; in North Africa, 4, 26; polo with Devers, 12; relations with British, 49, 53, 150–151; relationship with Devers, 15, 65, 85, 154–55; relationship with Eisenhower, 157–59; the Saar as objective, 195–205; in Sicily, 4, 26; supplying Third Army, 74; in WW I, 161–62; as World War II hero, 8, 14, 15

Peake, Charles, 185

Pershing, John, 160–61

Persons, Wilton, 152

Petain, 90–92, 122

Pforzheim, 132

Phalsbourg, 123

Philadelphia, 9

Philippines, 23, 24, 162

Plobsheim, 106

Pogue, Forrest, 140, 192

polo, 11–12, 34

Pommois, Lise, 185

pontons, 108, 112, 113

pontoon bridges, 3, 6, 110, 111–12, 114 130, 207

Pyle, Ernie, 41

**Q**

Quinn, William W., 96, 183, 185, 201

**R**

Ralston, Richard, 5

Rasp, Siegfried, 192–93

Rastatt: defenses of, 20, history of, 19, 129; logistical aspects of, 75; strategic significance of, 104, 119, 125, 128–29, 131, 143, 145–46, 162, 167, 171, 172, 190

Reeder, Russell, 27

refugees, 118, 183

regimental combat teams, American: 442nd, 80–81; 517th Parachute, 32

regiments, American, artillery: 4th Mountain, 11

regiments, American, engineer: 343rd Engineer; General Service regiment, 75; 40th Combat Engineer regiment, 36; 540th Engineering Combat Regiment, 116

regiments, American, infantry: 11th, 200; 30th, 65, 80; 109th, 174; 110th, 174; 141st, 64, 80–81, 186; 313th, 125, 188

Reilly, Pat, 188

Remagen, town of, 4–8, 133, 148–51; bridgehead, 163, 166, 169, 170

Remagen bridge: 4–9, capture of, 95–96, 146, 148–51, 199; river crossing point, 133

Remiremont, France, 57, 64

Reynaud, Paul, 90

Rhine River: advancing toward, 62–63, 65, 74, 85, 88; at Arnhem, 75; bridges, 2–9; near Colmar Pocket, 190–94; crossing points, 17, 20, 117, 150–51; cross–Rhine attack, 2–9, 53–54, 56–57, 60, 97–101; French arrive on, 18, 38, 66, 119, 125–27; geology of, 15, 36, 57, 61, 163; German reaction to, 169; history of, 18, 94, 96; planning an attack, 102–114; at Rastatt, 75, 129–44, 167; reached by Americans, 19–20; at Strasbourg, 66–67, 77, 125

Rhine River dams, 112–13

Rhone Valley, 15, 33, 35–37, 39, 45, 55, 70, 73, 

river–crossing schools: 95, on Doubs River 110–11; on Valbonne River 110–12

Roland, Charles, 163

Rome, Italy, 63–64

Rommel, Erwin: as bold commander, 158; inNormandy, 25, 40, 42, 53, 96; in North Africa, 4, 48, 49, 59, 122

Rooney, Andy, 6

Roosevelt, Franklin D.: appoints Devers, 156; as commander in chief, 23; complains of press coverage, 47; promotes Devers, 12, 157; relationship with de Gaulle, 184, at Yalta, 170

Rosenau, 127

Rouen, 44, 70

Ruhr: advance toward, 55–56, 75, 99, 117, 148, 150, 173; principal allied objective, 20, 25, 45, 82, 87, 95–96, 116, 139

**S**

Saar: advancing on, 54, 56, 116; as secondary objective, 45, 101, 195; importance of, 130, 142, 195

Saarbrucken, 130, 195, 197

Saar-Palatinate, 195, 198

Saint Paul's Cathedral, 21

Saint-Cyr, 90

Saint-Die, 77, 80–81, 118

Saint-Lo, 41

Saint-Mihiel Offensive, 66

Saint-Raphael, 31–32

Saint-Tropez, 30–31

Salerno, 31

Sambre River, 1

saphis, 91

*Saturday Evening Post,* 154–55

Saverne Gap, 62, 65, 67, 77, 83, 118,–19, 121, 123–24, 185, 187

SCAF (Supreme Command Allied Forces), 100

Schlucht Pass, 126

Schmidt, Dana Adams, 124

Schmidt, 163

Schnee Eifel, 172–74

Schonau, 106

Schreiver, Howard P., 187

Seppois, 127

Services of Supply, 72

Sfax, 159

SHAEF: broad front strategy, 97; on Colmar Pocket, 191–93; on cross-Rhine attack, 17, 37, 100, 140, 199; failure to exploit gains, 58, 74, 96, 138, 141–42, 147 182; in Germany, 203–204 190–93; logistical concerns, 68, 72, 75; opinion of Sixth Army Group, 16; overall planning by, 75, 87–88, 96, 103, 138, 166; plans for Sixth Army Group, 15–16, 74, 85–86, 97, 100, 113, 140; relationship with Devers, 141; relationship with French, 93, 132, 149, 185, 209; relationship with 6th Army Group, 45, 57, 65, 85, 87–88, 103, 112, 113, 116, 128, 167; transfer of 6th Corps, 65; at Wallendorf, 171–77

Shea, Jack, 40

shirttail allies, 2

Sicily, 4, 26, 34, 49, 115, 138, 159, 197

Siegfried Line: in combat, 124; as defensive line, 2, 42, 46, 56, 58, 77, 82, 88, 95, 97, 100–101, 107, 116, 117, 130–131, 139, 158, 163, 166, 171; as military objective, 40, 43, 118, 144; in Patton's sector, 149; at Wallendorf, 142

Sievers & Devers, 9

Simpson, William H., 117

Sions, Harry, 203

Sisteron, 68

Slim, William, 164

Smith, Robert Ross: advance into Germany, 193; conjecture by, 88, 130–32; on Colmar Pocket, 190; on cross-Rhine attack, 139; on Eisenhower, 135, 150, 167; on Northwind, 188; on Seventh Army, 138; on Wiese, 82

Smith, Walter Bedell, 53, 80, 82, 86, 147, 148, 173

smoke generating regiments, American: 69th, 112; 78th, 112

Sonderheim, 107

Soufflenheim, 125

Southern Group of Armies, 70

special forces, American: 1st Special Force, 32

Speyer, 107, 129, 131, 144, 201

Spotsylvania, 142

St. Jean du Marche, 64

Stalin, Joseph, 170

*Stars and Stripes*, 6, 34, 86
Stein, Gertrude, 28
Stillwell, "Vinegar Joe", 10
Strasbourg: advance on, 17–19, 60, 66–67, 77, 97, 104, 113, 119, 121–27, 129, 139; Eisenhower ancestral home, 9; bridges at, 132, 141; cross–Rhine attack, 58, 60, 103, 130, 143–44, 146, 158, 162, 169; Devers reaches, 58; in Northwind, 147, 187–88, 192, 196, 201; planned evacuation of, 184
Summersby, Kay, 148
supreme commander: in Colmar Pocket, 179, 190 193; as commander, 17; Devers as, 21; deficiencies of, 162, 212; difficulties of, 150; doubts about Devers, 24, 45–48, 156; Eisenhower named as, 23, 86; halts Devers's army, 178; in North Africa, 160; in Northwind, 183–184; relationship with de Gaulle 93; relationship with Montgomery, 53; role for Devers' army, 87; at USMA, 3; visits front, 134

**T**

task forces, American: 1st Airborne, 208; TF Butler 32–34; TF Harris, 187; TF Herren, 187; TF Hudelston , 187; TF Linden, 187
Task Forces, French: TF Massu 18, 123; TF Rouvillois 18, 123–24
Thomas, Lowell, 15
Thorpe, Jim, 3
Thumm, Hellmuth, 169, 192
tirailleurs, 91
Toulon, 25, 30, 32, 33, 37, 69, 70
Triumpho, Tony, 123
Truman, Harry, 205
Truscott, Lucian: at Belfort Gap, 126, 142; commands Fifth Army, 79, 204; as commander, 88, 159; relations with Eisenhower, 152; relations with French, 71; selected by Eisenhower, 86; in Sicily, 49; in southern France, 30–39; in the Vosges, 56–58, 65–67, 102
Tunis, 23, 115, 158
Tunisia, 4, 22, 38, 48, 91, 122, 158–59
Twelfth Air Force, 125
22–caliber, 166

**U**

U.S. Army Air Corps, 21
U.S. General Staff, 79
Ultra, 33, 129, 140, 183

**V**

V–2 rocket, 5
Van Creveld, Martin, 74, 75
Vancouver Barracks, 11
Vatterrodt, 130
Vera Cruz, 66
Vichy government, 38, 90, 92, 93, 122, 156, 159, 207
Villa, Pancho, 26, 160
Vittel, 61, 120, 135–37, 146, 152, 153
Von Kluge, Gunther, 42
Von Knobelsdorf, Otto, 59, 175–76, 179
Von Manteuffel, Hasso, 59, 82
Von Obstfelder, Hans, 186
Von Rundstedt, 96, 125, 173, 175, 193
Von Schlieffen, Alfred, 95
Vosges Mountains: advance into, 55–66, 78, 81–83, 87, 102–4, 116, 119–21, 123, 125–27, 180; at Belfort Gap, 36; as defense line, 20 34; logistics in, 68; in Northwind, 183–88, 191; retreat from, 93; at Saint Die, 77; terrain in, 163

**W**

Walker, Walton, 97, 196
Watzenan, 106
Wehrmacht: in Alsace, 18–19; Colmar Pocket, 190; condition of, 186, 199, 211; defense in Vosges, 59; generals in, 166; importance of Ruhr, 173; in retreat, 36, 42–43, 95, 116, 123–24, 142, 181, 196
Weigley, Russell, 85, 127, 142, 144, 148, 193, 107, 198, 202, 204
Wesel, 2, 148, 199
West Point, 3, 9, 10, 12, 23, 26–29, 39, 66, 79, 119, 140, 157, 165
Westminster, 21
Westminster Abbey, 22
Westphal, Siegfried, 96, 146, 176

Wiese, Frederich, in Colmar Pocket, 182; commands nineteenth Army, 25, 45; looses troops, 82; master at defense, 80, 120; organizes retreat, 33–38, 55–57, 60, 62, 63, 65, 93, 117, 145
wilderness, 142
Wilson, Maitland, 24, 86, 87
Wood, John S., 125
World War I, 5, 12, 27–28, 33–34, 37, 44, 51–52, 58

**Y**
Yalta, 170
*Yank,* 203
York, 9
York High School, 9

**Z**
Zhukov, Field Marshall, 170
Zouaves, 127

★ ★ ★ ★

# ABOUT THE AUTHOR

David P. Colley is an author and former journalist whose military histories include *The Road to Victory: The Untold Story of WWII's Red Ball Express,* which received the Army Historical Foundation's Distinguished Book Award in 2000; *Blood for Dignity;* and *Safely Rest.* Colley also has written for many national publications, including *Army, World War II, American Heritage,* and the *New York Times.* He has appeared on the History Channel and Eye on Books. He was a reporter for the *Baltimore Evening Sun* and an assistant city editor for the Trenton, N.J., *Trentonian,* and he served in the ordnance branch of the U.S. Army. He lives in Easton, Pa., with his wife, Elizabeth Keegin Colley, a photographer.